St. Louis Community College

Library

5801 Wilson Avenue
St. Louis, Missouri 63110

St. Louis Community College
at Meramec
Library

The Shoshoni-Crow Sun Dance

The Civilization of the American Indian Series

John Truhujo prays after doctoring a patient. Note directionality of medicine feathers. Pryor, 1941.

The Shoshoni-Crow Sun Dance

by

Fred W. Voget

University of Oklahoma Press
Norman

By Fred W. Voget

Osage Indians: Osage Research Report I (New York and London, 1974)
A History of Ethnology (New York, 1975)
The Shoshoni-Crow Sun Dance (Norman, 1984)

Library of Congress Cataloging in Publication Data

Voget, Fred W.
  The Shoshoni-Crow Sun Dance.

  Bibliography: p. 336
  Includes index.
  1. Crow Indians—Rites and ceremonies. 2. Sun-dance. 3. Sho-
shoni Indians—Rites and ceremonies. 4. Indians of North America
—Great Plains—Rites and ceremonies.
  I. Title.
E99.C92V63   1984   306'.08997   83-40332
ISBN 0-8061-1886-5

The paper in this book meets the guidelines for permanence and durability
of the Committee on Production Guidelines for Book Longevity of the
Council on Library Resources, Inc.

*Dedicated to the Crow People,
who have brought the past
forward into the present
and made the past a living
part of their adaptation
to changing times, and to
Ira, Frederick, Anthony,
Melvin, and Marshall Lefthand,
for their vital role in preserving
the Crow national patrimony and
heritage*

Contents

Preface   xv

Acknowledgments   xix

Chapter 1. The Crow Indians: A Short History

Historic Land and Livelihood   3
Crow Saga of Separation from the Hidatsas   4
Crows as Middlemen, 1740 to 1884   10
The Desperate Years, 1860 to 1884   12
Prelude to Reservation Life, 1870 to 1884   15
Adjusting the Old Life to the New, 1884 to 1950   16
Putting Political and Legal Machinery in Place   23

**Chapter 2. Traditional Crow Indian Culture and
    Society**

Two Primary Relationships   29
Family and Clan   31
Clan Bonds and Responsibilities   32
Kinship Rights and Obligations   33
Warfare, Individuality, and the Open Society   37
Building a Career Together: Mentor and Apprentice   40
Mystic Power, Dreams, and Individuality   43
Preparation for Individuality and Success   44
Reputation, Influence, and Political Power   49
Chiefs and the Political Process   50

Military Fraternities   54
Religious Organization and Ceremonialism   60
Informal Associations   61
Adoptive-Purchase Ceremonialism   63
The Adoption Process   66
Corporate Nature of Crow Medicine Societies and
    Worship   74

Chapter 3. The Traditional Crow Sun Dance

Introduction   77
Origins and Functions of the Sun Dance   79
Sun Dance Medicine Bundles in Tribal
    Ceremonialism   85
Description and Analysis of the Sun Dance   86
Crow Sun Dances: Comparisons and Commentary   105

Chapter 4. Introduction of the Wind River Shoshoni Sun Dance to the Crow Indians

In Search of Power and Meaning: William Big Day   129
Reinforcement, Dreams, and Christianity   136
Pathway to the Past: Personal and Cultural Factors   138
Dissemination of the Sun Dance Among the Crows   141
Secondary Disseminators of the Sun Dance   147
    Robert Yellowtail: Superintendent and Rancher   147
    Barney Old Coyote: Excommunicant and Peyotist   150
    Joseph Hill: Skeptic   156
Crow Sun Dance Leaders: Similarities and
    Differences   158

Chapter 5. Pablo Juan Truhujo: Shoshoni Innovator and Sun Dance Leader

Introduction   163
Early Life and Education   165
Marriage and Work Career   166
Religious Background and Sun Dance Career   167
Truhujo's Views of the Sun Dance and of
    Christianity   173

Christian "Reinterpretation" of the Shoshoni
  Sun Dance   181
Some Shoshoni Views of Truhujo in 1948   182
Establishing the Sun Dance Among the Crows   185
Postwar Disenchantment with Crow Leaders:
  A Second Laying on of Hands   189
John Truhujo as an Historical Person   194

**Chapter 6. The Shoshoni Crow Sun Dance: Ceremony
  and Symbolism**

Introduction   196
Sponsoring a Sun Dance: Dream and Vow   197
Organizing a Sun Dance   200
Consecrating the Sun Dance   203
John Cummins's Outside Dance, Lodge Grass, 1946   205
Building the Big Lodge   217
Ceremonial Entry of the Lodge   232
The Ceremonial Fire   241
Greeting the Sun Person   243
Sacrificing for Power: The Second Day   248
Paints and Medicines   252
Praise and Encouragement   255
Drummer-Singers and Dancers   258
A Dancer's Suffering and Visions   262
Terminating the Sun Dance   269

**Chapter 7. Integration of the Sun Dance into Crow
  Society and Culture**

Introduction   273
Crow Culture-History and Reservation
  Acculturation   274
Religion and Identity: The Spread of Peyotism   275
Peyotism and the Sun Dance in Cultural-Historical
  Perspective   281
The Sun Dance Then and Now: Comparisons   282
  The Sun Dance as a Tribal Event   282
  Sponsorship and Organization of a Sun Dance   283

Consecration   287
Pledger's Role and Authority   289
Ceremonial Pattern and Innovation   291
World View and Personalized Worship   294
The Sun Dance as a Power Quest   295
Interpretations for Whites: Correspondences and
    Legitimacy   296
Traditional and Contemporary Symbolism   297
Stellar Origins of the Sun Dance   299
Dwarfs, the Sun Dance, and Stellar Connections   301
Person-offering   305
Buffalo versus Little Man   307
Eagle and Thunderbird   307
Prayer Smokes and Pipes   308
Drumming and Singing   310
Old Needs in a New Setting   311
The Sun Dance as a Contemporary Institution   313

Appendix A

The Elk Lodge and the Full Moon Meeting   321
Elk Lodge Membership   328

Appendix B

Drummer's Cane and Rattle   330
Sponsor's Ceremonial Cane   331
Little Man or Person Offering   332

Appendix C

Crow Sun Dances by District, 1941 to 1946   334

Bibliography   336

Index   341

Illustrations

John Truhujo   *frontispiece*
Crow Tipis at Crow Fair, 1939   20
Camp Scene at Crow Fair, 1939   21
Woman on Top of the Ground and Well Known Writing   22
Sorting Goods for Give-away   23
Jack Covers Up Announces Gift of a Horse   35
White Arm and Blake White Man   36
Crow Men Playing the Handgame   37
Frank Hawk Signals in Handgame   38
Henry Big Day and Daughter   80
"War Party" of Four Old Men   96
Charlie Ten Bear   97
Henry and William Big Day   135
Tom Yellowtail   151
Truhujo Doctoring Horse   179
Truhujo Doctoring Old Men   180
Messenger Eagle   204
Consecrated Buffalo Head   205
Raising of Center Tree   221
Interlocking Rafter Poles for Sun Dance Lodge   222
Preparing to Attach the Buffalo Head   223
Dancers and Sun Dance Lodge, Lodge Grass, 1946   231
Sun Dance Lodge, Lodge Grass, 1975   232
Relatives Bring Cattails and Sage on Second Day   242

Interior of the Big Lodge, Pryor, 1941   243
Running at the Buffalo   244
Dancers at Crow Agency, 1941   245
Women Dancers at Lodge Grass, 1975   246
Greeting Grandfather Sun   249
Praying to the Sun   250
Tobacco Prayer by Thomas Lion Shows   251
Shoshoni Dancers Praying at Sunrise   259
Shoshoni Pledger Tom Wesaw   260
Dancers Resting After Sunrise Ceremony   261
Mr. and Mrs. Tom Yellowtail and John Truhujo   271

Photographs by Fred W. Voget except where otherwise noted

Maps and Figures

Map 1. Historic Crow Homeland   2

Map 2. District Sponsorship of Sun Dances, 1941–1946   160

Figure 1. Plan of Crow Encampment at Big Shadow's
Sun Dance, 1844 (reconstructed from Curtis, 1970)   99

Figure 2. Plan of Crow Sun Dance Lodge, after
Robert Meldrum (Morgan, 1959)   106

Figure 3. Plan of Big Shadow's Sun Dance Lodge, 1844
(reconstructed from Curtis, 1970)   112

Figure 4. Plan of Crow Sun Dance Lodge
(reconstructed from Lowie, 1915   116

Figure 5. John Truhujo's Lineage Relation to
Ohamagwaya or Yellow Hand (modified from
Shimkin, 1953)   154

Figure 6. Plan of "Outside Dance," Lodge Grass, 1946   206

Figure 7. Ceremonial Entry of the Big Lodge   233

Figure 8. Plan of Shoshoni-Crow Sun Dance Lodge   237

Figure 9. Plan of Wind River Shoshoni Sun Dance
Lodge (modified after Shimkin, 1953)   239

Figure 10a. Schematic View of "Full-Moon" Prayer
Meeting at Crow Agency   322

Figure 10b. Schematic View of Prayer Meeting at Pryor   323

Preface

In 1941, Crow Indians from Montana sought out leaders of the Sun Dance among the Wind River Shoshonis in Wyoming and, under the direction of John Truhujo, made the ceremony a part of their lives. The Crows in former times had their own Sun Dance but gave it up about ten years before moving to their present reservation in 1884.

In writing about the Sun Dance, I have tried first of all to describe the persons and circumstances that led to this singular event, as well as the nature of the ceremony and the place it now holds in Crow life and culture. Second, I have attempted to bring a cultural-historical perspective to the Sun Dance—viewing it as an acculturative event and analyzing the patterned features and processes involved. This approach prompted comparison of the contemporary Shoshoni-Crow Sun Dance with the traditional Crow ceremony in order to discover major continuities and changes in the Sun Dance in Crow experience. To appreciate the place of the ceremony in Crow life today also required comparisons to find out whether changes and persistences in the Sun Dance were comparable to those found in the composite reservation culture.

How and why the Crows borrowed the Sun Dance from the Wind River Shoshonis is their own story, for it is based on the narratives of friends and informants. Here I wish to express my special gratitude to the many Crows who contributed information and assistance, especially to William Big Day, Barney and Mae Old Coyote, Joseph Hill, John Cummins, David Bad Boy, Campbell Big Hail, Bird Horse, Al Childs, Charlie Ten Bear, Louis Walks on the Ice, Thomas Yellowtail, and John Truhujo (Shoshoni). Many of those to whom I owe thanks are deceased, as Peter Left Hand, who smoothed the path of my inquiries and helped with interpretations of announcements at public events and ceremonies. To Joseph Medicine Crow I owe very special thanks for generous and invaluable assistance in exploring word meanings and ceremony interpretations.

I owe much to those who dedicated themselves to recording and interpreting Crow culture, notably Robert H. Lowie, William Wildschut (edited by John C. Ewers and Peter Nabokov), Edward S. Curtis, as well as the fur trader, Edwin Denig, and Frank B. Linderman, the biographer of Plenty Coups and of Pretty Shield. Special thanks also are due Professor Robert Kiste for making available his manuscript field notes on Crow Peyotism, as well as Professors Rodney Frey, and Thomas H. Johnson, and to Richard Lowenthal for their respective papers on the Crow Sun Dance, the Wind River Shoshoni Sun Dance, and Crow public events. The Bureau of Indian Affairs regional office at Billings has been most helpful in making available special publications regarding the housing and economy of the Crows.

The beginnings of any work reach back in time, and I owe much to Professors Luther S. Cressman, George P. Murdock, and Ralph Linton; for it was the stimulus of their teachings that guided much of this study. I am deeply indebted to colleagues who investigated the clash of the American Indian and the invading European national cultures, especially those who focused on the role of réligion in culture-contact situations. Thanks also are due Professors Helmut Straube and Johannes Raum of the Institute for Ethnology, University of Munich, for the opportunity to extend my knowledge of religious and political movements as culture-contact phenomena during a summer semester in 1979.

My wife, Kay, has provided constant support, and this work owes much to her editorial skill. Cynthia Brooks and Janice Dyer contributed their stenographic skills and eased the burden of typing. I am indebted to the staff of Lovejoy Library for their unstinting cooperation in the tracking of sources, and to Southern Illinois University for making time available for research and writing. Diane Clements and Emily Brown have added their distinctive styles and special expertise to the maps and figures.

Books find their way into final print through the talent and competence of editors, and I am especially grateful to Joaquin Rogers and the staff of the University of Oklahoma Press for readying the manuscript for publication.

This book is not meant to be a final statement on the Sun Dance among the Crows. Basically it covers the period from 1941 to 1948, with observations at intervals between, and especially in 1975, added. There is much yet to be done, not the least of which is the investigation of the role of women in the contemporary ceremony.

FRED W. VOGET

Edwardsville, Illinois

Acknowledgments

For permission to reprint excerpts from copyrighted materials, the author is indebted to the following:

American Museum of Natural History, Anthropological Papers, New York City. R. H. Lowie, "Social Life of the Crow Indians," 1912, 9:179–248; "The Sun Dance of the Crow Indians," 1915, 16:1–50; "Minor Ceremonies of the Crow Indians," 1924, 21:325–65.

Harper & Row, Publishers, Incorporated. Frank B. Linderman, *American: The Life Story of a Great American, Plenty Coups, Chief of the Crows*, 1930; *Red Mother* [Pretty Shield], 1932.

Holt, Rinehart and Winston. Robert H. Lowie, *The Crow Indians*, 1935.

Museum of the American Indian, Heye Foundation. William Wildschut (ed. by John C. Ewers), "Crow Indian Medicine Bundles," 1960, vol. 17. By permission of the Museum of the American Indian, New York City.

University of Nebraska Press, Lincoln. Thomas H. Leforge (ed. by Thomas B. Marquis), *Memoirs of a White Crow Indian*, 1974, Bison Book.

Dr. Demitri B. Shimkin, University of Illinois, for permission to reproduce Figures 20 and 21, with modification, in "The Wind River Shoshoni Sun Dance," Smithsonian Institutions, Bureau of American Ethnology, 1953, Bulletin 151: 397–484.

The Shoshoni-Crow Sun Dance

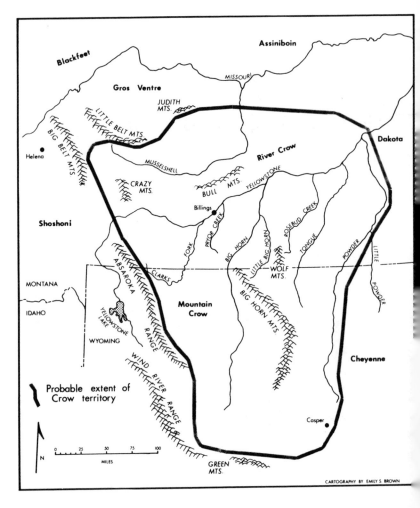

Map 1. Historic Crow Homeland

CHAPTER 1

The Crow Indians: A Short History

Historic Land and Livelihood

The Crow Indians were never a populous nation. During their buffalo-hunting days in the Plains, they probably did not exceed their present population of about six thousand persons.

In their traditional life, buffalo supplied the Crows with the basic necessities of food, shelter, and clothing. The horse, acquired early in the eighteenth century, added a special dimension to Crow culture. Men on foot were transformed into mounted hunters and into warriors who competed for wealth and reputation by raiding and trading for horses.

The clustering or dispersal of buffalo in their migratory grazing habits locked the Crows into a seasonal migration directed by band chiefs during eight months of the year. In late spring the bands usually came together and organized themselves under a Camp Chief. Summer was a busy time, involving much drying of meat for winter needs. It was also a happy interlude for visiting with friends and kin, as well as for adoptions into various fraternities, especially the sacred tobacco and military. At this time food, handcrafted objects, and horses changed hands, flowing along social axes in repayment for adoption, prayerful blessings, gifts of ceremonial rights, honoring of kin, and reciprocities associated with status

3

building. As summer gave way to fall, the Crows commonly reverted to their band organization in preparation for winter's snows, icy winds, and dispersed game.

In their wanderings, Crow bands maneuvered between the Rocky Mountains on the west, the Big Horn, Wind River, and Absaroka ranges to south and west, the Black Hills and Powder River to the east, and the Missouri River to the north. Mountain Crows usually wintered westward in the foothills of the Rockies; the River Crows north toward the Missouri and along the Yellowstone; and the Kicked-in-their-bellies southward into the canyons of the Big Horn River and the Wind River Mountains of Wyoming. Such were the territorial divisions of the Crows about the middle of the nineteenth century (See Map 1).

Separation from the Hidatsas

The Crows did not always live in their historic homeland centered in the Yellowstone and Big Horn river valleys. The history of their migration to the Yellowstone area began with a semi-legendary account of a quarrel between two Hidatsa chiefs over the succulent tripe of a buffalo's third stomach, called manyplies.[1] The time for this falling out must have been in early spring when buffalo sometimes were caught in ice floes as they struggled across rivers and were swept downstream. After the slim hunting of winter, even a drowned buffalo was inviting to village dwellers along the Missouri who otherwise were dependent on a harvest of cultivated beans, squash, and maize.[2]

[1] Edward S. Curtis, *The North American Indian: The Apsaroke, or Crows* 4:38–39, 44–45. Edwin T. Denig, "Of the Crow Nation," ed. by John C. Ewers. Smithsonian Institution, *BAE Bulletin* 151:19.

[2] Charles Mackenzie, "The Mississouri Indians, A Narrative of Four Trading Expeditions to the Mississouri, 1804–1805–1806," in *Les Bourgeois de la Compagnie du Nord-Ouest*, ed. L. R. Masson 1:337. In 1804, Mac-

The hero of the separation and migration to the Montana-Wyoming homeland was a chief called No Vitals. No Vitals not only led the people to their promised land, but at Devil's Lake in North Dakota he fasted and received a gift of sacred tobacco seeds. Crows commonly associated their holy tobacco with star spirits, sometimes with the seven spirits of the Great Dipper, and at other times with the Creator-Sun, or with Old Man Coyote, the amiable worldly trickster.[3] In Crow legend, No Vitals was not always the recipient of the gift, but there was agreement that the character and the destiny of the Crow people were linked to the sacred tobacco. "They believe," reported the trader Denig in 1852, "that as long as they continue to preserve the seed and have in their homes some of the blossom they will preserve their national existence."[4] In the Crow view, gift of the sacred tobacco assured the overcoming of their enemies, and hence they were destined to be a great and powerful people. Indeed, they

kenzie made the following observation on the use of dead buffalo by the "Mississouri Indians" [Hidatsas and Mandans]:

Buffaloes and other animals are in immense numbers destroyed every winter by the Mississouri Indians. In stormy weather, whole droves run from mountains and plains to seek shelter in the woods which form the margin of the Mississouri; many of them, attempting to cross when the ice is weak, sink and are drowned, and, in the spring, both sides of the river are in several places covered with rotten carcases and skeletons of buffaloes, elks, &c.

These dead animals, which often float down the current among the ice for hundreds of miles, are preferred by the Natives to any other kind of food. When the skin is raised you will see the flesh of a greenish hue and ready to become alive at the least exposure to the sun, and so ripe and tender that very little boiling is required. The stench is absolutely intolerable, yet the soup made from it, which becomes bottle green, is reckoned delicious. So fond are the Mandanes of putrid meat that they bury animals whole in the winter for the consumption in the spring.

[3] Robert H. Lowie, "The Tobacco Society of the Crow Indians," American Museum of Natural History *Anthropological Papers* 21 (1920):176–89.
[4] Denig, "Of the Crow Nation," 151:59.

sorely needed to cultivate much holy tobacco, for in their historic situation they found themselves surrounded and pressured by peoples three times as populous.

Narratives of the Hidatsas corroborate major details of the Crow separation. Their common descent is also supported by a close linguistic relationship (Hidatsa-Crow) which is distinctive from other Siouan speakers in the area. Archaeological and ethnological evidence suggests that the ancestral Hidatsas moved out of an Eastern Woodlands location in at least three migrations and reached the Missouri in the vicinity of Mandan villages at three separate times. The first of these ancestral Hidatsa emigrants may have reached the Mandan villages as early as 1615.[5]

No Vitals and his River Crows, as they came to be known after separation, were part of the last wave of migrants. Unlike the earlier migrants, the Hidatsa-River Crows were hunters rather than cultivators. They apparently moved about in the Red River Valley, and in myth are reported to have traveled northward into Canada to escape the devastating fire that came from the sky.[6] Perhaps a destructive forest fire set by lightning emptied the area of game and led the ancestral Hidatsa-River Crows to the large lakes over the border. Later they returned to Devils Lake, where No Vitals received the celebrated gift of mystic tobacco. Continuing southwesterly, they struck out for the Missouri and made contact with the Mandans, as had their predecessors, in their villages at Heart River.

The nomadic Hidatsa-River Crows liked the taste of Mandan corn and for a time took up cultivation to supply the major part of their food. The Mandans urged them to build a village to the north but within sight of smoke from the Mandan villages.[7] They relocated in a village on the north

[5] Alfred W. Bowers, "Hidatsa Social and Ceremonial Organization," Smithsonian Institution, *BAE Bulletin* 194:481.
[6] Ibid., 300.
[7] Ibid., 15.

bank of the Knife River, and while there, the legendary quarrel over the manyplies took place. The River Crows picked up a new sobriquet, "Those-who-quarreled-over-the-paunch," and they set out in a northwesterly movement following the Missouri. Before the migrations were over, according to an anonymous account, the Crows traveled to the present province of Alberta, thence south to Great Salt Lake, and finally back to Montana, passing through the place "where there is fire," perhaps Yellowstone Park or a fiery coal pit.[8] For some unexplained reason, the ceremonious planting and harvesting of the Sacred Tobacco to which No Vitals attached his own destiny and that of his followers did not take place in his lifetime. However, the first harvest was linked most fittingly to Cloud Peak, in the Big Horn Mountains, a most sacred place where Crows went to fast and still do.

Popular accounts of the Crows, Hidatsas, and Mandans are too hazy to give a firm date for the separation of the Crows from the Hidatsas proper, or Minnetarees. It probably took place not long before the horse transformed the pedestrian ways of Indian plainsmen. Observing that the Crows deviated more widely than the Hidatsas from a "common parental/Siouan/language," Lowie estimated separation at five hundred years ago.[9] This certainly is too early. Using a list of Crow chiefs and an average years-in-office formula, Curtis concluded that the separation took place about 1676.[10] Fur trader Denig placed the break about eighty years before his time (ca. 1850) or about 1770.[11] Archaeological evidence suggests that the Crows may have located themselves in their historic homeland as early as A.D. 1600 or as late as A.D. 1750.[12] Fragments of pottery and traces of a few earth lodges

[8]"A Brief History of the Crow Tribe." Mimeographed, n.d.
[9]Robert H. Lowie, *The Crow Indians*, 3–4.
[10]Curtis, *The Apsaroke, or Crows* 4:38.
[11]Denig, "Of the Crow Nation," 151:19.
[12]Michael Wilson, "In the Lap of the Gods: Archaeology and Ethnohistory in the Big Horn Mountains, Wyoming," *Archaeology* 17 (1976):33.

both at Hagen, near Glendive, Montana, and at nearby Ash
Coulee pointed to Mandan and Hidatsa connections and suggested to Mulloy that the Crows may have settled there tem-
porarily in their transition from part-time cultivators to full-
time hunters.[13]

It is tempting to link the separation of the Crows from
the village cultivators and their northwesterly migration to
the stimulus of the fur trade. The introduction of trade sent
strong ripples far beyond the presence of the trader himself,
strengthening existing exchange and even extending trade net-
works. Lewis and Clark were amazed to see tools and axes
that their blacksmith had made during their winter layover
at the Mandan village reappear among Shoshoni Indians in
Idaho.[14] The tools passed quickly along the trade network in
the plains and were on location when Lewis and Clark arrived about six months later. Trade induced tribes to move
about and jockey for favored trade relations and locations.
Traders were blocked on their way to tribal enemies, especially if these enemies possessed more furs, were superior in
numbers, or if trade would help make them even more of a
threat.

Late in the seventeenth century the northeastern plains
were in the process of being transformed by trade impulses
from British posts on Hudson Bay, as well as by French
traders and explorers entering Minnesota by way of Lake
Superior and through ascent of the Mississippi River. In all
probability, the Assiniboins broke away from the Yanktonais,
and the Atsinas from the Arapahos, during the last half of
the seventeenth century in order to get a share of this trade.
In the light of these trade stimuli, Curtis's figure of about
1676 for the separation of the River Crows under No Vitals

[13] William T. Mulloy, "The Hagen Site," Univ. of Montana *Publications
in Social Science*, no. 1.

[14] Meriwether Lewis and William Clark, *Original Journals of the Lewis
and Clark Expedition 1804–1806*.

from the Hidatsa proper seems reasonable. The lure of trade introduced a heady basis for differences in leadership that could easily precipitate a quarrel over a division of meat. Sometime between 1700 and 1725, the River Crows in all likelihood moved into place in the Yellowstone–Big Horn river drainage. This area was a central base from which they could get horses and craft goods from Shoshonis, Flatheads, and Nez Percés to exchange for the metal goods, guns, maize, beans, and squash available at the villages of their Hidatsa relatives and the friendly Mandans. The Crows themselves produced elkhorn bows, arrows, lances, shields, buckskin garments, tipis, and dried meat for the trade.

The visit of the La Vérendrye party to the "Mantannes" in 1738 indicates that the village tribes were the center of a lively and extensive trade that united nomadic horseriders of the western plains with Hudson Bay posts through the Assiniboins and Crees.[15] By the time French and American traders began to push their way into the middle Missouri region in the last two decades of the eighteenth century, Arapahos and Cheyennes already had joined Kiowas and Comanches in a trade network linked primarily to the Arikaras. Behind them came the Teton Dakotas, who, early in 1800, mediated the trade in horses between the Arikaras and the Eastern Dakota groups. Trudeau reported that the French trader, Menard, traveled westward several times with the Hidatsas to meet the Crows in trade, perhaps as early as 1780.[16] Larocque,[17] however, was the first to spend some time with the Crows, in 1805, and, in 1807, Manuel Lisa established a post at the mouth of the Big Horn River. Al-

[15]From their location the "Mantannes" visited may have been Hidatsas rather than Mandans. See H. E. Maxo, "The Journal of La Vérendrye, 1738–39," *North Dakota Historical Quarterly* 8(1940–41):242–71.

[16]A. Phineas Nasatir, *Before Lewis and Clark: Documents Illustrating the History of Missouri 1785–1804* 2:381.

[17]François Larocque, *Journal of Larocque from the Assiniboine to the Yellowstone*, ed. L. J. Burpee.

though Lewis and Clark passed through Crow country, they
did not meet with the tribe.

Crows as Middlemen, 1740 to 1884

In their role as middlemen, the Crows became the envy of
more populous and covetous neighbors. Trade was sensitive
to quality goods, and the Crows came to value for themselves and for their trade the superior crafted goods and
horses. Thus they became noted for the stylish quality of
their possessions and horses. Blackfeet to the north were
among the earliest and most persistent raiders against the
Crows. Both Larocque[18] in 1805 and Zenas Leonard[19] in the
1830s witnessed battles in this never-ending see-saw struggle.
Determined that the American Fur Company should not arm
their enemies, Rotten Belly led a force of River Crows to
Fort McKenzie, a new company post situated on the north
bank of the Missouri some six miles above the mouth of the
Marias River. When they failed to take the fort by surprise
according to plan, the Crows attempted to starve it out before the return of the Blackfeet. Their hopes were dashed
when scouts sighted the smoke of the Blackfoot camp not
far distant. Blackfeet earlier in the year had killed Chief Little
White Bear; and Rotten Belly, who was desolated by the
death of his relative and the failure to take the trading post,
ended his own life with a suicidal run at a warparty of Blackfeet intercepted on their way back from Crow country.[20]
    In the 1820s the Crows experienced increasing conflict
with tribes drifting southwestward in search of favorable
trade locations.[21] Teton Dakotas followed Cheyennes and

    [18] Ibid.
    [19] Zenas Leonard, *Adventures of Zenas Leonard, Fur Trader and Trap-
per, 1831–1836.*
    [20] Denig, "Of the Crow Nation," 151:55.
    [21] Joseph Jablow, "The Cheyenne in Plains Indian Trade Relations 1795–
1840," American Ethnological Society *Monograph 19.*

Arapahos into the Black Hills region, but their forays against the Crows assumed menacing proportions only after 1850. There were other rivals, some linked to the Crows with on-again, off-again alliances: Wind River Shoshonis, Flatheads, Nez Percés, Atsinas, Comanches, Kiowas, Assiniboins, and, on occasion, Pawnees and Osages.

The location of the Crows did not permit easy access to trade goods. Boating supplies up the Yellowstone was arduous and subject to the ever-present threat of ambush by parties of Assiniboins, Atsinas, or Blackfeet. Unless the Crows were constantly in the vicinity of a trading post for protection, there was no way to prevent hostile raiders from running off post horses and sometimes slaying post hunters. Within three years of its founding in 1810, Manuel Lisa abandoned his Fort Raymond post at the mouth of the Big Horn.

Assiniboins, Atsinas, and Blackfeet acted in restraint of trade and didn't care if traders were slain, since they wished to maintain their own trade monopoly with the village tribes on the Missouri, especially with the Mandans. The Crows had to get through to the Missouri trading centers, and did so, as Mackenzie's description of trade between the Hidatsas and the Crows in 1805 reveals. A "pipe of friendship" was smoked by the two parties to establish their peaceful intentions and procedures. While this was going on, the Hidatsas

. . . laid before them a present consisting of two hundred guns, with one hundred rounds of ammunition for each, a hundred bushels of Indian corn, a certain quantity of mercantile articles, such as kettles, axes, clothes, &c. The *Corbeaux* (Crow) in return brought two hundred and fifty horses, large parcels of buffaloes robes, leather leggins, shirts, &c., &c.

This exchange of trading civilities took place dancing; when the dancing was over, the presents were distributed among the individuals in proportion to the value of the articles respectively furnished; this dance therefore is a rule of traffic. The Mandan villages exchanged similar civilities with the same tribe.[22]

[22] Mackenzie, "The Mississouri Indians," 1:346.

With posts so difficult to maintain and supply at such great distances, Ashley's American Fur Company in the 1830s introduced a spring "rendezvous," a meeting and camp-out at a location convenient for traders and Indians or white trappers with pelts to exchange. Such new trade arrangements were convenient for the Mountain Crows. They began to carry their furs to the North Platte River, where they also chanced a meeting with independent traders who could supply some of their pressing needs. Despite continual harassment from their enemies, the Crows marketed about five thousand buffalo robes annually during the 1840s, and after 1850 they were on good enough terms with the Assiniboins to trade in relative peace at Fort Union on the Missouri, not far from the mouth of the Yellowstone. In 1875, according to the Report of the Indian Commissioner, the Mountain and River Crows brought in a total of 9,400 buffalo robes and 95,000 pounds of other furs for a combined value of $71,125.

The Desperate Years, 1860 to 1884

Surrounded by strong, persistent, and daring enemies, the Crows had need of the trader as an ally. Their magnificent courage and fighting prowess were not enough to stem the thrust of the numerically superior Teton Dakotas, who began to penetrate the eastern frontier of the Crow homeland in the 1860s. At mid-century their situation suggested to trader Denig that the Crows could not "exist long as a nation."[23] He forecast their early extinction or reduction to the role of freebooters hiding out in remote places in the Rockies.

When enemies are neighbors, those who lie beyond commonly turn out to be friends and allies. As their situation became more threatening, the Crows began to see the white man, located on the other side of the Teton Dakotas, as their

[23] Denig, "Of the Crow Nation," 151:71.

logical ally. Today they still point with pride to the fact that they never warred against the Yellow Eyes, as they called the whites.

In 1825 the Crows journeyed to the Mandan villages, led by their famed chiefs, Long-Hair and Rotten Belly, and agreed (Rotten Belly of the River Crows abstaining) to permit the United States government to construct roads and forts in their territory and send exploration parties into their lands without molestation. The government promised little more than peace, friendship, and trade. In 1851, at Fort Laramie, Wyoming, the government renewed the request for free passage and the construction of roads and forts. At the same time, the government urged the tribes assembled to define their national boundaries and maintain peaceful relations by staying within them. The annuity in goods promised for fifty years was cut back to five years by Congress. In 1868 the government offered territorial guarantees in exchange for land. In delineating their boundaries under the leadership of Chief Blackfoot or Sits in the Middle of the Land, the Crows ceded some 38 million acres in exchange for reserved lands of 8 million acres. This treaty included annuities and provisions for instruction in farming and the compulsory education of Crow children.

The Crows, as other Plains tribes, depended on dreams accompanying or following a solitary fast to bring mystic power and foreknowledge of what they might expect and do. Dreams that foretold success brought the confident knowledge that the good thing wished for would happen. Plenty Coups, chief of the Mountain Crows, had a dream of great prophecy. His dream foretold the spread and dominance of the whites. He saw a great storm destroy three of the four trees high on a mountain. Only the tree that housed a Chickadee survived. The Chickadee was Plenty Coups' Medicine Helper, and Yellow Bear, one of the Wise Ones to whom Crows turned when seeking advice or the meaning of dreams, observed,

He was told to think for himself, to listen, to learn to avoid disaster by the experience of others. He was advised to develop his body but not to forget his mind. The meaning of the dream is plain to me. I see its warning. The tribes who have fought the white man have all been beaten. By listening as the Chickadee listens we may escape this and keep our lands. The Four Winds represent the white man and those who will help him in his wars. The forest of trees are the tribes of these wide plains. And the one tree that the Four Winds left standing after the fearful battle represents our own people, the Absarokees, the one tribe of the plains that never made war against the white man.[24]

The Man Person who appeared to Plenty Coups in his fasting-dream took him to the top of a hill and pointed to a hole in the ground out of which countless buffalo emerged. The buffalo spread over the grassy knolls and all disappeared. After that he saw bulls, cows, and calves of another kind emerge from that same hole. They were spotted and did not lie down like buffalo. These strange and unknown "spotted buffalo" spread over the plains and remained, eating the grass.[25] All this forecast a change of life for the Indians, with their lands delivered into the hands of whites. There was only one safe course—friendship with the victors-to-be. This cooperation began in 1866 with the building of Fort C. F. Smith well up the Big Horn River to protect migrants on the Bozeman Trail.

During the turbulent and critical years that marked the passage from their free and independent life to the repressive, boring, and disheartening existence on the reservation, Plenty Coups emerged as the respected counselor of the Crow people. He was their great chief, the one to whom they listened, and also the one to whom many whites listened. Plenty Coups was also the last of the old chiefs. When he passed away in

---

[24] Frank B. Linderman, *Plenty Coups, Chief of the Crows*, 73–74.
[25] Ibid., 62–65.

1932, the Crows acknowledged no new chiefs in the old way. The peace policy with the Yellow Eyes proved advantageous. Crows scouted for Custer and continued to serve army posts after the Battle of the Little Big Horn. Within a few years, they witnessed the capitulation of their deadly enemies, the Teton Dakotas, Those-who-cut-off-our-heads. They also saw Blackfeet, Cheyennes, Arapahos and others reduced one by one to reservations as the Yellow Eyes filled up the land with cattle, homesteads, towns, and railroads. The Crows succeeded in keeping a piece of their old homeland—their beloved Big Horn River valley with the surrounding Big Horn and Pryor mountains.

Prelude to Reservation Life, 1870 to 1884

The Crows began a more supervised life in 1870 when they were required to report to the agency at Mission Creek, near present Livingston, Montana. They still maintained a seasonal search for buffalo and pelts for trade, with calls at the agency for head counting and annuity payments. They also received new foods issued as rations. Flour for pan-fried bread and sugar for sugary coffee or tea were instant favorites, but rice was another story. Rice looked too much like the maggots found on old meat, so they dumped it out on the ground and kept the sack cloth. First contacts with forbidden fruits lifted from the gardens of settlers brought roars of laughter. Two young men tried to cook a watermelon over an open fire, and the first of those who got their hands on cantaloupes scooped the seeds into their mouths and threw away the rest. Buffalo were increasingly scarce, and Yellow Eyes were all over the land, building log cabins, digging up the earth in search of yellow rocks, and running stagecoaches along dusty roads. In the meantime, raid and counter-raid against their old enemies the Dakotas and the Piegans, continued.

Relocation of the agency in 1872 to a site on Rosebud

Creek near Absaroka made little difference in Crow pre-reservation life. They were nearer their traditional enemies and were more easily reached for army service. Indeed, recruitment of Crows for the final campaign against the Dakotas and their allies was not far off. After Custer's defeat in June, 1876, Crows in increasing numbers were recruited at Forts Keogh and Custer to help the army cope with marauding Dakotas, Cheyennes, Arapahos, and Piegans.

Adjusting the Old Life to the New, 1884 to 1950

In 1884 the Crows moved to their present agency near Hardin, Montana. Reservation life now began in earnest, for the life-sustaining buffalo were all but exterminated by white hunters. By 1888, there was nothing to ship back East but buffalo bones for the fertilizer industry. Without the buffalo and the freedom to move and act as a nation, the Crows, as other Plains Indians, were a people in limbo. There was little meaning to life now except for visiting, drawing rations, and watching the building of schools and churches for their new life. Yet, when the Ghost Dance religion (1887–1895) swept across the plains and kindled hope for a return of the buffalo and the freedom of the old life, the Crows stood by virtually unmoved. In 1887, Wraps up his Tail excited some Crows with a claim that he had a sword with power to kill soldiers at a distance. Belief in his mystic power was quickly shattered with the death of the fugitive "prophet" at the hands of a Crow policeman.

From 1884 to 1935 the Crows experienced strong pressures to exchange their ways for those of their white brothers. Catholic and Baptist missionaries urged them to surrender "false" beliefs and to give up curious customs regulating marriage and social relations. Policy-makers in the federal government felt the need to establish an institutional base that would turn Crows into legal citizens. Since the Crows traced descent through females, the government early in the century forced them into the patronymic descent and legal practices of American society. Practice of the old religion was forbidden, and Crow children were sent off to a boarding school at Pryor. Land allotment and "certification of competency" to handle one's own affairs were used to encourage the economic objectives and habits of "ideal" American citizens. Families scattered to their allotments to take up farming and ranching—attempts which soon gave way to the leasing of allotment land to non-Indian cattle entrepreneurs. In their eagerness to get Indians down on the farm, government planners failed to consider the investment in land necessary to establish a family-based ranching economy. Further, by insisting on the division of the already inadequate family land base through inheritance, the government delivered the Crows into the hands of local cattle barons.

Indecision, arbitrary decisions, doubts, and divisions were an inevitable accompaniment of this period of initial adjustment. Religion became the primary determinant of where one stood—whether for the apparent truths and promises of the alien ways, for the truths and practices of their own ways, or for the intermediate ground of the abstainer, the wait-and-seer. Choice at first divided the Crows by families, but in time individual differences cracked the solidarity of early parental or grandparental choices. However, the impact of these divisive choices was softened by the extraordinary accommodations worked out between the demands of tradition and those of the alien culture.

The period from 1884 to the end of World War II was especially critical, since the Crows during this time put together an adaptive culture base that preserved the core of their own culture and still accommodated to American society and culture. A sense of dependency and self-doubt was aroused in many Crows, and there was much considered reflection about truths and procedures. This introspection led to conversions to the new as well as to a quiet and stubborn assertion of old values and ways. The Crows learned to live with the imperious demands of their white mentors, and, to some extent, the government learned to be more responsive to the differences expressed in Crow customs and to their needs as human beings. *That* sensitizing of government would not take place, however, until the 1930s, when Commissioner Collier sought to revitalize Indian communities by rebuilding the traditional value base.

Reservation life brought the Crows face to face with the coercive power of American society and culture and introduced them to their single option. Church and state combined in offering the image of the "saved" and the "competent" Indian. The Christian missionaries taught the "true" doctrinal interpretation of the world and instilled the morality that should govern relations with fellow men. Government representatives provided instructional skills essential to farm or wage work and penny-saving management. At the Indian Agency, in reservation stores, schools, churches, and hospital, the Crows gradually learned the rules. The world outside the reserve, however, was not as simple. It aroused a fearful sense of strangeness, of humiliation, and of hostility. The Crows were not allowed to enter some stores and restaurants —those that made their contempt public with signs, "Indians and dogs not served here!" or the more subtle sign of discrimination, "We reserve the right to serve anyone." The alienation and hostility of the outside world accented the reservation as a symbol of refuge. The Crows nevertheless resorted to local and sometimes distant towns for the excitement of chance meetings with friends, novelty, drink, and the purchase of necessities. In frontier and rodeo celebrations at Billings, Sheridan, and Cheyenne, they recaptured some of the glamour of their ancient image by showing off their Indian dress in gala parades and dances.

At home on the reservation, however, they continued to regulate interpersonal relations largely by Crow custom. Direct functional or doctrinal conflict between institutions of the dominant society and Crow culture did not threaten the persistence of traditions. The Crows bowed to legalized arrangements connecting them administratively, educationally, religiously, and economically with the wider society, but these conditions did not prevent the regulation of marriage, respect behavior between relatives, and attainment of public recognition in accordance with Crow custom and expectations. Church and traditional marriage practices were sometimes combined, or traditional marriages were arranged without benefit of legal or church certification. Such "common law" and at times polygynous arrangements existed outside the legal framework because of administrative ignorance or benign neglect. The key to the persistence of Crow tradition lay in the fact that membership in a church did not conflict with fulfillment of kinship reciprocities. There was no reason to feel guilty if one invited "clan uncles" to a feast or gave them presents in exchange for blessings that brought success, good health, and long life. No doctrinal issue was involved if clan uncles or aunts were thanked for prayerful blessings, whether they were of Catholic, Baptist, Peyotist, Sun Dance, or Sacred Tobacco persuasion. It took a strong Christian to refuse to publicly acknowledge and repay a Peyotist relative who prayed for recovery from a serious illness. Only some evangelicals, such as Pentecostals, made doctrine a basis for opting out of the reciprocity system. The informal passing of invitations for feasts and give-aways honoring kin minimized conflict by leaving attendance and participation to the convenience of the individual. Staunch Christians avoided direct participation in traditional religious ceremonies, but they found it awkward to refuse the help normally expected of kin when a relative put up a Peyote meeting or danced in the Sun Dance.

The persistence of traditional habits and customs among the Crows made them appear more conservative than neighboring tribes of Plains Indians. Perhaps it may seem ironic and curious that the long-time friends of the white man were the most loath to part with their old ways, but it was not

Crow Tipis with ramada-type shelter at Crow fair. Note the war-
bonnet attached to pole. Crow Agency, 1939.

easy for the Crows to divest themselves of their self-image as
a nation with a distinct history and culture. The Crows lived
out their strong sense of national pride and identity in day-
to-day institutional arrangements that constituted the core of
their traditions. In coming face to face with American society
and culture, the Crows, with traditional pragmatism, reaped
the advantages of a pluralistic outlook. Crow pragmatism
protected them from doctrinaire schisms and permitted a
joining of old and new. Christian sons-in-law still respected
their mothers-in-law by not mentioning names, by not looking at them, and by not speaking to them with the same ease
as Crows who adhered more closely to traditional belief and
practice. Basketball players used eagle or hawk feathers blessed
by "clan uncles" to help them make baskets, because what
worked was more important than differences in doctrine.

Camp scene behind the tipis, Crow fair. Observe the line of meat drying. Crow Agency, 1939.

Peyotists invited "fellowship" with Catholics and Baptists, but were turned back by priests and ministers. Crow tendencies to combine or alternate between hospital and traditional therapeusis plagued doctors insistent on proper medical procedures.

While such pluralism proved worrisome to white mentors, it gave the Crows the flexibility to live out their image of themselves as Crow Indians while adapting to the radically altered conditions of reservation life. By the 1930s this adaptive culture was widely accepted. About 1910, Peyotism was introduced and integrated into the exchange system that united an individual with paternal "clan uncles" in a transfer of wealth in exchange for prayers for health and success. In 1941 the Sun Dance was added to help in the curing of sick-

Woman on Top of the Ground and Well Known Writing visit while working hides. Lodge Grass, 1941.

ness and, when war broke out, to assure the safe return of victorious Crow youths. The Crows were constantly on the lookout for ways to express their prestige reciprocities in reservation situations, including outstanding performances in school, sports, and politics. A daughter who left to become a nurse or nun feasted "clan uncles" and "aunts" and showered them with blankets and other wealth for dream blessings. The parents and clan relatives of players on a winning team immediately began plans to celebrate the victory of their athletes by distributing wealth, in their names, to paternal kin. In honoring paternal kin, the matrilineal "child" also accrued prestige and honor, since "clan uncles" literally sang his praises with "praise songs" and publicly called attention to his deeds. In such ways the adaptive reservation culture ac-

Women sorting goods for give-away. Lodge Grass, 1939.

quired new customs and became ever more relevant to the present. Contradictions between Crow and American institutions obviously existed, but none so serious that they could not be plastered over, accommodated, reinterpreted, or simply ignored, according to individual or group belief and practice.

Putting Political and Legal Machinery in Place

In the history of the American economy, industry inexorably has overtaken the rural economy in one region after another. In the postwar period, industry in the United States absorbed previously bypassed rural pockets when managers found their labor costs congenial or that local mineral resources now could be mined and processed with profit. At the same time, the government encouraged private capital investment in Indian development and encouraged Indians to use funds from land claims settlements to develop their own resources.

World War II and its aftermath signaled a strengthening of economic and political-legal relations between the Crows and the industrial world. Yet at war's end, Crow culture lacked the political-legal base to adapt to the demands and transformations that this industrial world would bring. More was needed than the advice and supervision of the Bureau of Indian Affairs. The Crows needed experience and confidence to permit them to take initiative into their own hands and adapt to the spread of an industrial economy which now lay at their very doorstep.

The 1920s marked the beginning of their political-legal "readiness training" as the Crows were forced to defend against opening up their unused lands to white settlement. Robert Yellowtail emerged as their public defender, and through his persuasive eloquence and use of the political process, Crow territory was preserved. Commissioner Collier, between 1935 and 1945, sought to extend this legal training by proposing that the Crows organize themselves as a political-legal corporation under the benign jurisdiction of the Commissioner of Indian Affairs. The intention was to bring more autonomy to tribal government by providing the business organization and legal machinery for entering into contracts with private investors willing to capitalize economic development on the reserve. The Crows rejected this national corporate model, despite appointment of Robert Yellowtail as superintendent. Instead, in 1948 the Crows formally adopted a constitution modeled on their own political tradition of a tribal council. They modified tradition to meet present conditions by allowing every adult member of the tribe to vote. This general council was empowered to elect a chairman, vice-chairman, secretary, and vice-secretary as well as members to ad hoc committees organized around new needs.

The federal government fueled the political-legal process by permitting itself to be sued in a judicial setting, the Indian

Claims Commission. The Commission's primary task was to adjudicate the Indians' claim that they had not been fairly compensated for ceded lands. The year 1946 thus marked a turn in relations with the wider society, since from this time forward the Crows would be increasingly involved in legal processes when settling differences with the government of the United States. Lawyers and anthropologists were hired to research Crow title to their historic lands in order to assure that fair payment was made for lands previously ceded. Retaining legal counsel and hiring researchers and consultants became standard operating procedure. The tribal bureaucracy also expanded.

In the 1950s there were intensified government efforts to draw Indians into more complete participation in American society. The main elements of this fresh effort consisted of an urban relocation program and the development of reservation resources. Programs once again were aimed at a long-held objective, that of developing among Indians "the self-reliance necessary to conduct their personal affairs with the same degree of independence as other American citizens."[26] The programming of reservation development was no longer one-sided. Government representatives now indicated a willingness to listen to Indian ideas about what should be done and how it should be done. Human-and-natural-resource surveys accompanied the intensified effort to link reservation communities to the wider society. These studies covered population trends, housing, employment, labor skills, education, ranching, recreation, and water use, as well as special projects. Survey reports regarding reservation social conditions, resources, and resource management now became important reading for Crow political leaders. Leadership required a wide range of knowledge about the reservation community and

[26]Commissioner, "Programming for Indian Social and Economic Improvement."

what was happening in its relations with region, state, and federal government.

As settlement claims came in, the Crows were confronted with managing money on a large scale under the watchful eyes of the Bureau of Indian Affairs and of senators who did not wish to see funds drained away in per capita payments. Sale of the Yellowtail dam site and recreation area on the Big Horn River brought $2,500,000 in 1958, with another $2,000,000 added in 1964 by a suit brought against the government. Land claims produced a settlement of about $10,000,000. After payment of attorney's fees, the Crows had to decide within five years how to invest and distribute nearly $14,000,000. Other critical decisions loomed on the horizon as private oil and coal companies, spurred by the energy search, sent teams of experts to negotiate the mining and gasification of Crow coal. If coal mining became a reality, future planning could not be left to a simple distribution of royalty monies, since the Crow tribe would have an annual estimated income of between $8,000,000 and $36,000,000, according to a low or high yield development. Serious social and environmental impacts would accompany coal industrialization, including radical alterations in Crow society and culture.

In the 1970s coal emerged as the key to the economic future of the Crows and the future of the reservation community. Coal might, as one enthusiast put it, make them all "millionaires." However, coal income would not last forever. Intense coal mining would deplete reserves within forty years. A minimal-use rate would stretch out resources over ninety years. Under a minimal-use rate, per capita payments from royalties as contracted would amount to less than fourteen hundred dollars annually—hardly a millionaire's income! Moreover, the preliminary report on coal development emphasized repeatedly that the "contemporary culture of the Crow Indian people will almost certainly be irreversibly changed. . . ."[27] The report projected that coal mining and gasification operations would alter the land surface, raise air pollution levels, place severe demands on available water, alter the ecology of areas miles distant from the mines, and reduce wildlife and fish. An influx of mine families would increase population in and around the reserve by forty-five thousand. In particular, Lodge Grass and Wyola would expand, and more housing, educational, recreational, police, and shopping services would be needed. Large numbers of outsiders could shift political power and lead to dissolution of the reservation itself.

Coal as an energy resource thus brought the Crows to the very threshold of the industrial world. If they were to plunge ahead without any controls over the rate and kind of development, they could expect every manner of dislocation and a rapid deterioration of life as they knew it. Even with a controlled rate of development, Crow people would change, and their culture would change with them. The challenge of new job opportunities would add a mining labor profile to the administrative, clerical, road maintenance, mechanical, nursing, farming, and social service positions already available. Air pollution control, environmental conservation, water use, and legal expertise would offer other opportunities for Crows to acquire new knowledge and skills closely linked to the functional operations of American society. To meet the demands of the projected population increase would require an expansion of existing services. As many as four hundred teachers would be needed for the estimated ten thousand new students; and to maintain community health and law and order, some forty-three doctors and forty to fifty policemen would have to be added.

In 1975 the Crows met in district meetings to discuss the

[27] Bureau of Indian Affairs, *Projected Coal Development, Crow Indian Reservation*, 269.

implications of coal in their future. Men were the sole discus-
sants at Lodge Grass and Wyola meetings. For the moment,
discussion focused on the legality of present coal contracts
and royalties per ton. Some persons also voiced concern about
the impact of coal mining and the establishment of coal towns
on their life-style. Mining towns were apt to bring drinking
and other social troubles. Strip mining in the Wolf Mountains
would destroy a favorite hunting ground. For the time being,
no decision need be made about quality of life, for the Crows
possessed mineral rights to coal lands lying north to the Yellowstone. While surface rights were ceded in 1904, mineral
rights were not. Mines in operation there produced modest
royalties and employment for about forty-seven Crow men.
Momentarily, the future awaited the outcome of a legal review of the coal contracts. If justice could not be found in
the courts, then, as one district speaker who favored nullifi-
cation of the unfair contracts put it, they could take their
appeal to the World Court.

In the perspective of history, up to World War II the adaptive processes of Crow culture in contact with American
culture were rooted in traditional social values joined to a
mystical view of the world and of causation. The post-World
War II period stressed new processes: negotiation, contract,
judicial review. The adaptation was businesslike, secular, and
wholly derived from the dominant culture. It appeared that
Crow culture, with the implementing of mining in the offing,
was about to enter a new era.

CHAPTER 2

Traditional Crow
Indian Culture and Society

Two Primary Relationships

Man-buffalo and man-enemy relationships conveyed a distinctive character to the Crows and a culture shared generally with other Plains tribes. The first, centered in the buffalo, left its mark in economic, social, and political arrangements for the production and distribution of life necessities and comforts. The second relationship made its impact in specialized warfare that provided the booty and daring exploits by which pre-eminent status and political influence were achieved. Both the natural and human environmental systems stimulated trade and the formation of temporary alliances. From their Montana-Wyoming location the Crows continued a brisk trade with their corn-raising Hidatsa ancestors and their Mandan neighbors, especially after the introduction of European trade goods.[1]

In providing food, lodge covers, and robes for clothing and bedding, the buffalo touched all the basic aspects of Crow life. Elk, deer, bear, and antelope were hunted also, but the Crows set themselves in motion largely along paths followed by buffalo in search of grass. The tendency of buffalo to dis-

---

[1]For information about traditional Crow culture I have drawn heavily on Lowie's detailed descriptions, supplemented by Curtis, Wildschut, Crow biographies by Linderman and Nabokov, and my own field notes.

perse in herdlets meant better hunting and eating when bands, the basic ecological and political unit, went their separate ways. The River Crow and Mountain Crow bands, when first reported, maintained a high degree of independence under their respective chiefs, Rotten Belly and Long Hair, and each frequented separate regions to hunt. River Crows preferred the lower Yellowstone and Musselshell drainage, while Mountain Crows spent winters in the Wind River Basin, moving in the spring to the Pryor Mountains and the valleys of the Big Horn and Little Big Horn rivers. The bands probably did not unite every year, but the ceremonial planting of tobacco or the pledge of a Sun Dance furnished occasions for tribal get-togethers. The buffalo thus left an indelible impression on Crow social and political organization, since the band and not the tribe was the most efficient unit for accommodating to the migratory habits of buffalo.

Maintaining protection from tribal enemies probably influenced the size of bands. The population of the Crow bands, from two to three thousand, was comparable to bands, and, at times, tribal groups mustered by the Kiowas, Cheyennes, Arapahos, and Teton Dakotas, as well as to village bands of the Osages and Pawnees. The Crows also possessed an organizational flexibility common in the plains because they could break down into smaller ecological and political units according to need or to a leader's ambitions. Each of the thirteen Crow clans had its own chief, who sometimes led his followers to special hunting grounds. With a total population of about 6,000, Crow clans averaged some 460 persons. If five persons are taken as typical for each family, Crow clans consisted of some seventy to ninety tipis or families. There was a tendency for two Crow clans to establish close ties for mutual aid, sociability, and cooperation when on the hunt.[2] While intermarriage dispersed members of clans throughout the two bands, a nucleus of male clansmen remained together because

[2]Lowie, *The Crow Indians*, 15–16.

of a preference for patrilocal residence after marriage. The linked clans Newly-made Lodges and Big Lodges constituted a dominant membership of the Mountain Crows. References to the tendency of the Kicked-in-their-bellies to separate from the Mountain Crows in 1860s undoubtedly described a clan of the same name that formed the nucleus of an incipient band.

Family and Clan

The Crows conformed to a common inclination among the Plains tribes for brothers to unite cooperatively to form joint or extended families as the basic productive unit. Husbands provided raw materials in the form of meat and hides, which their wives processed. The drawing of water, gathering of firewood, and collecting of plant foods were all tasks allotted to women. The woman's domain was the camp and all the arduous work necessary to day-to-day existence. For men, life consisted of the challenges and hazards outside the camp. Courage shown by a woman threatened by an animal or enemy was always applauded, but women were not expected to have courage in the degree expected of youths and men. The productive and protective roles of men accentuated man's worth and woman's dependence. Women fortified the men by singing their praises for deeds of valor and scorning cowardice with ridicule.

The individual, more so than his family, was integrated into a clan organization that not only regulated marriage but also determined basic civil rights, obligations, and protections. Here a person found matrilineally related clan brothers and sisters who contributed labor and wealth voluntarily to assist a man when he married or when he honored his clan fathers with a feast and gifts. These clan fathers (today's "clan uncles"), men of the father's clan, conveyed dream blessings to a "son" to assure that he would be successful and live a long life. They followed his childhood career, blessed

him, and made public note of his successes with praise songs
as he brought down his first partridge, deer, and buffalo. He
in turn presented them with food, horses, buffalo robes, moccasins, and other material items for their comfort. Arrangements for the feast and repayment of clan fathers were made
by the boy's father and mother. As a youth moved into manhood and took up the warrior's role, clan fathers continued
to honor him by walking him around the camp, all the while
proclaiming his valorous deed and singing a praise song.

Clan Bonds and Responsibilities

Crow boys and girls found themselves at the center of two
converging axes of kin, the father's and the mother's matrilineal kinfolk. A main axis bound a person to his own maternal lineage and clan relatives, obligating him to contribute
material wealth on need, and to protect and revenge clansmen in case of death at the hands of non-clansmen. Clan
wealth could be used to outfit a bride, to repay a medicine
man for a cure, to help in payments when sponsoring a
ceremony, or when honoring clan fathers in a public repayment for their sacred prayers and blessings. Contributions
were left up to the individual, since word of the need or
occasion was spread informally. A liberal gift for services
rendered was a point of honor and a basis for invidious
comparison and gossip. The most spectacular distributions of
wealth occurred when repaying a ceremonial father for guiding the mourner-sponsor through the Sun Dance, or at the
"give-away" when honoring and repaying clan fathers. Parents
initiated the give-away for children and young warriors, but
as a man established himself he took over the responsibility
and in turn organized give-aways for his children.

The importance of war exploits and acquiring booty in
horses focused attention principally on men, but women also
were honored publicly in give-aways. Wives were the centers
of less lavish distributions of wealth, which accented and

strengthened ties between relatives by marriage and their clans. Man and wife shared a common destiny linked to the mystic power that the husband acquired and that he used to bring success and protection to his family. They were partners, and a give-away by a woman's sisters-in-law not only brought honor but also linked her to the husband's clan fathers, whose blessings were essential to his career. A brother demonstrated loyal respect for his sister by giving her husband a horse to reciprocate the honor accorded her by the husband and his maternal kin. The friendly and cooperative reciprocities between brothers-in-law added a special institutional mortar to marital bonds. Indeed, there was no better way to show respect for another and to maintain kinship loyalties than by periodic gifts. Wealth distributed as gifts enhanced status, and at the same time brought return gifts.

A war exploit established a kind of instant status for the warrior, opening the door to public affairs and membership in a military fraternity or cult group. A warrior's reputation brought invitations to bless and name a child, or to recite a war deed in a blessing for success of the public ceremony. Any conferral of sacred "capital" in a blessing required a liberal gift in return. A passage of wealth was necessary for the validation of any personal right exercised in public, whether the rights were purchased from another, dreamed, or acquired through war exploits. The validation of right ranged over a vast spectrum including the right to sing a particular song in a certain use of a ceremonial name, or the right to speak direct to a mother-in-law or son-in-law, which was contrary to custom.

Kinship Rights and Obligations

A child was the focus of attention from both father's and mother's clansmen. Responsibilities and privileges largely followed the lead of these two matriclans, and kinship terminology accented the relationship. A mother's brother ranked as a close and protective relation and was addressed as "elder brother." A senior among a group of brothers stood the best chance of inheriting the wife of a mother's brother on his death. A mother's brother's children were like son and daughter, just the same as a real brother's children. A mother's sister's children also were brother and sister, as were the children of a father's brother. A youth was taught early to show special respect to sisters, real and classificatory, and after age seven or eight it was not proper for a boy to play with his sister. The bonding of brother and sister was based on mutual respect and mutual aid. A man's sister was expected to make moccasins for his war journeys, while he acted as a protective brother to her children. After a father, a brother had a right to dispose of his sister in wedlock. Sometimes, in grateful enthusiasm, youths bestowed sisters on war buddies who either had saved their lives or magnanimously satisfied a desire for a particular horse. It was a brother's duty also to inform a brother-in-law of a sister's (wife's) infidelity.[3] Despite the formal restraints imposed by custom, the bonds between brother and sister developed considerable strength. Pretty Shield told of a woman who accompanied Crow scouts with General Gibbon. She sought revenge for the death of her brother at the hands of the Lakotas. At the battle of the Rosebud, she contemptuously struck coup on a Lakota with her coupstick and, when her "half-woman" (female) companion shot him down, jumped off her horse and scalped him.[4]

One learned to be most respectful of a father's lineal kin and to take seriously their advice and admonitions. A man was always their "child," as they were his "fathers" and "mothers," even if the "father" happened to be a baby in a cradleboard. It was the right and obligation of the father's lineage mates to see that a son grew up respectful of Crow

[3] Frank B. Linderman, *Red Mother*, 132.
[4] Ibid., 230.

Jack Covers Up, herald for Lodge Grass District, announces the gift of a horse and goods during a give-away. St. Xavier, 1940.

customs, married a hardworking and loyal girl of good family, and made his mark as a courageous warrior. Making all of a father's lineage mates "fathers" and "mothers," irrespective of age, underscored the respectful tone of the relationship. These same "fathers" and "mothers" dreamed the long life and success of a "child," and in turn he feasted them and showed his gratitude with gifts of horses, robes, and shirts.

The Crows used anecdotal narratives to instruct children about the world and how to get along in it. On one parable four brothers chose different paths to success. One prayed only to the Sun, another used the sacred sweat to pray, while another fasted and prayed to spirit persons in the mountains. The fourth brother elected to feast his clan fathers and to follow their advice when interpreting his dreams or conveying their medicine dreams. Each of the brothers achieved

White Arm, with Blake White Man to his right. Lodge Grass, 1940.

relatively similar successes, but only the one who paid dili-
gent attention to his clan fathers reached a ripe old age.

The instructional interests of the father's matrilineage were
kept alive on a day-to-day basis by a peer-group that corrected
faulty behavior with funpoking and ridicule. Children of men
of the father's matriclan were joking-relatives. They played
practical jokes on each other, and sometimes shamed a person by describing his conduct in public and laughing at him.[5]
The code specified tit for tat between joking-relatives, but
sometimes resentment spilled over, and a victim sneaked up
on his tormentor and snipped off a braid of hair. Such loss
of hair was a deep humiliation, and retaliation was certain to

[5]Robert H. Lowie, "Social Life of the Crow Indians," American Museum
of Natural History *Anthropological Papers* 9:204–205.

Crow men playing the handgame. "Hiding" is an occasion for intense competition between dancing fraternities, clans, and districts. Pryor, 1941.

follow unless it was forestalled immediately with a gift of one or more horses, according to the amount of hair removed. Such action usually meant no more joking between the persons involved.

Warfare, Individuality, and the Open Society

Crow society was an open society. Individuals moved up in society by building reputations based on conventional war honors and the possession and distribution of wealth, largely measured in horses obtained in raids against the enemy.[6]

[6] Ibid., 228–40; Frank B. Linderman, *American: . . . Plenty Coups;* Peter Nabokov, *Two Leggings: The Making of a Crow Warrior;* Fred W. Voget, "Warfare and the Integration of Crow Indian Culture," in *Explorations in Cultural Anthropology: Essays in Honor of George Peter Murdock,* ed. Ward B. Goodenough.

Frank Hawk signals location of elk tooth counters hidden by opponent in handgame. Medicine drumming and singing gives aim to his choice. Pryor, 1941.

Retired warriors known to possess powerful spirit guardians constituted an elite that shaped the careers of young men by offering counsel and the protective influence of mystical power, *maxpe*, for a fee. A warrior–medicine man often dreamt about the enemy—where he was located, how numerous, and how he would be slain. Dreams also pointed the way to an enemy's horses and the numbers and kinds to be captured in the raid. Fortified with a prophecy of success and a talisman of power, a protégé went forth against the enemy confident that he could overcome the foe. Speaking of dreams with which Sees the Living Bull blessed him, Two Leggings recalled that "The events he foretold always came true. He had given me his medicine and now he gave me his dreams and visions which brought me many victories as the summers and winters passed."[7]

The reputations of great men thus were sprinkled profusely with "miracles." Medicine men discovered in dreams the exact number of days a Crow war party would take to find the enemy and the number that would be killed by the avenging party. With mystic powers men also lured buffalo into camp and drove rain clouds away from the Sun Dance. Men blessed with mystic powers drew others around them, like Iron Bull, whose sister's sons ate at his table daily and rode his fine steeds in exchange for herding Iron Bull's many horses. Iron Bull also generously fed a number of old men in his lodge daily, supplying the meat through his own skill as a hunter.[8]

Successes against the enemy built reputations and wealth in horses, a prime currency for strengthening social relationships and getting married. Success measured mystic capital and led to invitations to perform invocations for the public welfare. Four conventionalized war deeds measured a man and inducted him into the company of chiefs: striking first coup on the enemy; wrestling a weapon from an enemy; cutting loose a horse picketed in front of a tipi in the enemy camp and walking away with it; and leading a war party that brought back horses or scalps without loss of life.[9] The primary aim of warfare was not to take scalps but to build wealth and reputation by daring actions in which something was taken from the enemy in a way that demonstrated possession of an invincible mystic power.

There was an acknowledged, though sometimes disputed, ranking of chiefs according to number and kinds of exploits. Usually the most renowned, and consequently the one possessing the strongest "medicine," was recognized as chief of all the Crows. When the tribe gathered, he served as camp chief. As "He-who-leads-the-moving-band," he ordered their

[7] Nabokov, *Two Leggings*, 166.
[8] Curtis, *The Apsaroke, or Crows* 4:51.
[9] Lowie, "Social Life," 9:238–40; Curtis, *The Apsaroke, or Crows* 4:12–13.

movements and hunting until disasters at the hands of the
enemy signaled that he no longer possessed medicine powerful enough to protect the people.

The number of chiefs who completed the four conventionalized war deeds was never large, perhaps no more than
six to ten at any one time. They constituted an elite whose
advice was always given and respected in public council. Men
without war deeds were not permitted to speak, since without
successes against the enemy there was no sign that the advice
was supported by medicine helpers and would end favorably.
A chief or respected warrior enhanced his reputation by increasing the number of his horse raids, war parties captained,
coups struck, and scalps taken until he retired at about the
age of forty. After this time he continued his successes vi-
cariously and built his wealth through the careers of young
men upon whom he conferred dream blessings. A respected
warrior and chief was free to carry an eagle-wing-feather
fan as a public mark of distinction. His most prized possessions, however, were his medicine talismans and his medicine pipe wrapped in buffalo hide and stored in a cylindrical
rawhide container. This was the supernatural capital upon
which his reputation rested and through which he maintained
relations with younger men as well as with the society at
large.

Building a Career Together: Mentor and Apprentice

The Crows built their careers largely through a mentor-apprentice relationship. The apprentice "son" passed horses,
choice food, and other wealth of a material nature to his
mentor "father" in exchange for the mystical key to success.
Occasionally a ceremonial father obtained sexual privileges
with a son's wife, usually for giving ritual instruction.

A young man's petition for a share of the mystical power
was usually granted if the older man soon dreamt about a

successful war party.[10] Loan of a medicine feather or other talisman entitled the "father" to some of the horses taken by the "son." This loan-use relationship ended after the apprentice carried the medicine on four expeditions and rewarded his "father" with a horse or other wealth. Then the "son" became full owner of the feather or other talisman.

Power dreams and talismans bestowed by a medicine father were persuasive in leading others to join in and give the ambitious youth a chance to try out his leadership and war skills. An enterprising young man fortified his petition for more talismans, especially use of a medicine pipe, by striking a first coup or performing another conventionalized war deed. A medicine pipe was the coveted goal and prime symbol of an acknowledged war captain, or pipe holder. Sees the Living Bull, Two Leggings's clan father, to whom he had turned for power and instruction, finally promised to make a "great medicine that would permit me to go out as a war leader."[11] During the ritual conferral of power feathers, songs, face paintings, painted rocks, and weasel and horse-tail attachments, Two Leggings's medicine father told him that "he would give me something to make me a chief."[12] What Sees the Living Bull gave his "son" was his medicine pipe. He advised Two Leggings to put aside the pipe he was using, since he held the mistaken belief that he (Two Leggings) already was a chief.[13]

Every man on the warpath needed some token of power to protect himself and others. Without a talisman obtained from a renowned kinsman, a man was a nobody and fell into the category of a helper. As a helper he was ordered to get water, firewood, and meat for the comfort of others, and he had no right to any of the booty.[14] On the other hand,

[10] Lowie, "Social Life," 9:233.
[11] Nabokov, *Two Leggings*, 150.
[12] Ibid., 151.
[13] Ibid., 153.
[14] Ibid., 134–41.

a captain and pipe holder exercised complete authority over his followers and held the right to dispose of the booty obtained. The pipe holder organized the war party, obtained use of the medicine, and arranged for his followers to be present at the transfer in order to learn about the power of the medicine, sing the power songs, and take note of any taboos associated with the powerful talismans. The bond between the owner of the medicine and the captain who borrowed it, and his followers, was solemnized with a sacred smoke and a gift by each member to the owner. A captain's gift was hardly less than a fine horse.[15]

The authority of a pipe holder was seldom disputed. On the march a trusted friend sometimes carried the medicine bundle at the head of the column. At the appointed spot designated in a dream the captain halted his party, opened the bundle with appropriate ceremony, and offered a prayer smoke to get confirmation of the original dream. Strengthened by rehearsal of the bundle ritual, the sacred prayer smokes, songs, and face paintings, the party made itself ready to test the enemy and to turn the prophecy of success into reality.

While war offered the most frequent and striking examples of the mentor-apprentice relationship, the institution was invoked in almost every social relationship where mystical power was transferred. Religious ceremonials and fasting with bodily torment commonly involved the mentor-apprentice relationship. A mourner who sought revenge against the enemy by sponsoring a Sun Dance sought the assistance of a Sun Dance bundle owner and put himself under the instruction and guidance of his ceremonial father. By taking the proffered pipe, a "father" solemnized the relationship with his "son," who, along with his relatives, was bound to give wealth to the medicine father. The obligation to feast a father's clansmen and to give them wealth simply institutionalized the mentor-apprentice relationship within the kinship structure.

[15] Ibid., 136.

If a father passed a medicine bundle on to a real son who by descent belonged to a clan different from the father, the son was expected to pay a fee.

Mystic Power, Dreams, and Individuality

"Medicine" was not only the key to success, it also was the key to the individuality prized by the Crows. A man found individuality in the horse tracks he painted in yellow on his cheeks, in the short red lines drawn from the outer edges of his eyes, in the personal medicine song, and in the wolf tails trailing his moccasins, symbolic of first coups struck. A woman experienced much of her individuality in public ceremony through her husband, who, by warrior's right, decorated her face.

It was *my* face that he painted when he had gained that right by saving a Crow warrior's life in battle. And it was I who rode his warhorse and carried his shield. Ahh, I felt proud when my man painted my face . . . . After this I had the right to paint my face whenever there was a big feast or a big dance; and I did it because it was only showing respect for my man, Goes-ahead.[16]

For most Crows, the power that guaranteed success and public acclaim was sought in dreams and visions. Only a few persons seemed naturally blessed with power. On his own initiative a person sought out a medicine helper in a lonely fast, but a more reliable procedure combined the power quest with the purchase of power and guidance from a warrior of reputation. The necessity of offering some material inducement to the power giver was emphasized by offering to the spirit helper a finger joint or strips of skin carved from an arm or leg. The quester, fasting and wailing, conveyed the image of a pitiable pleader; and in offering a morsel of him-

16Linderman, *Red Mother*, 131.

self to the Sun, addressed that supreme spirit as if he were a father's clansman.[17] A seeker of power tethered to a post, or to the dragline of a horse, or to a series of buffalo skulls, always relied on a reputable mentor to insert the skewers in his flesh, to pray for him, and to look after him.

Women, too, had their medicine helpers obtained in fasts. There was Strikes-two, who put the Lakotas to flight by waving her root-digger and singing: "They are whipped. They are running away."[18] A Lakota captive, Feather Woman, obtained power from the mountain lion and taught her Crow husband, Two Faces, "how to make other people do as he wished by looking at them."[19] With the aid of her wolf medicine song, "I'm doing as you told me to do," Pretty Shield's mother stirred a dark cloud that rushed past them and thundered over pursuing Lakotas, permitting mother and daughter to escape.[20] Day-to-day hazards brought a touch of the miraculous into every person's life, and by his own actions a person became a vital part of that miracle.

Preparation for Individuality and Success

The individuality so highly prized by the Crows was set in motion, usually four days after birth, with a name-blessing ceremony. A warrior, preferably someone who had struck coup recently, was invited to bless and name the newborn. The infant was lifted through incense three times and then named after a striking war deed, such as Takes the Gun, or Takes the Horse. Such a name-blessing required payment as for any service or token of the sacred. Names were personal property, just as song and paintings, and men changed their names to call attention to war deeds. Men also were

---

[17] Lowie, *The Crow Indians*, 240.
[18] Linderman, *Red Mother*, 203.
[19] Ibid., 179.
[20] Ibid., 171–72.

given nicknames, as in the instance of Big-Shade, who was big and fat. When his "son" achieved a warrior's status, the younger man also took the name of Big-Shade, paying his clan father a horse. Girls picked up nicknames for their idiosyncracies just as young men did, but seldom changed their names. Sometimes a daughter's nickname followed not from her own quirks, but from those of a mother or other relative. Hits Herself over the Head received her name because her father's sister had hit herself over the head in anger with a stone-headed club.[21] On the other hand, a father, wishing to give his daughter the right start in life, might invite a renowned warrior to give her a name based on the strongest coup he had made.

Parental attitudes and actions encouraged assertiveness by a minimum of interference with a growing child's exploratory tendencies. Parents redirected the crawling child away from the dangerous fire, but in the case of an older active child, they introduced fear of the enemy and of underwater beings. Fear was useful in holding children at play close to camp. A child who cried or whined constantly received little sympathy, and they poured water up his nose. Parents and grandparents followed a principle of readiness and did not force walking or other skills on the growing child. They watched for clues that revealed the eager interest of the child to learn the bowman's art, or the skill of tanning, and then provided the necessary tools and relaxed supervision. Childhood playgroups supplied skill incentives and role playing as boys rode stick horses, hurled mudballs, sometimes loaded with hot coals, and counted coup, while girls pitched and packed their play tipis. Older brothers and sisters served as confidants, mentors, and protectors, for this was the obligation of older to younger, emphasized by the Crows in their personal relations.

Besides teaching a younger brother skills, the older was

21 Lowie, "Social Life," 9:216.

expected to supply his brother with tools as needed, whether lariat or horse. A grandfather also stepped in and organized a play group of boys into a war party of "magpies." He took them to the river, where they disguised themselves with mud, some wearing wolf skins, the symbol of scouts, momentarily borrowed from a father's gear. Then they stealthily made their way back to camp, where each attempted to filch some of the meat drying beside a mother's or other relative's tipi. If successful, a youth was given a stick symbolic of a horse, and he then recited his horse-coup before his fellows down by the riverbank, followed by the praise of his peers and grandfather. If he was caught in the act of making off with the meat, the magpie's mother rubbed the mud off his face, and he had only the solace of encouragement on the next try. The name magpie was appropriate for this group of poachers, since this fat blue-colored bird was very cheeky, ever hovering around, ready to lift a piece of meat from rack or campfire. Cooking and eating the filched meat was always a pleasure for the human magpies.

Warrior magpies never knew when to expect a real test of body or courage. On a cold and stormy morning they might be called from the warm fire in the tipi to a river filled with floating cakes of ice. Their mentor "tossed out a handful of peeled sticks into the water, calling out, 'Go get them Magpies!'"[22] Pulling off shirts and leggings, the magpies plunged into the icy waters, and he who brought out the most sticks claimed the coup. They learned, too, that grizzly bears possessed that cool, fierce courage, strength, and mastery of self so vital to a warrior's success and long life. The grandfather who named Plenty Coups one day held out the raw meat of a grizzly bear's heart to the eight-year-old. By eating some of the grizzly's heart, a boy took on the character of the fearsome bear. Later, it was this same grandfather who also called out Plenty Coups and some twenty other youths

[22]Linderman, Plenty Coups, 25.

to challenge a huge buffalo bull that had been wounded in the hunt. The bull was the center of attention for a circle of mounted hunters, and, as the youths entered the ring, the buffalo charged and scattered them. Then his grandfather ordered all youths off their horses and advised: "A cool head, with quick feet, may strike this bull on the root of his tail with a bow."[23] The first to do could count coup! Plenty Coups was off his horse in no time, and, getting out of his shirt and leggings, he advanced on the buffalo. He dodged the charge of the maddened beast twice, and each time struck him on the tail as he thundered past. No other youth was able to match the feat of the nine-year-old Plenty Coups.

The persistent challenge of physical danger and pain brought out the character of youths. All this, however, was a prelude to the dream-fast, the real test of success and of individuality. The vital importance of the dream-fast burst upon Plenty Coups when he was still nine years old. His older brother, whom he adored, was killed in a raid against the Lakota. Plenty Coups described his feelings: "My heart fell to the ground and stayed there. I mourned with my father and mother, and alone. I cut my flesh and bled myself weak. I knew now that I must dream if I hoped to avenge my brother, and I at once began to fast in preparation, first taking a sweat-bath to cleanse my body."[24]

The maternal uncle, a very special "elder brother," also helped and encouraged a "younger brother" to polish his riding, hunting, and war skills, and to fast. When going on a horse raid, a maternal uncle took a sister's son along to give him a chance to learn the arts of war. An older brother sometimes checked the wavering aspirations of a younger by forcing him to accept a reputation-making challenge he was on the point of refusing. This happened to Young Jackrabbit

[23] Ibid., 29–30.
[24] Ibid., 34.

when he was reluctant to commit himself to carry a no-retreat staff for his military fraternity.

All declined to smoke, then they came towards me. Someone asked them, "Whom are you looking for?" They answered, "Young Jack-rabbit." I was seated in the rear and tried to hide. They brought the pipe to me, but I refused to accept it. One of the pipe-carriers was my own older brother. He seized me by the hair, struck my chest, and said, "You are brave, why don't you smoke the pipe?" He wished me to die, that is why he desired me to smoke the pipe. He said, "You are of the right age to die, you are good-looking, and if you get killed your friends will cry. All your relatives will cut their hair, fast and mourn. Your bravery will be recognized; and your friends will feel gratified." I took the pipe and began to smoke. They asked me whether I wished to have a straight or hooked staff. I chose the hooked staff. My comrade also smoked the pipe.[25]

This was no actual death wish on the older brother's part, but, in conventional language, pointed the younger man to the challenge of a warrior's courage and reputation.

When things did not go right in the building of a young man's career, a concerned father or a father's clansman took the problem to his bed and came up with a prophetic dream or vision. This happened to Bull Chief, who at the time carried the name of Bull Weasel, bestowed by a father's clansman. A buffalo helper spoke to Bull Weasel's father and outlined what he should do. His father called Bull Weasel to him and said, "I will make a man of you."[26] First Bull Weasel sweat-bathed and purified himself in the smoke of his father's incense. Next his father covered Bull Weasel's body with yellow ochre and tied a red eagle feather in his hair. Then he drew two lines [in red?] diagonally across both arms. These would bring good luck, one for striking coups, the

[25]Lowie, *The Crow Indians*, 177–78.
[26]Lowie, "Social Life," 9:217.

other for taking guns from the enemy. His father explained to the young man that "These two things are what we like among our people. If you perform these deeds I will rename you. The first time you strike a coup that is not disputed . . . and also get a gun, either at the same time or later, I will give you a new name. Bull-weasel is not a good name for you, so you had better have it changed."[27] Following his father's vision-instructions, Bull Weasel accompanied the first war party going out. He not only captured a gun from the enemy but also counted a coup on him. His father then renamed him Bull-Chief, and under this name he went on to distinguish himself as a war leader and pipe holder.

Reputation, Influence, and Political Power

Human and environmental factors, together with the social mobility made possible by free access to the mystical capital of success, tended to diffuse the bases for political power among the Crows. The unity of the tribe was always compromised by ecological rhythms that dictated dispersal throughout nine months of the year. The band thus was the primary unit for day-to-day living and decision-making, and the tribe was a temporary federation united by a need to repel hostile neighbors with populations greater than the Crows, and to get together for social and ceremonial activities. Since food was always a prerequisite for congregating, the grazing habits of buffalo and the four seasons were paramount considerations. Band leaders of the Mountain and River Crows governed some two thousand to twenty-five hundred people, mustering five or six hundred tipi households. In the winter, clans often separated from the band and sought out favored shelter and winter hunting areas. Family and clan visiting added and subtracted the population of

[27] Ibid.

bands from year to year. While patrilocal preferences localized the male population of a matriclan, exogamous marriage
sent their sisters into other clans, sometimes affiliated with
the same band, sometimes with another band. The dispersal
of sisters to other clans at marriage meant that each band
mustered some representation from each of the thirteen clans.
It was the localized male population of the matriclan, however, which provided a support base for a clan chief. Intermarriage between affiliated clans facilitated concentration of
a stable male population for the band.

A band thus functioned simultaneously as the primary unit
in their seasonal migrations and as the primary political and
military unit. A divine hand, the medicine father, was behind
every leader, guiding him to ample food for his people, giving
him victories over powerful enemies, and keeping his people
free of disease. Failure to find food on the hoof or disasters
at the hands of the enemy instantaneously dissolved the mystic charisma enshrouding the leader and led chiefs voluntarily
to relinquish their places at the head of the moving band.

Clan, band, and tribe provided a tiered organization in the
concentration of political influence and power. Military fraternities and the acquisition of war medicine bundles provided competitive challenges and peer acceptance for a warrior ambitious to build a career from clan to band and then
to tribal chief.

Chiefs and the Political Process

A chief automatically wore a number of hats. First, he belonged to a matrilineal clan, of which he was the head. Next,
he wore the hat of a band chief. Then, if his career and mystic
charisma warranted, he was chosen to lead the nation during
the summer hunt and act as its political head and protector.
At this time a Sun Dance and other religious and social
ceremonies usually took place. In some degree, band and

tribal chiefs exerted influence and control according to the forcefulness of their personalities, strengthened by the popular view of the success of their mystic powers. Crows recall the bullying tyrannies of One Heart and of One Eye, but in each instance the person wronged turned on and bested the tyrant, who was intent on taking a wife or making off with choice cuts of a kill.

The diffusiveness of power-bases and the fact that the Crows followed only a winner meant that the ambitious had a hard time building a set of followers to seize and maintain power. Chiefs did not govern simply because they were born into populous clans or bands or belonged to military fraternities with large memberships. People connected outstanding successes with possession of mystic power. When daring horse raids and coups struck on the enemy followed one after the other, a warrior's chances for invitations to perform public service and eventually to lead a clan or band increased. A string of successes suggested that the man was specially favored by his spiritual medicine father. Invitations to public leadership usually were mediated by older men of enduring reputation, the wise ones of powerful medicine dreams. The Crows always looked for the man with the right mystic power for the task at hand. Even the famed Red-bear (clan-band-tribal chief), when leading the Mountain Crows, gave way to a leader of a buffalo hunt selected by the military police. Their choice fell to a man who not only was a good warrior and hunter, but also had power to control the wind, which Red-bear had not.[28] In a confrontation with the Lakotas, Chiefs Blackfoot (clan-band-tribal chief) and Iron Bull deferred to old White on the Edge, who possessed the greater medicine. White on the Edge thus carried the pipe at the head of the moving camp at this moment of danger and smoked with the chiefs to learn what lay ahead while the stragglers

---

[28]Curtis, *The Apsaroke, or Crows* 4:112.

caught up.[29] Band and tribal chiefs also surrendered the direction of the camp during important religious ceremonials, such as the Sun Dance.

Wise leaders commonly relied on the counsel of wise elders and war captains with powerful medicines. Informal councils usually were held in the tipi of the band chief and were started with an invocation of spirit beings through the offering of a prayer smoke. A herald of good voice and warrior reputation announced the decision to move the camp. He called upon the women to strike their tipis and be ready to move out at sunup, and he reminded the military fraternity in charge of the camp to arrange for scouts and a rear guard to keep stragglers in line. On the move, a band or tribal chief carried his medicine pipe at the head of the column, surrounded by his wise medicine counselors. At the predetermined campsite, his tipi became the center of the encampment, but the Crows were not inclined to make use of a circle unless enemy attacks were feared. Halting at noon was customary in order to make camp—the pitching of tipis and the attendant chores of preparing a meal and watering the horses. If people needed meat, the chief called upon trusted scouts and told them where they should look for buffalo.

Public confidence in a chief rested in large part on the example of his life and successes, and in his wise counsel. At times a chief mounted his horse and exhorted his young men as he passed by their tipis. He advised them, in effect, to "keep their powder dry" and to put trust in their medicine fathers.

Young men, to cut sticks is easy; to dry them is easy. See that your quivers are full of strong arrows. . . . Have extra sinew with you; if one bowstring breaks and you have no other, the enemy will kill you. Now your hearts may feel at ease, but you know not what may come at noon. . . . These bows and arrows and guns

[29] Ibid., 93.

are our teeth [in analogy to animals]. Have them good. You are young; your bodies are yet pure, and the spirits are looking down upon you. I have brought you to the foot of the mountains that you may climb where the air is pure—go there and fast. We have heard that the spirits are looking for their children; perhaps you are the ones they are seeking. Behold those who have many horses and large lodges; see how well they live; think how they do it. As you climb the mountains and fast, make offerings that someone may grow up among you strong enough to carry on what I am doing. You must remember that I cannot always be with you.[30]

A wise chief invited his young men to his tipi and beside the warmth of his lodge fire, he counseled them about life matters. They were told to look upon him and note his face. "All men have flesh, all men have hearts, all men know what death is."[31] The Crows were surrounded by enemies, and when the enemy charged they must remember their hearts. Let them look around and they would see that old men were few. Whether they were to live long or to die young was up to the mighty spirit powers. Taking care of their horses was important, and they should see to it that their wives had clean horses to ride. They should look after the old people and share meat with the poor, avoiding the foolish behavior of peoples around them. They should remember that a wife is a devoted follower and nurse in sickness. While a brother sleeps blissfully on, a wife eases the suffering of a sick husband. Wives should be treated kindly and never beaten. "Only the wise will hear my words; the foolish will hear them now, but when I pass they will forget," was a final admonition.[32]

A chief's reputation was measured in great part by the size of the war parties his intentions generated. Those in deep mourning for a son or husband lost to the enemy commonly petitioned noted chiefs to undertake a revenge expedition.

[30] Ibid., 10.
[31] Ibid.
[32] Ibid.

Petitioners brought wealth in horses and leather goods as inducement, and sometimes a wife-to-be. Everything was solemnized with the offer of the pipe, an old man of the party making his petition by laying his hand on the head of the warrior chief. A wise man usually invoked his medicine father to discover a prophecy of success before he accepted. In 1858, Red Bear led a war party of some two hundred men against the Wind River Shoshonis, accompanied by the wives and sisters of those to be avenged.[33] As a battle loomed, lesser men turned to a leader with outstanding medicine and promised him a horse, were he to wrest a gun from the enemy or to count coup. The promise of either feat called for a blessing on the spot, and leaders held a stock of dreams ready for such occasions, as Crows do today. Among the Crows, success instilled confidence, and the desire to share in this success started a flow of wealth to the successful.

Chiefs controlled the camp and maintained order in the hunt, but had no part in settling private wrongs. Family and clan prevailed in fights and even homicides. The personal reputation, influence, and mediatory skills of chiefs always were factors in keeping the peace. A murderer could take temporary refuge in a chief's tipi while relatives collected horses and other gifts to avert revenge. The better part of wisdom, however, was for the offender to get out of camp until tempers cooled.

Military Fraternities

Historically the number of military fraternities varied. About 1860 there were six: Hammer Owners, Lumpwoods, Foxes, Muddy Hands, Big Dogs, and Bulls. The youngest and oldest warriors belonged to the Hammer Owners and Bulls, which is as close as the Crows came to an age-graded organization. Those between seventeen and fifty were active in the other four societies. Membership in the Lumpwoods and Foxes, and

[33] Ibid., 83-91.

probably in the Muddy Hands and Big Dogs, was divided into younger, middle-aged, and older men. In 1860 the Lumpwoods and Foxes were dominant both in rivalrous competition and in numbers. The Foxes may have numbered about a hundred and the Lumpwoods "considerably higher."[34] As reservation life approached and then became established, the military fraternities gave way to the Hot Dancers and Crazy Dogs, the Crows purchasing the songs, dances, and regalia from the Hidatsas about 1875.[35]

Military fraternities constituted an important focus of power, since they united men in companies of warriors without regard to family, clan, or band. A man counted on fraternal comrades in clans and bands other than his own. Each military fraternity had its own leaders, insignia, dances, songs, and decorative paintings for body and paraphernalia. Each year at springtime, when the Crows got together as a nation, the warrior fraternities selected new officers and learned which of them would police the band on the move, on the hunt, and in camp. During this springtime reorganization the "soldier" societies competed fiercely to see who had the greatest number of war honors, horse raids, and even seductions. At the first snowfall, however, competition slowed as the warrior societies settled in for pre-winter feasting and socializing.

Fraternities actively recruited promising warriors with the lure of horses and other wealth. When a member was killed by the enemy, a man's comrades-in-arms were prominent mourners and displayed their grief by jabbing arrows into legs and arms. To fill the place of the deceased with a son or brother was a frequent thought and desire. If a man lost horses to the enemy, or if his tipi was damaged in a runaway, he counted on his comrades to make good much of his loss.

[34] Lowie, *The Crow Indians*, 173.
[35] Ibid., 206–207.

In the company of his peers a man found not only loyal comrades but also the challenges that brought out his courage, endurance, skill, and leadership. Exemplary bravery was expected and cultivated. Those honored with straight or hooked staffs among the Lumpwoods, or a bearskin belt among the Big Dogs, took on obligations not to retreat in battle. The otter wrappings of the Lumpwood and Fox staffs were constant reminders to the bearers that they must live up to the fighting heart of this small but tough animal. A young warrior could refuse the pipe offered, but on the fourth offering he usually touched his lips to the stem and smoked, unable to resist the praise and bullying of comrades and older brothers. Bulls who drank at a watering "trough" during a fraternal dance publicly gave notice that they would stand strong against the enemy. In exchange for taking on the enemy challenge they were entitled to wear buffalo-head masks and to snort and charge the crowd.[36] Usually two or four men in each fraternity let their comrades know that they would be exceptionally brave in the face of the enemy. These men were considered as "made to die," and through their bravado the fraternities maintained a lively competition for courage and coup counts. Though not a fraternity, the Crazy-dog-wishing-to-die persons expressed an ultimate disregard for body and life ideally expressed in the military code. A man became a Crazy Dog because he could not live with humiliation suffered at the hands of a girl friend or a bully, or because of a crippling injury that kept him from a warrior's life.[37] He dramatized his distinctiveness by doing everything the opposite of what was normal. To get a Crazy Dog to mount his horse, he must be told to dismount. The vow to die brought not only momentary public acclaim but also the solace of girl friends.

Striking out in a blaze of glory rather than living in the

[36] Ibid., 205–206.
[37] Ibid., 331.

shadow of public shame was the warrior ideal. Famed chiefs Rotten Belly and Red Bear followed this code when, frustrated by failure and humiliation, they made suicidal runs into the midst of the enemy.[38] All vows for extraordinary bravery ended with the beginning of the new year and winter season, when snow and cold cooled tempers and ambitions to joust with the enemy. Leaders and standard bearers of the fraternities now relaxed and waited for the springtime elections when fresh candidates could take up the enemy challenge. Now they feasted and smoked together and got ready for the spring competition, especially rivalrous between Lumpwoods and Foxes. If the Lumpwoods counted more horse raids, picketed horses taken, guns captured, and coups struck, they could "capture" the wives of Foxes with whom Lumpwoods had carried on affairs. Mortified husbands tried to maintain a demeanor that signaled a cool lack of concern. For parading the captured wives, the Lumpwoods had to have a horse that had been used to rescue a comrade from the very midst of the enemy. Wives so captured seldom were kept long. The competition kept the camp in turmoil, and women who expected to be captured sometimes sneaked out of camp to the shelter of a widow in mourning.[39] When the wife-capturing ended, the military fraternities sent out war parties to see who could strike the first coup. The competition between Lumpwoods and Foxes was so intense that they usually staked their songs and dances. The losers faced a slow social life, since their rivals had the use of their songs and dances for the season. The fraternities had their heroes, and these men focused competition, as between Bull of the Lumpwoods and Crazy Pend d'Oreille of the Foxes. Crazy Pend d'Oreille, following his vow, clashed with the Cheyenne enemy and fought

[38]Denig, "Of the Crow Nation," 151:54–55; Curtis, *The Apsaroke, or Crows* 4:50.

[39]Lowie, *The Crow Indians*, 186–91; Thomas B. Marquis, *Memoirs of a White Crow Indian*, 195–97.

his way out, while Bull was killed. Since that time Bull's songs have remained the property of the Fox society."[40]

The fraternal military system carried out important public functions. First, it provided an organization for instructing youths in the ideals and skills of warfare and of career building. Second, it served as the proving ground for leadership. Third, the military fraternities controlled conflict by policing the camp and hunt.

Youths in their early teens began a formal introduction to the martial arts by joining the Hammer Owners. Their officers imitated the warrior fraternities in having two leaders at the head, two at the rear, four bearers of staffs ornamented with the hammer emblem, and four members dedicated to exceptional bravery, the "made to die." Hammer owners carried out sham battles in which staff-bearers fulfilled no-retreat obligations, and those "made to die" counted coups on animals encountered in their forays.[41]

Most Hammer Owners were fifteen or sixteen years of age. They accompanied war parties and were capable of fighting beside their elders. Bravery was paramount, for to die in glory was a thing to be remembered, while to live without public acclaim and wealth obtained by raiding was no life at all. To be selected as a staff bearer brought the first public recognition and a company of associates who voluntarily followed one of the staff bearers. During the dancing and festivities at the annual reorganization, the father of the chosen staff bearer feasted his company or offered them a smoke prayer from his war medicine pipe.

The Old Bull society, according to Leforge, was "made up of the ultra-moral people, the uplifters, the conservative and well-behaved element among the Crow."[42] The Old Bulls served as a public conscience, since they warned against med-

[40] Curtis, *The Apsaroke, or Crows* 4:18–20.
[41] Lowie, *The Crow Indians*, 202–204.
[42] Marquis, *White Crow Indian*, 197.

dling in family affairs and spoke out against "vicious habits in general."
The officers of all military fraternities were expected to exhibit a warrior's courage and public sacrifice. The very organization of the military fraternities linked to inter-fraternity competition provided the constant challenge by which the qualities of leadership could be elicited and kept in fine tune. There was little opportunity to rest on one's laurels, because the challenge was constant and intense.

The military fraternities shared power with the chief, since they were given the task of keeping people in line on the march, in the camp, and on the hunt. A chief belonged to a military fraternity, and it is possible that this influenced the choice of the fraternity to serve as police for the year. Since decisions regarding movement of the camp and where they would search for buffalo were left to the chief and his wise counselors, the military fraternities acted as the executive arm of chief and council. They controlled conflict in camp by thrusting a medicine pipe between those fighting. In a surround hunt, they restrained hunters until the hunt chief gave the order to charge the buffalo. Before the hunt they watched the herd to prevent poachers from making early kills and running the buffalo off. If they met with resistance, the police could kill the poachers' horses and even the poachers themselves.[43] Leforge once joined two sportive Crows in inciting buffalo to run into the camp. Found out, they were escorted by the "dog-soldiers" to a distance outside the camp and told to stay away from camp for one moon.

It was a distressing penalty; but we stayed out. We should have received much worse treatment had we violated the order. We often hungered for food as well as for society. A few times our sweethearts slipped out at night and placed food where we could find it, but they too were watched and were subject to penalty if dis-

---

[43] Lowie, *The Crow Indians*, 5.

covered, so this could not be depended upon as a regular comfort to us. In addition to our ostracism, our people had to pay fines by gifts to other people, particularly to the families whose lodges had been damaged. My adopted father had to give away many ponies as a consequence of my indiscretion. . . .[44]

A Crow who murdered his companion on a war party was whipped by the police, his horses were confiscated, and his relatives gave horses to the relatives of the murdered man.[45]

The hunt for buffalo during the summer and ceremonies like the Sun Dance required a host of able-bodied men. The summer also was prime time for trying one's medicine and luck in a horse raid against the enemy. Chiefs sometimes banned warparties and depended on the military fraternities to hold the young men in camp, but some always slipped past the guard.

Political-legal restraints usually arose where a collective need existed. For the Crows, the buffalo hunt, camp, and line-of-march represented three domains where their collective welfare was at stake. In these three areas they empowered chiefs and military fraternities to exercise stern controls backed by fines, ostracism, and even death.

Religious Organization and Ceremonialism

Authority was no less diffuse in Crow religious organization than in the political domain. Medicine bundles grounded in individual revelations, with transfer fees, turned religion into the exercise of private rights to ceremonial rites and the sale of same. Crow religious organization was diffused among a number of cult groups. These cult groups were of two kinds: the informal association and worship of those possessing special medicines, whether received as a gift from a spiritual or

[44] Marquis, *White Crow Indian*, 145.
[45] Ibid., 183.

human medicine father, purchased, or obtained through inheritance-purchase; and the worship of those joined by virtue
of adoptive-purchase of right to membership.

Informal Associations

Activation and use of mystic power in the service of a private
or group need was fundamental to Crow religious belief and
practice. The Cooked-meat Singing and Bear-song Dance illustrated worship by an informal association of those who
shared the same mystic power, although the specific manifestation might be different.

The Cooked-meat Singing belonged to those with rock
medicines given to the Crows by the famed Dwarf and his
companions who inhabited the Arrow-shooting-rock toward
Pryor Gap. An owner, man or woman, usually received a
dream communication in which a bear might be dancing and
eating wild berries and chokecherries. A stick was given to
those invited to take part in the ceremony, and at the time
of invitation these persons would confer a dream and blessing favorable to long life.[46] Not all rock-medicine owners
were invited, but the intention was to get together those noted
for their medicine fasts, dreams, and success.

The singing was designed to assure a plentiful supply of
food in the months ahead. They chose a time when there was
plenty. The chokecherries and berries were ripe and many
buffalo were at hand. Getting meat ready for the ceremony
required those persons invited to form hunting parties. They
needed chokecherries to mix with the tender flesh of the buffalo's backbone and fatty bone marrow when making pemmican for distribution. Handling the individual rock medicines

[46]Robert H. Lowie, "Minor Ceremonies of the Crow Indians," American
Museum of Natural History *Anthropological Papers* 21:353; William Wildschut, "Crow Indian Medicine Bundles," ed. John C. Ewers, *Contributions
from the Museum of the American Indian Heye Foundation* 17:100.

and praying for good luck, health, and wealth in horses was a central feature of the ceremony.

After the first singer has finished his songs, he passes his bundle to the next person on his left. As the medicine passes from one to the other, it is held in both hands and each one present presses it to his heart with a prayer for good luck, health and happiness; kisses the rock, and passes it to the next one on his left. The bundle is handed to both men and women, and even to children who may be present. As it is passed a bead or two is given to it and the hope for good luck is voiced. Some people donate feathers, hoofs, beaver tails, etc. The feast-giver is given blankets and larger donations, including horses.[47]

Rock-medicine owners were obligated to honor paternal clansmen since an owner could not sing his medicine songs until he had given a gift to paternal clansmen who were present.[48] Only someone with bear medicine was allowed to mold the bear effigy out of pemmican and distribute the pemmican balls that were eaten to end the ceremony.

Those with a spirit helper inside their bodies were the main performers of the Bear-song Dance. It took place in the fall when the berries were ripe and bears danced among them. Pemmican was distributed. In all probability someone dreamt of bears and berry patches.

A cottonwood post was set up in the middle of the dance ground and decorated with a bearskin with claws.[49] After painting and dressing themselves in a special tipi, the spirit dancers were led in procession by a woman, with men bringing up the rear. Each danced to the bearskin post to the beat of the bear song. At some point the spectators saw horsetails, weasels, buffalo tails, shells, feathers, bear teeth, red paint, bullets, and eggs issue from the mouths of the performers, a

---

[47] Wildschut, "Medicine Bundles," 17:103.
[48] Lowie, "Minor Ceremonies," 21:355.
[49] Ibid., 21:358.

sure sign of a spirit inside a person. To get the spirit back inside, a dancer had to be smoked with sweetgrass, bear root, or some other special incense.[50] Those with horsetail spirits were noted for their many horses, while those with buffalo tails were noted for healing wounds.[51]

The ceremonial opening of any medicine bundle brought together a temporary group of invited or interested worshippers. The tipi of any Sun Dance, Rock, War, Shield, Skull, Pipe, Hunting, or Curing medicine owner thus at some time was turned into a house of worship.[52] Medicine bundles effectively decentralized religious ceremonialism among the Crows.

Adoptive-Purchase Ceremonialism

The Crows possessed three adoptive-purchase ceremonies, notably the Tobacco, Horse Dance, and Sacred Pipe. Of these the Tobacco was uniquely their own, whereas the Horse Dance ·and Sacred Pipe were obtained from the Assiniboins and Hidatsas respectively.[53] THe northern range of the River Crows brought them into more frequent contact with their Hidatsa ancestors and northern tribes like the Assiniboins. Historically, the River Crows were well-positioned to transmit ceremonies and dances from the northeastern sources to the Mountain Crows. However, the Sacred Pipe ceremony was introduced to both the River and Mountain Crows at the treaty meeting at Knife River (1825), when Rotten Belly and Red Feather at the Temple were adopted by the Hidatsas.[54] The primary aim of adoption was to obtain a share of

[50] Ibid., 359.
[51] Ibid., 356.
[52] Nabokov, *Two Leggings*, 109–11; Wildschut, "Medicine Bundles," 17:109.
[53] Lowie, "Minor Ceremonies," 21:329, 335.
[54] Curtis, *The Apsaroke, or Crows* 4:179.

mystic power in association with a medicine bundle. Usually the adoption was carried out by a bundle owner and spouse. Adoption established a protective "father-" or "mother-child" relationship that endured throughout life and extended the range of kinship support for both parties. If "father" and "child" were of different bands, there was always a home away from home. Adoption also brought admittance to an exclusive group, which owned the same medicine and was privileged to exercise all rights thereto. There may have been as few as six and as many as thirty who owned the horse medicine at any one time. In 1910, some twenty-six persons were said to be holders of the Sacred Pipe.[55] No estimate of membership for the Tobacco "chapters" can be made, although thirty of these developed. Not all, however, were operational at the same time.

The Horse Dance medicine brought wealth, principally in horses, while the Sacred Pipe was meant for curing. Tobacco was given to the Crows to overcome their enemies, and extraordinary success in horse and scalp raids was a common element in the lives of those who started up Tobacco chapters. Sore Tail, who began the Eagle chapter, had but seven mules to move his tipi before a visitation from eagle, the Sun's messenger, that came to him during a fast. Afterward he "came to have a herd of from seventy to a hundred horses," and the mountain-sheep dress of his daughter was loaded with "elk teeth down to her feet. . . ."[56] Sore Tail's tipi furnishings were covered lavishly with buffalo hides and red flannel trade cloth. He was so rich that a constant stream of ambitious young men came to his tipi. He tied a blue medicine feather to the necks of his "children" and sent them forth to count many a success. Indeed, Sore Tail was so saturated with good luck that even a woman whom he blessed returned victorious from the war trail.[57]

[55] Lowie, "Minor Ceremonies," 21:329, 347.
[56] Lowie, "Tobacco Society," 21:129.
[57] Ibid., 129–30.

Despite the specificity of power associated with medicine bundles, the Crows were inclined to test through a vow the mystic power associated with medicine bundles in all kinds of personal contexts. Vows fulfilled thus added new powers to a medicine bundle or ceremony. For example, a man with a sick relative vowed to join the Tobacco society if recovery occurred; and at times a man vowed to have a secular dance performed at his expense if he succeeded in a war raid.[58] In this way outstanding medicine bundles and ceremonies took care of three basic human needs: plenty of good things to eat, good health, and a good supply of wealth for comfortable living, social reciprocity, and status.

Adoption was initiated by either the "child" or the "father." If a "child" had a dream or could point to a vow fulfilled, a "father" was more easily persuaded to carry out the ceremonial adoption. Competition, or perhaps a need to get more wealth at the time, was important in determining the direction of initiative for adoption. Tobacco chapters actively recruited members with spontaneous gifts of horses, clothing, and invitations to take food.[59] Gray Bull arranged a trade-off. If his "father" would give his war medicine, Gray Bull would consent to adoption.[60] While adoption involved an exchange of wealth, adopters usually counted on a fourfold return at least. Gray Bull mustered thirty-three horses with the aid of his relatives and those of his wife when the two of them were adopted.

Without wealth at hand, the poor still purchased a share of the mystic power by performing routine services. Strikes at Night tanned fifteen buffalo hides for a Horse Dance bundle owner who wished to put up another tipi. Strikes at Night's husband was blind and they were poor, so he suggested that she not specify any payment but request adoption. This she did at the moment of accounting, and though the bundle

[58] Lowie, "Minor Ceremonies," 21:363.
[59] Lowie, "Tobacco Society," 21:134.
[60] Ibid., 135.

owner was not very happy, she consented. The adoption paid
off, for many horses and other wealth flowed into the hands
of Strikes at Night and her husband.[61] A man without available wealth usually hunted for his adoptive father-to-be. During one winter Lone Tree bagged ninety buffalo and some deer
for a Horse Dance bundle owner who consented to adopt him.
He, too, became a rich and lucky person.

One night my wife and I were singing Horse society songs. I wished
to win something. The next morning I went for my horses and as
soon as I got to my herd I saw two new race horses among mine
with brand new saddles and blankets. I knew they had belonged
to Sioux Indians. On another occasion my wife and I were singing
at night and the following morning I found a similarly equipped
horse. I sang another tune and found a stray horse in my herd.
Still another time I got a stray mare. On another occasion I sang
and a short time afterward I killed an enemy and struck a coup.
Another time I sang with my wife, using the dewclaw rattle. The
following day there was a big fight and I captured the prettiest
horse ever owned by a Sioux, a red-eared pinto, and in addition,
a perfectly white horse. The people crowded around to look at my
horses.[62]

Since Lone Tree obtained some of the root for keeping up the
strength of horses, he sold his power to make a horse a race
winner. It only took a small portion placed in the horse's
mouth.

The Adoption Process

While specific elements of adoption varied with regard to the
Horse Dance, Sacred Pipe and Tobacco societies, there were
patterned similarities that are best followed through Lowie's
more detailed account of the Tobacco adoption, drawing upon

---

[61] Lowie, "Minor Ceremonies," 21:330–31.
[62] Ibid., 333–34.

other societies for comparison and illustration. Leaving aside the origin revelation that served as a charter for the ceremony and the exercise of ceremonial and transfer rights, events were ordered as follows: first, the formal invitation or request to be adopted; second, preliminary instruction in the songs and dances; and finally, formal adoption and transfer of medicines.

The protocol of an adoption-invitation called for a giving of wealth and was usually sealed with food made as a gift at a sit-down feast with the adopter and members of his society. While among the River Crows, an old man from another band called to Bear Gets Up that he should come on over and eat. Suspecting something, Bear Gets Up took along a horse as a gift. They feasted him and gave him buckskin leggings and moccasins, which he later learned were given in hope of adopting him into their Tobacco chapter.[63] At the name-blessing of a newborn, parents sometimes vowed that, if the baby lived, they would consent to adoption into the Tobacco chapter of the namer. Although the warrior who named Cuts the Picketed Mule was killed on a war raid, the man who had initiated the slain warrior brought food and clothing to the deceased's wife and obtained her parents' consent for adoption of the boy into his own Tobacco chapter.[64] Bird Above's son was so sick that he became impoverished paying out horses and other wealth for doctoring. Finally, when the boy was deathly sick, Bird Above told those present that he would let himself be adopted into the Pipe society by the first pipe owner who asked him. When none extended an early invitation, Bird Above requested initiation. Apparently he was prompted by the suspicion that the son was falling sick again because the vow of adoption was unfulfilled. The adoption was carried out the same day.[65]

By taking food together, the adopter and the initiate struck

[63] Lowie, "Tobacco Society," 21:134.
[64] Ibid., 134–35.
[65] Lowie, "Minor Ceremonies," 21:340–41.

up a special relationship in which the adopter became the "father" or "mother" of the initiate, who in turn became a "child," "son," or "daughter."[66] The procedure was carried out in four sessions, at each of which the initiate was presented with the larger amount of food to take home.[67]

These preliminary sessions during the winter initiated the adoption with feasting and the selection of four songs that were given to the "child." The "father" usually chose the medicine songs displayed by members of the adopter's society. At the fourth meeting, following the Tobacco procedure, "the father asked some man to sing a certain one of his songs, saying, 'I want my child to have that one.' He thus selected four songs. As each song was chosen, the owner sang it, and then rising took the candidate's arm and danced with him while the other members sang. The candidate was now pledged to pass through the initiation in the ensuing spring."[68]

The formal adoption and transfer of medicine usually took several days. The procedure was divided into eight stages: (a) consecration of the novice(s) and medicines in a special tipi; (b) ceremonial exit from the consecration tipi and procession to the adoption tipi; (c) consecration of the adoption tipi with coup blessing and prayer smoke with a pipe by the adoption-lodge owner or pipe lighter; (d) public transfer of songs and dances, with the novice dancing between or with donors; (e) payment of wealth to adopters and to fraternal brothers who have contributed wealth or services for the novices; (f) invocative purification and good-wish blessing of the novice through a "washing" or sweating, including the medicines; (g) display of medicines and the taking hold of the medicines by the initiate, presented by the "father" or secondary donor-sellers, thereby indicating that he is not afraid

---

[66] Ibid., 341.
[67] Lowie, "Tobacco Society," 21:137.
[68] Curtis, *The Apsaroke, or Crows* 4:63.

and can manage the power within; (h) feasting of the medicine-sellers and ceremonial parents by the initiate and his relatives, to terminate the proceedings.

In the Sacred Pipe preliminaries, two pipestems were stuck in the ground about a foot apart and an ordinary calumet was laid before them. A pipe bundle containing the pipe to be transferred was displayed also in the middle of the "father's" tipi. Other pipe holders came on invitation, and one acted as a pipe lighter. He was an important ceremonial figure, since he initiated prayer and consecrated the paraphernalia. Smoking together in prayer was an essential preliminary to acting together in any enterprise, just as the "smoking" of pipe and drums in the fragrant incense of sweetgrass was a prerequisite to their use. While the drumming and singing of four medicine songs went on, the "father" and "mother" gently swayed the "son" and "daughter" from side to side as if handling babies, for adoption called up the notion that the initiate and his wife were about to be born.

A childbirth theme was pervasive in much of the adoption ritual. "We will let this boy be born" was a signal for building the adoption tipi in the Tobacco ceremonies.[69] In the Sacred Pipe, a warrior feigned with awl in hand the ear-piercing normally carried out on the fourth day when an infant was named with a coup blessing. At the feast given by the initiate in gratitude to the adopters, the adopter came as a father to greet his newborn and brought choice meat, along with fine moccasins and leggings.[70] The "father" fed the initiate as if he were a young eagle, as the "novice throws out his hands/as wings/ and four times moves his mouth in imitation of the young birds."[71] On the fourth try, he actually took the meat and all then partook of the feast.

The painting and dressing of the candidate and his wife in

[69] Lowie, "Tobacco Society," 21:137.
[70] Lowie, "Minor Ceremonies," 21:347.
[71] Ibid., 343.

accordance with ceremonial rights owned by the adopter took place in a special tipi. In the Sacred Pipe, the novice escaped from his "father's" tipi to the consecration lodge, where he was finally tracked down. Four warriors recited their deeds, and the first must have struck coup on the enemy inside a tipi; otherwise, no one could enter.[72] Tobacco members assembled in the consecration lodge, resplendent in their finest dress and ornamentation, with medicine bags slung down their backs. Those with the right to paint the tobacco plant insignia, validated by dream, vision, or inheritance-purchase, set to work. Women usually painted women and men painted men, but there were some members who had the right to paint both sexes.[73] At the request of the "father," a member painted the initiate, and then the "father" undressed his "child" and reclothed him in a fine outfit. Now they were ready for the procession to the adoption lodge, led by the wife of the owner. She feinted leaving at each of three songs, and exited on the fourth. At each of four stops along the way they sang a medicine song and then they entered the adoption lodge with its centered altar-replica of the original tobacco planting ground.[74]

As in the Sacred Pipe, only a warrior who had surprised and scalped the enemy in his own tipi could pronounce the coup blessing upon entering the adoption lodge. He alone was qualified to set fire for the kettle of boiling tongues that young men of budding reputation claimed by thrusting red-striped sticks through the lodge walls.

The accent was on success in war, growth, and the good things of living. A warrior gave his coup blessing and brought back a cupful of water for the owner-builder, who gave him some fruit. The owner-builder or another designated warrior consecrated the occasion by pointing out how well-off the people were at the time. The sacred tobacco was coming up,

[72] Ibid., 345.
[73] Lowie, "Tobacco Society," 21:149.
[74] Ibid.

there were plenty of berries, and everyone was free of sickness.

A pipe lighter circulated a pipe in prayer among the men and the candidate to solemnize the occasion and bring good luck to the transfer. Following a brief interlude of singing and dancing by women, the candidate arose and danced to each of his four songs. This was the moment for payment, and a herald told relatives to bring the wealth forward— stick tokens for horses, blankets, quilts, money, and other valuables for the "father." The lodge owner usually claimed two pieces of the red cloth preferred in offerings to the Sun. All ended this portion of the Tobacco adoption drama by taking up a green branch and, to the accompaniment of a special song, moving the branch up and down to make the leaves dance as if growing.[75]

In the Sacred Pipe the "father" brought his "child" into contact with growth and the continuous renewal of life by placing him on crossed blades of grass, symbolic of spring. The candidate's birth was dramatized in a ceremonial washing and by the feigning of ear piercing by a warrior who offered a coup-blessing. The washing and ear piercing were repeated four times, in accordance with the Crow ceremonial number. The "father" symbolized the good luck and wealth that would follow his "child" by drying his head with quilts, blankets, strips of red calico, and even money, each of which was thrown away to the assembled guests after use.[76] Prayer sweating in the Tobacco adoption was the counterpart of the baptismal-cleansing of the Sacred Pipe. Both ceremonies expressed good wishes for the newly adopted.

A "child" furnished willows for the sweat lodge according to instructions of the "father." The number was in sets of four, perhaps as many as ninety-four willows or more, according to the rights of the sweat-lodge owner. He also brought stones from the mountains. Four warriors, who built the

[75]Ibid., 139.
[76]Lowie, "Minor Ceremonies," 21:347.

sweat lodge, received four pieces of red calico from the wealth brought by the candidate's relatives.

Medicine bags of members sweating were placed on top of the buffalo hides or quilts covering the sweat-lodge frame. Usually the owner began the singing after four cups of water were poured on the four heated stones. This was a time for singing medicine songs and telling good dreams. From four cups of water they went to seven, then ten, and finally paid no attention to the count. At each interlude a respected warrior handled the water and four songs were sung. Before each start the cover was raised with a good wish—for life until winter, for plenty of berries, or a spring free of sickness and death. The "father" had a special wish for his "child." After washing him with bear-root and water, or rubbing him down from head to foot with the sage so sacred to the Sun, the "father" wished a full life for his "child." "All you above, let him live to be an old man."[77]

Before the fourth and last good wish, the medicine bags were taken down and faced to the mountains. The men plunged into the water after the prayer-sweating to assure that sickness or any other thing which threatened well-being or life would be carried downstream away from them.[78] All that remained was for the candidate to claim his medicines from the bags placed atop the sweat lodge by members of the adopting society. The timing of the prayer sweating usually determined whether the newly adopted claimed his medicines in the afternoon or the next day.

The newly-adopted Tobacco member selected power tokens from medicine bags displayed in a large tipi. He chose mystic tokens from any bag, a choice that usually included four bags of the sacred tobacco itself. Frequently the four who gave songs during the preliminary instruction were ready with sound advice on the stronger medicines. Whatever was chosen—eagle

[77]Lowie, "Tobacco Society," 21:141.
[78]Ibid.

tails, a shell, a wolfskin, a whip, or an otter skin—was paid for with a horse or other valuable. Each item was accompanied by a song, which would be taught to the initiate.[79]

In transfer of the Sacred Pipe, the "father" rubbed his "child" and family down with a corn cob. A dancer who carried and danced the pipe during the transfer preliminaries began the assembly of parts for the bundle by "smoking" the pipe in sweetgrass or bear-root. The pipestem of red willow in its red tassels, red flannel strips, or red-headed woodpecker skin recalled the sun or sun's glow on the clouds at sunset. The eagle-tail-feather fan linked the pipe to the most powerful of birds and messenger of the Sun Person. The duck-headed mouthpiece was shaped in memory of the duck who succeeded in bringing mud from the deep waters to build the earth. A tubular stone pipe usually was a part of the medicine-pipe bundle. Always there was a corn cob, which stood for the "first fruit of the earth."[80] Wrapped in red or black flannel, with buckskin and otterskin ties, the bundle was placed on the back of the candidate's wife. In the future she carried the Sacred Pipe from camp to camp, always well dressed and riding a fine horse.[81] This was the moment when the skull bearer and those he had initiated gave expensive clothing to the wife, including elk-tooth dresses, and received horses and other valuables in return.

The physical transfer of medicine was almost matter-of-fact, as in the selection made by the candidate in the Tobacco adoption. When someone with an indwelling spirit was a "seller," the initiate sometimes took fright. This happened to Strikes at Night in her Horse-medicine adoption. Her "mother" had an eagle inside that popped out of her mouth as she danced.

At the fourth song she whistled and made the eagle wobble. I could hardly move. I stopped dancing when she got close, seized her by

[79] Ibid., 142, 157–61.
[80] Wildschut, "Medicine Bundles," 17:115.
[81] Lowie, "Minor Ceremonies," 21:346.

the armpits and gently rubbed down her arm. Everyone was glad and I heard expressions such as, "The poor woman got it after all." The woman told me to return the medicine to the spread. Then they smoked and sang four songs they wanted to give us, whereupon all got up to dance. They gave me a rope for the left hand and a whip for my right and bade me make a circle with my right. Then I and my sons, one on each side, danced to the four songs. After the fourth song . . . I got the medicine bundle . . . , which I carried on my back. I received instructions how to burn incense and how to hold the eagle. . . . .[82]

At some point all candidates were told to make ready a grand feast for the adopting members and others in attendance. It was the Crow way to send everyone home filled with food and good feelings for others. The feast for Sacred Pipe members was the scene for a final episode in the transfer of the medicine bundle. The adopter came as if he were a father greeting his newborn son and symbolically fed him. When all were feasted, the newly-adopted was instructed to get a lodgepole and to place the pointed end inside the tipi. In turn the "father" pointed the pipe toward his "child" for him to grasp. Enfolding his "child's" hand around the stem, the "father" sang four songs and formally announced, "Now I give it to you."[83] The initiate attached the medicine pipe to the lodgepole and raised it among the poles of the tipi. To effect a proper transfer, the "father" on four successive days raised the pipe on the pole and took it down at night. On the fourth night he wrapped the pipe in its bundle and tied it to a lodgepole above the seat of the new owner, at the back.

Corporate Nature of Crow Medicine Societies and Worship

It is not far-fetched to view the Crow medicine societies as corporations from which the candidate purchased common

82 Ibid., 332.
83 Ibid., 344.

or preferred stock according to his ambitions and means. An original visionary, according to the rules, sold shares of his mystic capital three times. At the fourth sale, he sold out. Through purchase-adoption, a person became a stockholder with the right to sell shares. All members of the corporation participated in any sale arrangement, but convention restricted them to the sale of a single medicine song, or to a selection of private medicines initiated by the purchaser with the aid of the "father" or other member-consultant. There seems little doubt but that the procedure of purchase-adoption accounted for the association of a group of worshippers sharing stockholder rights in a mystic capital, as manifested, for example, in the Horse Dance, Medicine-Pipe, and Tobacco societies.

Purchase-adoption conveyed an exclusive membership and opened the door to participation in all the ceremonial and public activities of the society. For Tobacco adoptees it meant the right to take part in the worshipful cultivation of tobacco, planting in a plot assigned to the Otter, Weasel, Strawberry or other "chapters" according to membership. There was also a sharing in the personal and family well-being, which the prayerful cultivation and worship of the medicine tobacco, with all its good wishes, conveyed. There were further rights and social perquisites for the ambitious. One acquired the right to build the adoption lodge, or to build the medicine sweat lodge through purchase from their owners. There also was the right of mixing the tobacco seeds for planting, following a special formula. Rights to songs, ceremonial drumming, singing, and painting also awaited those who dreamed, for a dream was a sign portentious of a future purchase.

The diffuse quality of Crow religious organization thus issued from a development of ceremonial associations organized around the sharing of mystic powers by members recruited through purchase-adoption. The Crows forged a tight fit between religion, career, and social standing. Those with surplus mystic capital to sell were warriors, or retired warrior-dreamers whose successes against the enemy and dream predictions affecting life and well-being, came true. The curing of illness was a right conveyed by a spirit medicine father at a time of fast, or by purchase from an established curer. In final analysis, worship among the Crows was a right acquired from a spirit or human owner of power by fasting, dreaming, or purchase. A dream communication usually was a prerequisite for taking the initiative or considering that the power association was validated. Worship thus was a highly individualized expression of personal success, social reputation, and personal well-being. However, this individualized worship always coincided with traditional ceremonial conventions and instruction given to the original owner of a medicine bundle. In the Medicine-Pipe adoption, the "father" transferred the pipe by attaching it to a lodgepole because of Tattooed in the Face's exploits in connection with the medicine pipe, in which he rescued a Crow marked for sacrifice to Sioux war arrows during a Sun Dance. Confronting the Dakota with their own medicine pipe, he won release by jumping safely from one buffalo skull to another and then walking along a lodgepole that joined the last of the seven skulls, all the while carrying Young Buffalo Calf Head on his back.[84]

[84] Wildschut, "Medicine Bundles," 17:117–19.

The Traditional Crow Sun Dance

Introduction

The Arapahos, Cheyennes, Crows, Blackfeet, Sarsis, Teton Dakotas, Kiowas, Atsinas, Assiniboins, Plains Crees, Plains Ojibwas, Sisseton Dakotas, Wind River Shoshonis, Comanches, Utes, Hekandika Shoshonis, Poncas, and even the Kutenais west of the Rockies shared a ceremony commonly classified as the Sun Dance. The Hidatsa *NaxpikE* and Mandan *Okipa* ceremonies likewise exhibited elements that related them to the Sun Dance ceremonial complex.

The origins and history of the Sun Dance in the Plains are unknown and can not be reconstructed adequately from a comparative analysis of traits shared or absent in the individual tribal ceremonies. From his comparative analysis Spier determined that the Cheyenne, Blackfeet, and Atsina Sun Dances were the most elaborate of all, hence these peoples may have originated and developed the ceremony.[1] Tribal traditions are useful in following probable lines of borrowing suggested by trait-comparisons. The Kiowas acknowledge that

[1]Leslie Spier, "The Sun Dance of the Plains Indians: Its Development and Diffusion," American Museum of Natural History, *Anthropological Papers 16.* See also, Harold E. Driver and Alfred A. Kroeber, "Quantitative Expression of Cultural Relationships," Univ. of California *Publications in American Archaeology and Ethnology 31.*

they took over a Sun Dance mannikin from the Crow.[2] Shimkin, using the narrative of trader Alexander Ross, traced the Wind River Shoshoni Sun Dance to the Kiowas.[3] A Comanche who was familiar with the Kiowa Sun Dance joined the Shoshonis and introduced the ceremony to them. The Comanche was Ohamagwaya, or Yellow Hand, who reputedly came to the Shoshonis about 1800 and was recognized as one of their chiefs in 1820.

The rationale for the Sun Dances of the several tribes varied. It included the themes of seasonal renewal, growth and replenishment, and the acquisition of mystical power. While these themes received differential emphases in the individual tribal ceremonies, the acquisition of mystic powers and the mobilization of power for war commonly were intermingled with private intentions and public concerns. This was the case especially for tribes in the high plains. Although associated with the Sun, the spirit person at the hub of the universe, a buffalo spirit commonly appeared as the figure who bestowed the ceremony.

Among the Crows the Sun Dance was the primary instrument for mobilizing mystical power to effect personal revenge against the enemy. A fasting mourner, overwhelmed by loss of a beloved brother or father, received supernatural direction to pledge the ceremony. Hence, the Sun Dance was performed at irregular intervals, perhaps every three or four years.[4] The last Crow Sun Dance took place about 1875, and is said to have ended disastrously when the pledger rushed from the lodge, no longer able to bear the torment of his fast.[5] Some

[2] Hugh L. Scott, "Notes on the Kado or Sun Dance of the Kiowa," *American Anthropologist* 13 (1911). James Mooney, "Calendar History of the Kiowa Indians," BAE *Seventeenth Annual Report.*

[3] Demitri B. Shimkin, "The Wind River Shoshone Sun Dance," *BAE Bulletin 151*, 409–14, 472–73.

[4] Lowie, *The Crow Indians*, 297.

[5] Robert H. Lowie, "The Sun Dance of the Crow Indians," American Museum of Natural History *Anthropological Papers* 16:5; Nabokov, *Two Leggings*, 80.

sixty-six years later, in 1941, the Crows borrowed the Wind River Shoshoni Sun Dance in its entirety.[6]

Origins and Functions of the Sun Dance

The precise point in time when medicine bundles associated with the Crow Sun Dance originated, is not known.[7] Ewers considered Sees the Tent Ground's bundle to be quite old, with a projected date of about 1775.[8] On the other hand, Scott estimated the Kiowa borrowing of the Crow Sun Dance mannikin as early as 1760.[9] Use of a Sun Dance effigy was reported to Lewis Henry Morgan by Robert Meldrum, a trader who knew the Crows in the 1820s.[10]

From the Crow point of view, the important thing about a ceremonial bundle was not its antiquity but its record of successes—the true sign of a gift from powerful supernatural helpers. Crow narratives are not clear concerning who first received the gift of power in the Sun Dance from a spirit

[6] Fred W. Voget, "Individual Motivation in the Diffusion of the Wind River Shoshone Sun Dance to the Crow Indians," *American Anthropologist* 50 (1948):634–46.

[7] The Crow Sun Dance undoubtedly sprang from the ceremonial and mourning complex shared with their Hidatsa relatives. The Hidatsa *NaxpikE* (Hide-striking) ceremony contained various elements, including volunteer skewer-fasters, found in the Crow Sun Dance. However, the Hide-striking was pledged by someone who wished to effect the transfer of a sacred arrow medicine bundle and its rights through a dream sanction and adoption purchase. Since the Crow ceremony was pledged by a mourner, the stimulus for the Crow Sun Dance probably came from the self-mortifying mourning conventions shared with the Hidatsas, and which extended to leaders whose parties had suffered disaster. A Hidatsa pledger of the Hide-striking could undertake the skewer-ordeal, but a Crow pledger of a Sun Dance did not torment his body beyond fasting and dancing before a supernatural figure attached to a pole (see Bowers,"Hidatsa Social and Ceremonial Organization," *BAE Bulletin* 194:234, 247, 308–23).

[8] Wildschut, "Medicine Bundles," 17:30, n. 2.

[9] Scott, "Notes on the Sun Dance of the Kiowa."

[10] Lewis H. Morgan, *The Indian Journals, 1859–1862*, 185–86.

Henry Big Day with daughter. Note medicine bag hung to receive power from sun.

helper. Lowie's informants favored either Four Dances or Iakac as the originators, while Wildschut attributed the origin to the so-called duo, Prairie Dog Man and Big Bird, following the account of Two Leggings.[11] Four Dances was personally known to Two Leggings and could have been born about 1800. Quite obviously Four Dance's bundle would not meet the estimated antiquity of that of Sees the Tent Ground. Wildschut, unfortunately, gave no indication of how old the bundles of Prairie Dog Man and Big Bird were.

At any one time, some four to eight Sun Dance bundles were in use. Each was validated by a vision experience and included, as the central figure, an idol in human form fashioned out of buffalo or deer hide. Sweet grass, white pine needles, special roots and herbs, and tobacco were used as stuffing for the mannikin. The effigy bodies were simple triangles, with

[11] Lowie, "Sun Dance of the Crow Indians," 16:13–14; Wildschut, "Medicine Bundles."

eyes, nose, and mouth crudely outlined in black. A profusion of feather plumes, commonly from a screech owl, enfolded the head at the back and sometimes encased the whole figure. A bundle normally included a skunk-skin necklace and skunk-skin strips, which were attached to the ankles of the pledger, who was referred to as the whistler. According to the particular vision, buffalo-hide effigies with legless, triangular human bodies, or buffalo-hide rattles might be prominent elements of the bundle.

The rectangular hide containers for these medicine bundles usually were decorated with triangular human figures or circles symbolizing human beings. The morning star, indicated by a square cross, was a prominent decoration. Sun was the father of Morning Star. Known as Old Woman's Grandchild (i.e., Moon's grandchild), Morning Star heroically overcame various monsters infesting the earth. However, he left the earth for the sky when some men tried to get him to eat a buffalo fetus and thus aroused his fear.[12] Things related to birth and young animals were ritually offensive to Morning Star, and he never appeared in the sky until late in the spring, after young animals were born.

The vision experiences of Four Dances, Iakac, and Prairie Dog Man were like other supernatural contacts described by Crow visionaries to legitimatize belief and practice. Revenge for the death of a near relative, frequently a son or younger brother, was the central theme of the Sun Dance vision. In the longer narratives of Four Dances and of Prairie Dog Man, the use of core symbols, forms, and practices, including the mannikin, were legitimated and explained.

On his vision quest, Four Dances made contact with seven men (linked to the Big Dipper) and a woman who wore an elk-hide robe and held a man effigy before her face. The woman was none other than Moon, otherwise known as Old

---

[12] Robert H. Lowie, "Myths and Traditions of the Crow Indians," *American Museum of Natural History Anthropological Papers* 25:52–74.

Woman or Grandmother. As Four Dances stood face to face with the supernaturals, he saw the head of the little mannikin pop out of the buckskin wrapping just as the Seven Brothers began the first of four medicine songs. During the second song, Moon shook the bundle at him, and Four Dances saw the arms of the little man. By the third song the waist came into view, and at the fourth song the mannikin changed into a screech owl and alighted on Moon Woman's head. Four Dances now lay on his back, looking skyward in the usual manner when fasting and hoping for a visitation. The owl flew to this breast. Then:

Suddenly one of the men loaded and cocked a breechloader, then he stepped toward the boy and sang a song. The woman said to the screech-owl, "Now, little screech-owl, this man is going to shoot you, you must make your medicine." It stood up on his feet and began to flap its wings. The man drew closer, and shot at the owl, which entered his [Four Dance's] breast and began to hoot inside. Andicicopc [Four Dances] looked towards the northeast. In the valley he saw a sun dance lodge. The seven men and moon got up, singing and beating their drums. They moved towards the lodge, making four stops on the way and singing a song each time. After the end of the fourth song, they entered the lodge. Andicicopc looked through the lodge and saw the doll attached to a cedar tree on the north side of the lodge. At the foot of the tree he saw the whistler lying flat on his back. The seven men sang four songs again. Moon went to the whistler, and seized him by both hands. At each song she raised him slightly, then put him back in his former position, but the fourth time she pulled him up completely. Moon then stepped up to the doll and gave it to the whistler, who held it in both hands. After a short time he put it back in its place. They sang and danced, facing the medicine doll. Thus the doll was discovered, and whenever anyone wished to have a sun dance he requested the visionary to direct the ceremony. The doll represents the moon-woman, and the lodge the sun's lodge.[13]

[13] Lowie, "Sun Dance of the Crow Indians," 16:14. The owl is a sinister bird, a harbinger of evil and even death. If an owl enters a house, death

Prairie Dog Man was mourning a young son killed by the enemy when he heard a voice from above command: "Build a structure for the sun. Those who killed your son are forest people."[14] In his vision Prairie Dog Man saw prairie dog mounds turn into tipis and one of the prairie dogs became a human being. On call, the prairie dog spirits assembled at a structure made for the sun. A person appeared carrying a pine tree. At its top was attached a willow hoop decorated with seven feathers. The tree was presented to a man and wife who approached from out of the sunset. On command from a voice, the man and woman sang a song and gestured as if striking at something.

Suddenly there appeared a little screech owl of the kind that lives among the prairie dogs. It flew straight to the pine tree where the hoop was fastened. There it changed into an effigy. The man and his wife were nearing the structure when the voice from within, which represented the dancer, was heard to say, "I have no skunk skin yet, nor any deerskin, nor a whistle, nor eagle plumes."[15]

Returning to the Crow camp, Prairie Dog Man told the people that they should move camp to Bear Dance, where he intended to construct a Sun Dance lodge. At this point an orphan and known skeptic of religious power came forward and joined in the ceremony. The skeptic, Big Bird, quieted the surprise of the people by stating, "You people should know that I am the originator of this ceremony. I have two friends who told me all about it." Big Bird had the people gather buffalo tongues, and he also carved a doll out of ash and covered it with deerskin.

This was the first sun dance effigy. On the cover . . . Big Bird

---

to someone will follow. The screech owl is the worst of all. As an ultimate symbol of impending death by mystical power, the screech owl was a fitting helper for a mourner bent on revenge.

[14] Wildschut, "Medicine Bundles," 17:22.

[15] Ibid.

painted crosses. Then he took some owl feathers and, after tying them in a bunch, fastened them to the head of the doll. All he would say was that he had been given these instructions by the two boys. And the Indians understood he meant the two boys who had been given the sweat lodge by First Worker.[16]

On seeing the little man made by Big Bird, Prairie Dog Man exclaimed, "That is exactly the effigy I saw in my dream."[17]

Big Bird now supervised construction of the Sun Dance lodge and guided Prairie Dog Man through the dance. Before the dance started, Big Bird predicted that down the Rosebud they would come upon some Forest People hunting buffalo, and these enemies would be slain in retaliation for the killing of Prairie Dog Man's son. This is precisely what happened. The Crows surprised four Forest People hunting buffalo and killed them. At this time one Crow initiated the coup system by striking the dead enemies and taking their bows and arrows.[18]

One woman was credited with acquiring a Sun Dance man-being, but none knew how. She made a figure of the little man, which was supposed to have entered her body. The woman never removed it until just before her death. As a woman, she was not expected to pledge a Sun Dance, but she did make four replicas of the little man, which she passed on to her son. The son then transmitted one of the effigies to a brother, who likewise passed it along to his son, Bear from Above. Although Bear from Above never sponsored a Sun Dance, he periodically burned incense and unwrapped the little man—but only to where the head and shoulders were exposed. "The face looked like that of a doll baby; it was painted yellowish and red."[19] Bear from Above then attached the mannikin to his tipi. All this ritual was in re-

[16] Ibid., 24.
[17] Ibid.
[18] Ibid., 25.
[19] Lowie, "Sun Dance of the Crow Indians," 16:15.

sponse to dream communications, and when his wife died, Bear from Above buried the mannikin with her.

Lowie's informants never made clear the relation between sun, moon, and the Sun Dance.[20] The ceremony was referred to as "making a little tipi," that is, a miniature of the Sun's big lodge. Today, probably as of old, a pledger sets the time for the dance when Grandmother Moon is in full phase. As the sun sets in the west, the red-hued moon rises dramatically on the eastern horizon, directly in line with the entrance that has been oriented to the rising sun.

Sun Dance Medicine Bundles in Tribal Ceremonialism

Although the Crows commonly united in putting on a Sun Dance ceremony, there was no tribal Sun Dance bundle in the custody of special ritualists, as among the Cheyennes. Sun Dance bundles were private property, and Lowie's informants recalled from four to six bundles, each of which had been validated by a vision revelation. At any one moment, however, one bundle usually took precedence over others in the minds of the public. About 1850, Wrinkled Face possessed the most sought-after Sun Dance medicine bundle. Following Crow practice, sacred Sun Dance objects commonly passed from an original owner to a brother or son. Women could acquire Sun Dance bundles through inheritance, but they were restricted from sponsoring a dance or serving as a ceremonial supervisor. Ritual restrictions sometimes even prevented a woman from unwrapping the effigy and praying to him.

Sun Dance medicine bundles were especially dedicated to killing the enemy. Warriors sought protection by giving a horse or other valued goods to the bundle owner for a replica of the little man. Unwrapping his bundle, the owner

[20] Lowie, *The Crow Indians*, 297.

made a copy of the mannikin, tied it to a willow hoop adorned with eagle feathers and consecrated it in the smoke of sweetgrass. The warrior wore the talisman suspended from his neck, and each time he was successful, he gave the owner a horse and returned the effigy. After the fourth time, the little man became the property of the user.[21]

Description and Analysis of the Sun Dance[22]

Viewed in terms of its processes, the Sun Dance can be divided into two parts: first, acts that consecrated the pledger, ceremonial leaders, and the lodge; and second, the quest for a vision in which an enemy was visualized as dead. Programmatically the Sun Dance progressed through the following stages:

1. initiation of the Sun Dance cycle by vow of a man who was mourning a loved one slain by the enemy;
2. public announcement and consecration of the tribal venture through four buffalo hunts;
3. selection of a Sun Dance bundle owner to supervise the ceremony;
4. construction and consecration of the lodge; and
5. the dance for power before the sacred effigy.

Consecration of the pledger and the instruments for revenge were vital preliminaries to attainment of the vision essential to success of the mission. Much of the Sun Dance ceremony, in consequence, centered on rituals that sanctified

[21] Lowie, "Sun Dance of the Crow Indians," 16:13.

[22] Lowie's detailed descriptions have been used to define the core features and ceremonial pattern of the traditional Crow Sun Dance. Other descriptions by William P. Clark, *The Indian Sign Language;* Curtis, *The Apsaroke, or Crow;* Morgan, *The Indian Journals 1859–1862;* and Nabokov, *Two Leggings,* have supplied additional elements and a basis for comparison with Lowie to bring out similarities and differences, and possibly new elements.

the pledger and his dress, the effigy, and the Sun Dance lodge. In overview, the consecratory preparations might seem to overshadow the vision, but all of these preparations were indispensable to the mobilization of powers in order to attain supernatural attention and favor, of which the vision was the symbol.

Initiation and Consecration of the Sun Dance

In the metaphor of "cutting ankles" a man communicated his pledge of a Sun Dance to the Camp Chief and thus solicited the cooperation of the whole tribe. A herald carried this vow to the assembled camp and informed the people of a buffalo hunt in which nothing but tongues and choice meat were to be taken. The pledger, dressed in moccasins and a buffalo robe, led the hunters on foot. Companions of the dead warrior usually collected the tongues, moving from tipi to tipi. Arranged in sets of ten, the tongues were distributed to twenty outstanding warriors. The distributors of the tongues dramatized their entrance into the camp as if they were a returning war party, and they called out the names of the distinguished pipe holders and other warriors whose virtuous wives would cook the tongues.

After the hunt for the tongues, the pledger took a pipe filled with tobacco to the Sun Dance bundle owner whom he wished to guide him through the ceremony. By smoking the pipe, the medicine man adopted the suppliant as a son. From that time forward all Sun Dance activities and direction of the camp were the responsibility of the medicine bundle owner. The people now moved in stages to the site of the dance, collecting tongues along the way. The dance ground marked the fourth stop.

Sanctifying the Whistler-Pledger

The process of sacramentizing the "whistler," carried out by the bundle owner, probably began right after the first hunt and was repeated at each ceremonial stop enroute to the dance ground. The whistler's own tipi provided the staging for the consecration process. Ground cedar was brought in to carpet the floor, and sage was used to make up a bed in the rear. The bundle owner seated himself to the right of the whistler and received old men who inquired about the whistler's intentions, tested the strength of his convictions and the validity of the dream, that sanctioned the ceremony. With pipe they added their prayer smokes and blessings.

The visitation of the old men undoubtedly was designed to get at the truth or falsity of the dream. If false, a man probably withdrew and waited for a clearer signal. If the interpretations of the old wise men agreed with a pledger's conviction, he reaffirmed his intention to go ahead with a simple statement to his ceremonial father: "Sing for me tonight, and I will dance for you."[23] This set the bundle owner in motion to get together the kilt, moccasins, buffalo robes, eagle-bone whistle and other gear required. The owner's wife assembled a tanned deerskin for the kilt, an unused buffalo robe, and buckskin for the moccasins. Before the manufacture of any item, the owner purified with incense the materials, tools, and persons involved. The ceremonial father himself cut the hide for the kilt, feinting three times before putting the knife to the hide. A virtuous woman prepared the kilt and the woman who sewed the moccasins qualified only if her husband had killed and scalped an enemy. The moccasins were blackened with charcoal as a sign of victory and were decorated with buffalo hair to represent a scalp taken from the enemy.

Consecration of the whistler was symbolized in the ceremonial drama of painting and dressing for the Sun Dance, undressing, and sleeping beside a buffalo skull. This ritual called for four singers with their hand drums and two women accompanists. All dress paraphernalia were assembled within

---

[23] Lowie, "Sun Dance of the Crow Indians," 16:20.

easy reach by the effigy owner, including a cup of white clay, ground cedar, eagle-bone whistle, buffalo-hide rattle, two feather plumes, skunk-hide necklace, kilt, robe, moccasins, and sage. Taking some clay, the ceremonial father began to sing, accompanying himself with the rattle. His wife, who acted as his assistant, sang along with him and put cedar on the fire of smoldering buffalo chips. After the fourth rendition of the song, the owner carefully smoked the kilt. He then repeated the four songs and gently raised the whistler, grasping only his thumbs.[24] As the whistler came erect, he extended his left foot over the cedar incense and stepped into the kilt. The wife then raised the kilt into place and tied it with a leather cord. During the donning of the kilt, the drummer-singers offered prayer smokes.

The whistler next was painted with white clay in the manner of a buffalo when rolling in a wallow. First, however, the best drum was purified in fresh cedar incense by the bundle owner's wife, while her husband sang a medicine song. In returning to his place, the consecrated drummer with his drum made a (clockwise?) circuit to avoid crossing in front of the whistler. After consecrating his rattle, the ceremonial father sang softly and with the fourth song sang aloud, at which time the drummer-singers joined in. After smoking his hands in the cedar incense, the father outlined the whistler's body from head to toe. He did this three times, and then, on the fourth song, feigned the painting of the whistler with white clay—first from the front, head to toe, then the back, followed by the left and right sides. Following the same order (E, W, N, S), the wife-assistant applied the paint to the whistler, using a bundle of sage. Next the ceremonial father drew a square cross on the whistler's breast and back, to signify Morning Star. With a zigzag line from each eye, he symbolized the whistler's tears. A zigzag lightning mark applied

---

[24] Raising a supplicant by the thumbs probably was a ceremonial convention in the communication of mystic power.

to the forehead imitated the painting used by the Sun himself.

To complete his "son's" dress, the ceremonial father hung a skunk-hide necklace around his neck, tied a feather to the back of his head, and attached eagle plumes to the little fingers of each hand. Both the skunk skin and the feathers were daubed with white clay. The moccasins were smoked in fresh cedar and put on, first the left (N) and then the right (S). This was done by the owner's wife. After smoking the buffalo robe, the owner three times feigned placing it on the ground. On the fourth song he put the robe in place and guided the whistler to his seat. The wife adjusted the robe and drew the ends around the pledger.

The bundle owner next smoked and daubed the final item of dress, the eagle-bone whistle, with white clay. To the accompaniment of song, the "father" danced in a squatting position before his "son." Three times he feigned the insertion of the whistle, and on the fourth song he inserted the whistle into the pledger's mouth. The pledger then danced in imitation of his mentor.[25] To end this drama, the owner took the whistle and draped it around the whistler's neck.

Upon completion of the ceremonial dressing, the drummers ended their singing, took up a pipe, and offered prayer smokes. All during the dress-consecration the cover of the tipi was raised for all to see. Four warriors now entered from the left, and four from the right. Each carried a wolfskin to indicate that he had served as a scout, and each had moccasins tied to his belt as if in readiness to set out on a war expedition. Only the weaponry of war was missing, since it was forbidden at this stage of the ceremony. Two women sang a song that indicated return from a successful war venture: "Woman

---

[25] A squatting or kneeling position probably identified the dancer with the eagle, since the eagle medicine man commonly kneeled when dancing in the "nest" at the top of the Sun Dance lodge. The ceremonial seems to emphasize a mystical transfer from eagle-father to eaglet.

friend, sing my song, my house is here!"[26] As the drummer took up the song, the men sounded a war whoop and flirted with the women. After the fourth rendition, the warriors individually recounted war deeds and left. Thus began the mobilization of the mystic powers of renowned warriors to overwhelm the enemy.

To the accompaniment of prayer smokes and songs by the drummer-singers, the bundle owner ceremonially undressed the whistler. Feigning three times in each case, he removed the head plume, skunk-skin necklace, little finger plumes, whistle, and moccasins. The kilt was not removed. At the call, "Bring in his quilts!" two bundles of sage and cedar were brought.[27] After shaping the cedar into a pillow and the sage into a mattress, the owner lowered the whistler to his bed, with feet to the fire and with palms up. Following three feints and songs, the owner on the fourth song covered the whistler with the buffalo robe. Now he called out, "Bring in the buffalo bull!" This horned skull he set close to the whistler's head, facing the fire and the east.

Consecration of the pledger now was ended, and he soon was left alone to sleep and, it was hoped, to dream of power. The owner and his wife-assistant made public where they would next encamp, perhaps only a few miles away. At this time they also selected one of the military fraternities to organize transport of the ramada-type structure erected to house the sanctified tongues and the pledger's tipi. The military fraternity also raised a pile of wood some fifteen feet high at the chosen site, to mark the location of the pledger's lodge.

At the second, third, and fourth camps the police awaited the people, and, as they arrived, directed them into a circle with the pledger's tipi and the shade structure containing the tongues in the middle. At each stop the bundle owner repeated the ceremonial dressing and undressing of the whistler

[26]Lowie, "Sun Dance of the Crow Indians," 16:24.
[27] Ibid., 25.

and more warriors recounted their coups. With the fourth consecration the preliminaries ended. The next task was construction of the "little tipi" in which the pledger would receive a vision granting his revenge.

The Buffalo Bull Hunt

A Sun Dance required pine poles larger than the usual lodgepoles and two buffalo bull hides to tie the poles together. First came the buffalo hunt, for which they selected two men, a noted marksman and a skillful butcher. Both were qualified warriors.

The bundle owner not only selected the hunters but also told them where they would make their kills, according to dream instruction. The warrior-hunters were up before dawn, since the two bulls must be shot before sunrise. Only one arrow, or shot, was allowed to bring down the buffalo. The hide must show only one hole where the arrow penetrated. The second kill required the hunter to tie an eagle feather to the bull's tail and one to his horns before the buffalo fell to the ground. The hunters were not permitted to eat or leave any of the meat from these animals behind.

Two scouts adorned with wolf-skin sashes scouted the hunters as they approached camp. On sighting the hunters, the scouts painted themselves with white clay and rushed toward camp howling like wolves. A crowd gathered, and individuals tried to count coup on the wolf-scouts, exclaiming, "Here I take a horse," or "I take a bow," or "I strike the enemy!" The scouts gave the best of reports: the hunters had not only killed an enemy, but also returned with his scalp and with good horses.

As the hunters made their way down a path lined with people and carpeted with cedar, the bundle owner approached to get their account. He wore a headband of cedar and a blackened face as a sign of victory. With rattle and song he approached the hunters, who duly reported that they indeed had killed two enemies, i.e., the two buffalo. Singing a song of victory, the bundle owner escorted the mounted hunter and butcher in four stages to the pledger's tipi. Here they were taken from their horses by four renowned warriors, who placed them on separate plots strewn with cedar. Two war captains then proceeded to cut up the meat, which was distributed to the assembled people.

Getting the Lodgepoles

Camp police forced every able-bodied person to take part in the ceremonial killing and couping of poles for construction of the lodge. An outstanding warrior selected the lodgepoles of cottonwood or of pine, in accordance with the owner's vision. However, the first of the four-pole frame usually was of cottonwood, and it probably was the northeast pole of the frame.

The pledger and the bundle owner led a procession to the trees and consecrated them. In preparation, the owner constructed a handled hoop interlaced with twelve, or seven, willows. To each of the willows he attached eagle feathers supplied by the whistler. The feathers and willows were painted black as a symbol of victory. The little man effigy was placed in the center of the feathered hoop. Standing to the right of the whistler, and facing the whistler's wife, the bundle owner told her to sing her "song of joy" and to set about cooking the tongues. The pledger's wife sang four times and then placed the tongues in a kettle, beside which she arranged some willow sticks that had been sharpened, painted black, and decorated with real scalps.

The pledger, carrying the effigy-hoop, took his position well in advance of the procession and moved toward the timber where the poles were located. Next in line came the ceremonial father and his wife, followed by drummer-singers, police and four women carrying the cooked tongues. The entire camp straggled behind, with police closing up from the rear. Only the sick and enfeebled remained in camp.

On coming to the tree selected as the first pole, the whistler took a position facing east. A shelter was constructed and the whistler seated himself, facing east with the effigy-hoop. Beforehand, the police, acting on instructions, sought out a virtuous woman and presented her with the best of the buffalo tongues. Acceptance meant that she would initiate the cutting of the tree and pray for success of the venture. Acceptance meant, too, that if her husband died, she could never marry again. For that reason a woman might refuse, even though by accepting she and her husband gained status and were the first to receive food in any distribution.

A virtuous woman to the Crows meant one who had been duly married by exchange of wealth and had remained steadfast to her man. The quality of faithfulness was difficult to maintain because of the casual approach to premarital and extramarital affairs linked to a high level of competition among men. If a woman had a secret love affair, she excused herself with the convention, "My moccasin has a hole in it." Young men, using the same convention, challenged pretenders. Considering the awesome responsibility assumed by a woman regarding success of the Sun Dance and the good fortune of the people, deception was dangerous. A woman called upon the Sun to witness her virtue, and, as in oaths taken by men when coups were in dispute, supernatural punishment was expected to follow falsification. Besides a virtuous woman, the tree ceremony included a male transvestite and a captive, preferably a woman from the hated enemy. Each was given a sacramental tongue.

In the ceremony of pole-notching, the chaste woman stood to the west of the tree, facing east. She was armed with a stone maul and a blackened and pointed elk-antler prong. The berdache, axe in hand, stationed himself to the north, while the captive woman positioned herself to the east of the tree. The bundle owner and his wife stood behind the virtuous woman. Singing and rattling, the owner nudged the woman, who then touched the tree with the antler prong and made the motion of driving it into the cottonwood with the maul. The berdache and captive made similar motions according to their tasks. This symbolic drama was repeated at the end of each of three songs. Each time the virtuous pole notcher silently wished for success over the enemy. On the fourth song the woman struck the antler with the maul and drove it against the tree, while the berdache touched the tree with his axe. The captive, hands smeared with grease and charcoal, drew a black band around the tree and wished for success: "May the poor Indians have a good war the next time, may they kill a Dakota and take captives."[28] As the berdache set to work cutting the tree, young men gave the war whoop and shot at the limbs of the tree. Even as the tree feel, they rode up to count coup.

Young men and women had the task of dragging the twenty poles of the lodge to the dance ground. They, as others, dressed in their finest outfits and rode on their best lionskin saddle blankets. First, however, the police captured twenty young men to sit on the poles. The four poles making the foundations of the lodge were the most important, and the four youths selected for these were committed to a no-retreat obligation.

Pandemonium broke out as young men sought escape in all directions, with police in hot pursuit. As the four no-retreat honorees were brought in, the whistler approached and touched each with the medicine hoop. This act collapsed all resistance, and with a sigh of distress, each accepted with the convention, "My lodgepole is heavy." Each then sat down on the assigned pole. Sixteen others were selected because they were from wealthy families. Immediately their relatives brought beaded work, buffalo robes, moccasins, shirts, horses, and other property. These goods were deposited before the bundle owner, who distributed some items to the hunters, scouts, and others who performed services, but reserved most of the

28 Ibid., 32.

"War party" of four old men gathers to charge Sun Dance timbers.
Crow Agency, 1941.

gifts for himself. As the herald announced that everything
was ready, young women ran to the poles of their favorites
and attached lines for dragging the poles. Each of these young
men, riding double with their girls, dragged a pole back to
camp. For this service each received a buffalo tongue.

The first to get back with his pole was given leadership
of a party to get willows. Girls went along to cut the willows, tying them in bundles, for use in covering the Sun
Dance lodge. Members of the military fraternities arranged
the willow bundles in a ring surrounding the poles, which
were placed at the lodge site like spokes of a wheel, perhaps
to represent the sun's rays.

The whistler and his ceremonial father received a constant
stream of people who came to visit and to offer prayer smokes.

Charlie Ten Bear armed with coupstick for striking coup on the Sun Dance timbers. Crow Agency, 1941.

The whistler and his mentor smoked with a straight tubular pipe associated with sacred prayer in the Sun Dance. After the visiting ended, the bundle owner had a herald announce that the lodge would be constructed on the morrow, and that the young people should be up early to help out. The owner also searched out a small cedar tree and set it up behind the buffalo skull, alongside the pledger's bed of sage. Another buffalo skull, corresponding to the two obtained in the ceremonial bull hunt, was brought in. Finally, the pledger was ceremoniously undressed and left to his dreams.

Building the Lodge

Early in the morning a party of young women and men went out to bring in firewood and brush to cover the lodge. The leader of the brush gatherers was a virtuous young woman, selected with the offer of a tongue. She walked, leading the horse of a brave warrior, with other members of the party riding behind.

Upon return of the brush party, young men prepared sets of two tipi poles linked with rawhide for use in raising the four-pole frame of the lodge. The four-pole frame was arranged on top of the firewood, tied, and then wrapped with willows.

The bundle owner made himself into a symbol of victory by painting his chin, cheeks, and forehead with charcoal and setting a cedar band atop his head. He also blackened his moccasins. Then it was the turn of the whistler to be blackened. Next came the two buffalo hides, which were blackened and cut to form the eagle's nest at the top of the lodge. The knife and whetstone were furnished by a female relative of the pledger.

After singing four songs, the bundle owner blackened the buffalo hides and sharpened and blackened the knife. He then feigned slitting one of the fore and hind legs of each hide, and made holes along one side of each hide in order to join them with foot-long willows. A warrior noted for his skill in taking horses collected the willows, and then two warriors recited coups and sharpened and blackened them. In all the cutting the owner simply indicated where the hide was to be cut or filled with holes, and left the work to his wife-assistant.

The "nest" was formed by slipping the four-pole frame through the slits of the hides to a point below the willow wrappings. Consecration of the nest required a man with eagle medicine. He painted himself according to his power-vision, carried a feather fan in each hand, and tied his medicine to the back of his head. He began to whistle and to imitate the behavior of an eagle as soon as he stepped out of his tipi. Songs were sung at each of three stops. If a dog got in his path, or a person crossed in front of him, he returned to his tipi and started his ceremonial procession again. The nest was his fourth stop, and at the end of his fourth

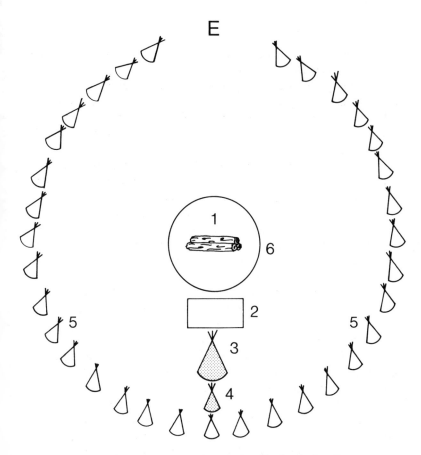

E

Figure 1. Plan of Crow Encampment at Big Shadow's Sun Dance, 1844 (reconstructed from Curtis, 1970).

Legend

1. Woodpile marking center of Sun Dance Lodge to be constructed.
2. Ramada-type shelter for storing consecrated buffalo tongues. This shelter probably was covered with brush on top and sides, or with buffalo hides, according to season. The entrance faced east.
3. Pledger's tipi.
4. Tipi of bundle owner and director of the Sun Dance. The band chief, who was a medicine man, reportedly located his tipi at this point when making camp. However, another "priest" directed the dance, and it is quite probable that the bundle owner used the chief's tipi for ritual preparations.
5. Tipis formed in circle facing east.
6. Area where Sun Dance Lodge will be erected.

song, the bird man continued his eagle imitations as he and the nest were raised into position. As the eagle man was raised, people whooped as in victory. The eagle man and his nest were raised and lowered three times, each time moved a bit higher, before being brought into position on the fourth try. As the eagle man scrambled down, the remaining poles were quickly set into position. The eagle medicine man now reported a vision prophetic of success against the enemy, relating how he saw the actual killing of an enemy. For his services and blessing the eagle man was entitled to four articles brought to the bundle owner by families of the young men selected to drag the lodgepoles.

The woodpile that supported the four-pole frame was removed, and willow bundles were tied around the lodge as a cover. Leaving an opening for public viewing, the workers continued the willow covering to the top of the lodge.

War leaders next added their special consecration and blessing to the lodge. They followed the prescription of Morning Star, who instituted the No Fire Dance, or coup recitation. In imitation of war parties, scouts led pipe-bearing captains and their followers into the lodge. Circling to the right of the entrance, the pipe holders paused near the fire, blew their eagle-bone whistles, and looked up at the nest in hope of getting a vision. Continuing to the back of the lodge and facing east, the captains reported their visions, if any. Each announcement was made to the accompaniment of drumming, which interrupted and accented each sentence of the narrative.

After the war blessings, people were reminded to rise early to get white clay for the whistler's bed and dance ground. The party of young men and women was led by a young man who never had played the game of touching the genitals of sleeping women, a common nighttime challenge of youths. Picking up a bit of clay at the quarry, the virtuous leader spoke somewhat as follows: "Because I never touched the genitals of a woman while she was sleeping, I wish that you kill an enemy."[29] On the return, the young man walked, leading the horse of the best-looking woman in the party. He made a circuit of the camp for all to see before depositing the load of clay at the back of the dance lodge. For their services and blessings the young man and woman received a sanctified tongue.

Before making the white clay bed for the whistler, a warrior who had captured an enemy recounted his deed. Using a buffalo-scapula hoe supplied by a female relative of the whistler, the military fraternity smoothed a rectangular area and spread the white clay in some thickness. Finally, all was ready for the whistler to begin his vision quest in the consecrated lodge.

Dancing for Power

Eight days had passed since the whistler gave notice of his intention to undertake a Sun Dance. This was ritually in order, since the sacred number of the Crows was four or multiples of four. Four days were devoted to collecting tongues, and at the same time to consecrating the whistler and his paraphernalia. One day was consumed in the hunt for bull hides, another for getting the lodgepoles, and still another for building and blessing the lodge. The journey for white clay marked the eighth day, and it was on this day that the whistler formally entered on his vision quest. During all this time, and even before announcing his intention, the pledger was on a partial but rigorous fast. The bundle owner joined him in this partial fast, as did other older men. Once the whistler entered the Sun Dance lodge, his fast and that of his associates, was complete.

The cedar tree and buffalo skulls still had to be set up behind the whistler's bed, and black paint had to be applied

[29] Ibid., 42.

to the butt of the cedar. When the owner and his wife ceremoniously carried the tree and skulls into the lodge, the whistler readied himself for his entrance. Standing back of the doorway of his tipi, the whistler thrust the effigy-hoop outside and
pretended to leave, just as the drummer-singers completed a
first song. At the end of the second and third songs he showed
more of his person. With the finish of the fourth song, he
stepped forth, dancing and blowing his whistle while gazing
fixedly on the sacred hoop. He interrupted his dance four
times before he entered the lodge and proceeded to the rear.
At this point the owner took the hoop and tied it to the
cedar tree, placing it on a level with the eyes of the whistler.

Members of the dead man's war party prepared a fire in the
center of the lodge and erected a simple tripod frame for
suspending kettles, in which buffalo tongues were cooked.
Adorned with cedar headbands, virtuous women, including
the wife of the whistler, came with wooden forks blackened
and decorated with scalps. Young warriors claimed tongues
with long thrusting poles, sharpened and ringed with yellow
bands. A claimant usually gave the tongue to his sweetheart,
just as a married woman honored with a tongue gave it to
her husband.

Before the whistler began his dance, renowned warriors
again entered to recite and to dramatize their coups in sham
battle. Wives came along burdened with guns, bows, and
knives taken from the enemy. These trophies were deposited
in front of the coup reciters, facing the entrance.

Fasters and visionaries who intended to suspend themselves
from rawhide ropes dangling from the twenty poles of the
lodge now arrived. They were painted with white clay and
usually were assisted by a father's clansman. After reciting a
war deed the warrior-sponsor made a prayer wish: "This man
wishes to do what I did."[30] He then pierced either the breast

[30] Ibid., 44.

or back flesh in two places and attached the skewers. At times more than twenty visionaries volunteered to sacrifice themselves. Those unable to suspend themselves from the lodgepole lines dragged seven buffalo skulls until the flesh broke. Or a suppliant suspended himself from a pole set up inside or outside the lodge. Self-torturers usually were suspended during the day, and, if the flesh was not broken, were taken down at night. During the night they rested in small four-post shelters covered with brush and leaves.

The drummers began singing after the coup recitations. At this time the bundle owner danced and whistled and then transferred the whistle to the pledger's mouth. With gaze riveted on the little man, the whistler danced in place on the clay bed. The start of the drumming and singing also set the self-tormentors in motion, running and struggling to break the flesh.

The dancing of the whistler was interspersed with coup recitations. Coup reciters usually numbered four or more, and singing continued between the war-narrative blessings. When all were finished, the owner undressed the whistler and put him to bed.

The second day of the whistler's full fast was approached with great anticipation. This could be the day when the whistler obtained his wish! Before dawn a herald aroused the young people and instructed them to eat and dress up in fine clothing. The ceremonial father dressed the whistler and painted him again with white clay and drew crosses symbolic of Morning Star. Coup recitations again supported the whistler's quest. After a coup striker told of his deed, a clan father of the whistler sang a praise song for his "son." In turn, the father received a stick, for which he later traded a horse.

The alternation of dancing and coup recitations went on all day except for four breaks in the drumming and singing. At the second and subsequent interludes, relatives of the whistler brought gifts for the ceremonial father. These breaks were never uniform in timing, since the intention was to force the whistler to go "crazy" and fall down. If he appeared near the vision state, the singing of a particular medicine-song was prolonged. As the whistler tottered, the bundle owner noted the direction of the fall and shook his rattle over him until the heavy breathing subsided. He then dragged the whistler to his bed and covered him with the buffalo robe. The whistler hoped to see lots of dead enemies in the vision given by the little man in the hoop. Precisely what he saw was not disclosed at this time, but the bundle owner, who interpreted the vision, told the waiting people that the vision was good.

When visions of the dead enemy came hard, the owner might induce the vision. The request usually was made by the whistler's relatives. In Lowie's words, the ceremonial father

took a rattle, approached the doll, made incense of cedar leaves, and made the whistler smoke himself with it. Then he ordered him to look at the doll, while he himself took a seat at the foot of the pole to which the doll was suspended. He shook the post and looked at the whistler, who began to dance, riveting his eyes on the doll, while the owner began to chant his songs. After a while, the dancer saw the doll painting its face black, and promising that he should kill an enemy at such a season of the year and under such circumstances. Suddenly, the whistler ceased to dance, and fell down in a swoon, his eyes still fixed on the doll.[31]

The whistler's vision brought the dance to an abrupt end. All spectators received a consecrated tongue and departed. One by one, the fasters left. The ceremonial fathers of those suspended each recited a war deed blessing and then withdrew the skewers. Young boys retrieved the lines and gave them to the suppliants. Meanwhile, the bundle owner offered

[31] Ibid., 50.

a final prayer smoke and undressed the whistler, smoking each piece of attire in turn, including the buffalo robe. The whistler usually was in such pain and so weary that he needed the support of relatives when walking to his tipi. The bundle owner had the medicine hoop and his gifts removed to his tipi. At a later time the hoop was taken by a relative of the whistler and offered to the Sun Person. The lodge was left standing, while the people moved on to their next camp. Proof of the vision would come during the designated season, when the war party, led by the pledger, set out for the enemy.

Crow Sun Dances: Comparisons and Commentary

Descriptions by Morgan, Curtis, Clark, and Nabokov provide additional information on traditional Crow Sun Dances and a basis for limited comparisons with Lowie's account. Since dream revelations validated an individual's right to possess a Sun Dance bundle and direct a performance, dreams offered a natural base for variations on ceremonial conventions. Mourner-pledgers, too, might introduce minor variations according to their dreams, as in the substitution of pine for cottonwood — a variation that may happen today.

After Lowie, Curtis provides the most precise account of a Sun Dance, and the order of events and ceremonial elements are more easily compared. Robert Meldrum's description, reported by Morgan, is the more divergent of the ceremonies and may represent variations found among the River Crows, whose position brought them into more frequent contacts with northern and northeastern tribes than was the case for the Mountain Crows. Reconstructions of Sun Dance lodges bring out interesting variations as well as core features. However, for any description, omissions and ambiguities necessitate inferrences about locations and ceremonial elements, using common ceremonial form and procedure as a guide.

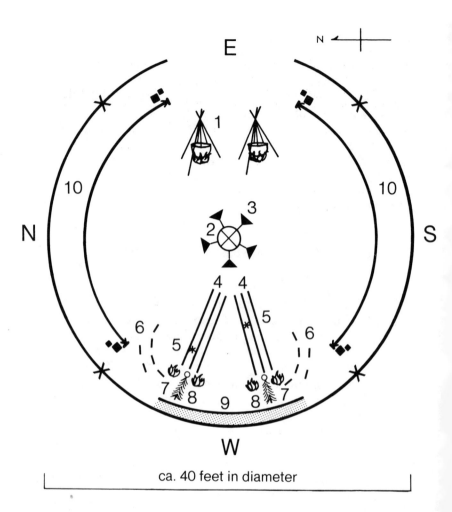

ca. 40 feet in diameter

Figure 2. Plan of Crow Sun Dance Lodge, after Robert Meldrum (Morgan, 1959). The Sun Dance lodge was a very large tipi with a center pole set in the ground for support and raised on a four-pole foundation. The two pledgers make this Sun Dance unique, and probably account for the extra poles, thirty-six as against twenty-four, used in construction. Meldrum noted that as many as twenty votaries might be hung from lines attached to the center pole, and fifty to sixty might drag buffalo skulls, with lines tied to skewers in their backs, around the lodge on the second day.

Legend

X. Four-pole foundation.
1. Pots with buffalo tongues.
2. Center pole.
3. Skewered votaries hanging from lines dropped from center pole.
4. Three rows of white sand, about one foot in height.
5. Pledger dancing between sand rows.
6. Drummer-singers, with female singers behind.
7. Perpetual incense fire.
8. Cedar tree to which hoop with mannikin is attached.
9. Position of mourners, probably either behind a willow screen or in booths.
10. Position of renowned warriors and wives.

Seasonal Performance of the Sun Dance

Early spring, when the grass was greening, and summer were
the usual times for putting up the Sun Dance lodge. Meldrum
spoke of winter performances when buffalo hides were used
as covering in place of brush, but any performance before
trees had leafed out necessitated a cover other than foliage.[32]
In the spring of 1844, a hundred buffalo were slain to provide cover for the dance lodge pledged by Big Shadow. The
hide cover was made into "four large wedge-shaped pieces,
hair side out, and drawn over a willow-bundle thatch inter-
lacing the poles."[33]

Pledging a Sun Dance

Mourners, prompted by dream revelations, were the pledgers
of Sun Dances. Through the Sun Dance, pledgers marshalled
the mystical power resources then in the hands of outstanding
tribal members in order to revenge the slaying of a loved
relative. On occasion, two mourners apparently pledged a
Sun Dance together and sought a prophecy of revenge in the
same dance lodge, but whether under the same or different
bundle owners is not indicated.[34] Dual pledging automatically introduced variations in that each pledger had to have
a separate dance area and ceremonial paraphernalia (Figure 2,
Meldrum reconstruction).[35]
    A mourner's dream of a lodge to the Sun was a powerful

[32] Morgan, *Indian Journals*, 183.
[33] Curtis, *The Apsaroke, or Crows* 4:68, 74.
[34] Morgan, *Indian Journals*, 185.
[35] Reconstruction of the Sun Dance lodges presents problems because
none of the descriptions gives sufficient detail on all items. Locations of
ceremonial structures and positions of participants are approximate. Cross-
referencing sources brings additional precision, and at times I have applied

and sufficient sanction for mobilizing the people behind the pledger's determination for a revenge-victory. However, in such a nation-wide enterprise, the Crows undoubtedly relied on their wise elders, as Lowie indicates, to test the validity of the mystic communication and to sound out the pledger's own capabilities and determination to carry out the mandates of the dream.

A pledger communicated his intentions first of all to the head chief. Big Shadow made his intention known "to the people through the chief medicine-man, who at the time was the head-chief Hair on Top. . . ."[36] Hair on Top was chief of the Mountain Crows, and Big Shadow's ceremony in all likelihood was representative of Mountain Crow Sun Dances.

The head chief probably remained in control of preliminaries until establishment of the camp at the dance site. He thus was responsible for gathering the buffalo tongues and hides for the lodge cover, and the location and setting up of the camp. At Big Shadow's Sun Dance, Hair on Top, "Being the medicine-man and chief, . . . pitched his lodge west of the pile of logs. . . ."[37]

Establishment of the camp at the dance site would appear

my own knowledge of Crow ceremonial practice to set locations.

The location and orientation of the pledger's bed illustrates the problems commonly faced in reconstruction. The bed is described as located toward the back of the lodge. A power-faster normally slept on his back, facing the rising sun, placing the foot of the bed to the east. In all probability the pledger's bed was aligned with the rising sun, with the perpetual fire located at the east end, or foot, of the bed. Meldrum makes no mention of a bed and has two fires on either side of the cedar tree, to which the hoop-mannikin was attached, located toward the back of the lodge, that is, to the west.

Location of the foundation poles presents another problem, but here Crow practice in raising a tipi as given by Campbell can serve as a guide. See William S. Campbell, "The Tipis of the Crow Indians," *American Anthropologist* 29 (1927).

[36] Curtis, *The Apsaroke, or Crows* 4:67.
[37] Ibid., 68; see Figure 1.

a logical moment to transfer ceremonial authority from the chief to the Sun Dance bundle owner. At White on the Neck's Sun Dance, the band chief of the River Crows led his people up the Big Horn to where cottonwood trees for the lodgepoles were plentiful.[38] The chief also was in charge of the hunt in which buffalo tongues were gathered, and this event signaled that "preparations for the Sun Dance had begun."[39] While Lowie is not clear on the moment when the Sun Dance bundle owner assumed full control over the camp, he implied that it was after the hunt for tongues. After establishment of camp at the dance site, Big Shadow came to Hair on Top and promised him presents for his help up to then, and instructed him to "select what chiefs you need to help you, and they too shall have presents."[40] With these instructions, Hair on Top apparently selected a Sun Dance bundle owner to "paint the dancer and to do the other sacred things in the sun-lodge."[41] Perhaps Hair on Top's reputation and status both as medicine man and as chief led Big Shadow to rely more than usual on the wisdom of his choices and the protection of his power. Hair on Top probably was in charge until the poles for Big Shadow's Sun Dance were consecrated and cut down, since the "priest" of the Sun Dance did not appear on stage until he was given wealth by relatives of young men honored with assignments of lodgepoles.[42]

Construction of the Lodge

According to Meldrum, the Crows endeavored to complete the gathering of tongues and movement of the camp to the dance site by the evening of the seventh day.[43] Once everyone

[38] Nabokov, *Two Leggings*, 81.
[39] Ibid.
[40] Curtis, *The Apsaroke, or Crows* 4:70.
[41] Ibid.
[42] Ibid.
[43] Morgan, *Indian Journals*, 183.

was in camp, with all tipis aligned to the rising sun, the bundle owner took charge of directions in consecrating and building the Sun's lodge. Lowie alone in his description focused attention on sanctifying the pledger and ceremonial paraphernalia. Consensus on the construction of the lodge in the several accounts was striking, although the order of events varied. For example, it is not clear whether they first consecrated and killed the two buffalo used for tying the three- or four-pole foundation of the lodge, or proceeded to the forest and killed the lodgepoles symbolic of the slaying of the enemy.[44] In all likelihood, either might come first, reflecting the flexible ceremoniousness of the Crows following individual revelation rather than a rigid ritualistic form of ceremony.

Before building the lodge, the bundle owner was paid for the services of his mystic power. By constructing an eagle's nest and consecrating it with eagle medicine, they sent a special signal to the Sun Person that they were going to worship as he had instructed them. Men of power also consecrated the lodge by recounting successful strikes against the enemy, and by conveying dream prophecies of success to the pledger's revenge mission. The pledger danced for power under the direction of the bundle owner, while other suppliants fasted or tormented themselves by either suspending themselves from lines attached to poles or by dragging buffalo skulls. At some propitious moment the revenge party, protected by the dream or vision of the pledger, set out, and its triumphant victory celebration brought the cycle to an end.

Buffalo Hunt

The leader of the hunt for buffalo consecrated to the lodge probably assembled his hunters for a sing to call the buffalo. They used buffalo-hide rattles, and the leader drew buffalo tracks on the ground of the special tipi in which they met.

---

[44]Lowie, "Sun Dance of the Crow Indians," 16:26; Curtis, *The Apsaroke, or Crows* 4:71; Nabokov, *Two Leggings*, 82.

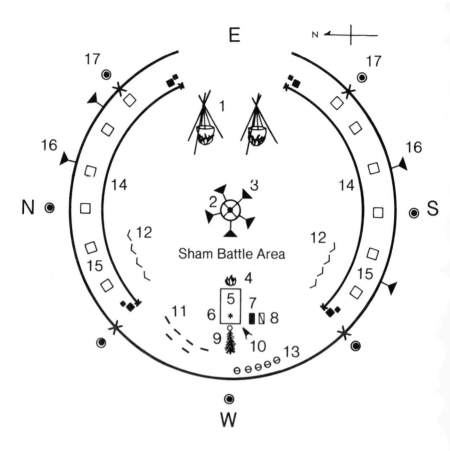

Sham Battle Area

Figure 3. Plan of Big Shadow's Sun Dance Lodge, 1844 (reconstructed from Curtis, 1970). The lodge was a large tipi raised on a four-pole foundation.

Legend

X. Four-pole foundation.
1. Pots with buffalo tongues.
2. "Eagle's Nest."
3. Skewered fasters, suspended from lines dropped from four-pole foundation.
4. Perpetual incense fire.
5. White clay bed.
6. Pledger, or "whistler."
7. Bundle owner.
8. Praise-singer.
9. Cedar tree with hoop and mannikin.
10. Buffalo skull.
11. Drummer-singers, with female chorus behind.
12. "Good young men," who, in pairs, reenact battle successes.
13. Mourners (?).
14. Renowned warriors and wives from second day of dance.
15. Willow booths where those who pledged a skewer-fast took position after pledger entered the lodge, and where they rested at night.
16. Skewered dancers outside lodge, suspended from four-pole foundation and "eagle's nest."
17. Post-dancers, skewered with two rawhide lines tied to posts twice the height of a man.

They sang all night until dawn, when older, experienced hunters scouted the buffalo and brought the designated hunters to them.[45] As usual in the solicitation or impressment of "volunteers," the military fraternity in charge of the camp selected four highly-skilled hunters to consecrate the buffalo for Big Shadow's Sun Dance lodge. Big Shadow supplied the horses, ". . . two for packing the hide and meat, two for riding, and one for chasing the buffalo."[46]

The hunters went in pairs, and each struck down a young bull with an arrow that did not go through the animal. Before the bull fell to the ground, one man tied an eagle-down feather to the tail, the other to the head. The eagle feathers were given by the bundle owner and indicated that the "whole lodge was offered to the Sun."[47] The hides were used in constructing the eagle's nest. The hunters were instructed to bring hides and all meat back to camp, leaving only the heads behind. Four scouts, painted white and disguised with coyote skins, rode in a circle and yipped like coyotes to indicate the war party with the enemy, that is, the hunters, had been sighted. The hunters entered the camp from the east only after a messenger came for them. Here they were met by a special praise-singer, who owned a creation song and who led them between two rows of people to the shelter housing the sacred tongues. At this point two warriors narrated coups and gave wish blessings for the revenge mission. As in Lowie's account, the hunters were not allowed to touch foot on soil, but were removed from their horses and placed on a robe. Old people who had assembled now were rewarded with choice pieces of the buffalo, including the liver, which was quickly cooked.[48] Two Leggings reported that the pledger, with hands painted white and face black, took up a knife blackened in token of

---

[45] Nabokov, *Two Leggings*, 81–83.
[46] Curtis, *The Apsaroke, or Crows* 4:71
[47] Ibid., 72.
[48] Ibid., 73.

victory and cut the meat into small portions to make it go as far as possible. To end this day's ceremony, the pledger sang four songs and cut the buffalo hides in half.[49]

Buffalo hunt narratives reveal the minor variations expected in Crow ceremonial performances. For example, Lowie emphasized two as the ceremonial number, while Curtis and Nabokov accented four. There were two hunters to kill two buffalo, two scouts signaled the hunter's return, and two war captains cut up the buffalo and distributed the meat. The Crow desire to find the best-qualified individual opened the door to variability concerning who performed a specific act. Some of this apparent flexibility undoubtedly was a product of missions in the descriptions at hand. For example, the praise-singer who controlled a creation song was a constant companion and assistant to the bundle owner in Curtis's account. Lowie accorded more direction and participation to the bundle owner, who selected the hunters and told them where they would find buffalo. He also met them at the camp entrance and received their reports of killing the buffalo-enemy. It was he, with face blackened, and not the praise-singer, who escorted them in four stages, while he sang a song of victory, to the pledger's tipi—not to the tongue lodge—where they were carried from their horses.

Consecrating the Lodgepoles as Slain Enemy

None but the ill or infirm escaped the pole-collecting task. Actually, it was not an onerous burden, but an adventure against the enemy. The cottonwood and pine trees for the Sun's lodge symbolized the enemy to be slain, and hence they were scouted and couped. Everyone dressed up in his best and put on a festive spirit for this victorious moment. Basic events accented in the primary descriptions reveal a consistent pattern:

[49] Nabokov, *Two Leggings*, 82.

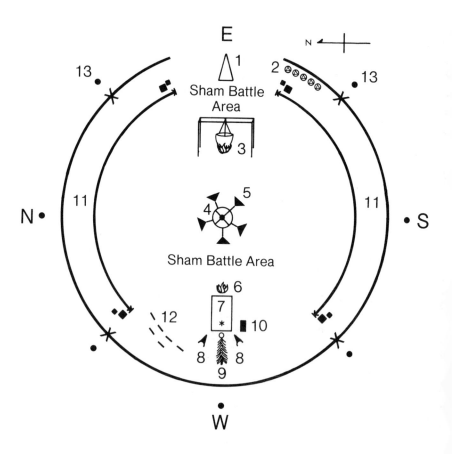

Figure 4. Plan of Crow Sun Dance Lodge (reconstructed from Lowie). The Sun Dance Lodge was simply a large tipi raised on the traditional four-pole foundation. Use of a three-pole foundation may have been more characteristic of the River Crows.

Legend

X. Four poles marking foundation of lodge.
1. Position of coup narrators at consecration of the lodge, first night.
2. Fire tenders.
3. Consecrated buffalo tongues heated in pot.
4. "Eagle's nest" below apex of intersecting poles.
5. Skewered votaries hanging from lines dropped from four foundation poles.
6. Incense fire at foot of pledger's bed.
7. Pledger and white clay bed.
8. Buffalo skull.
9. Cedar tree with hoop mannikin.
10. Probable location of bundle owner.
11. Renowned men and wives.
12. Probable location of drummer-singers.
13. Posts for skewered votaries.

1. Scouting of the poles as enemy, especially the first or main pole, by a renowned warrior, who reported that he had found the enemy.
2. Selection of a virtuous woman who blessed the venture and symbolically killed the enemy by mimicking the cutting of the tree, using an elkhorn prong and stone maul.
3. The ceremonial procession to the main tree and the consecrative slaying and couping of the tree as if it were the enemy.
4. The honoring of young warriors who were assigned one of the poles for the lodge. Parents and kin provided wealth for the bundle owner.
5. Under leadership of the first to drag a pole to the dance ground, young men and women gathered willow bundles for binding the foundation poles and providing a partial thatch.

The Crow penchant for selecting the most qualified person for a public duty led them to choose a pipe holder who had completed with distinction the four conventional coups to perform the task of scouting the enemy-poles.[50] This war captain's task was to find the three or four foundations poles, and then report in metaphor that he had located an enemy who could be easily slain.

At times the Crows made sexual virtue a qualification for carrying out a ceremonial act. This was the case for the tree notcher. The bravest of the camp police usually were sent in search of a woman of virtue; but sometimes a pledger had a certain woman in mind and sought her out himself. He painted himself white, a sign of ceremonial purity, and led a group of men who promised to fast during the Sun Dance.[51] The search party carried the choicest of the sacred tongues, and if the

[50] Curtis, *The Apsaroke, or Crows* 4:68.
[51] Lowie, "Sun Dance of the Crow Indians," 16:31; Morgan, *Indian Journals*, 183.

woman accepted it, she faced a public challenge and risked humiliation if she was a pretender. With tongue in hand she went to the center of the camp and told the Sun, and one and all, that she had been rightfully married with a gift of horses, and that she had remained true to her husband.[52] The camp police led her around the camp to accept challenges to her virtue.[53] If a women felt she could not meet the qualifications, she used the time-honored convention, "My moccasin has a hole in it." The selection of a tree notcher came right after setting up camp at the dance site, delayed until the enemy-poles had been scouted; or, it took place either before or after the procession to the enemy-trees.[54]

In all likelihood the distinguished pipe holder who scouted the enemy-poles reported back to the pledger in his tipi, and doubtless the bundle owner and camp chief also were there. The order of the processional to the enemy-poles is not detailed clearly in the descriptions. The virtuous woman probably rode at the head, followed on foot by the pledger, bundle owner, chiefs abreast, and then the remainder of the camp closed up in a grand arc. Undoubtedly, mounted camp police brought up the rear, and it is quite probable that young warriors also were mounted.

At the tree, the tree notcher validated her virtue anew before the Sun, the Old Man Above, and blessed the revenge venture. After feinting three times, she tapped the elkhorn prong with the maul, which was the signal for young men armed with lances, bows, guns, and coupsticks to whoop and rush to count coup on the enemy-tree.[55] A captive woman marked the tree with either a red or a black ring, and, as soon as the young warriors counted the first coup, a berdache

[52]Nabokov, *Two Leggings*, 81.

[53]Curtis, *The Apsaroke, or Crows* 4:69.

[54]Ibid.; Lowie, "Sun Dance of the Crow Indians," 16:30; Nabokov, *Two Leggings*, 81.

[55]Curtis, *The Absaroke or Crows* 4:69; Lowie, "Sun Dance of the Crow Indians," 16:30; Nabokov, *Two Leggings*, 82–83.

cut it down. As the tree fell, the warriors again rushed to strike a second coup and to wish that all enemies might so die.[56] Meldrum implied that the virtuous tree notcher cut down the first tree, which served as a center pole for the lodge.[57]

After the ceremonious felling of the first tree, any one could cut the rest, although Lowie implied that sweethearts of the pole draggers did so.[58] This followed the usual division of labor, which assigned the getting of firewood and poles for tipis to women. All poles might be of cottonwood, or the first of cottonwood and the remainder of pine, according to a pledger's dream instructions, or those of the bundle owner. The total number of trees used in the lodge varied. It might be eleven,[59] or twenty,[60] or twenty-four,[61] or even thirty-six.[62]

Poles were assigned to brave men whose relatives generated wealth to recompense the bundle owner and reflected the Crow view that anyone honored with a public role should distribute wealth. A distribution signaled a genuineness in feeling and intention, and it also evoked more blessings for the sacred task ahead from those who received the wealth. This was a conventional procedure among the Crows to generate and to circulate wealth. Pole assignment in the Sun Dance probably was an honor that could not be refused, since it promised a share in the good luck that the pledger gained, and perhaps that of the bundle owner also.

Meldrum noted that the center pole was given to the bravest of warriors, and that it was "his property although it remains standing with the lodge."[63] Nine other brave men

[56] Curtis, *The Absaroke or Crows* 4:69.
[57] Morgan, *Indian Journals*, 183.
[58] Lowie, "Sun Dance of the Crow Indians," 16:33.
[59] Nabokov, *Two Leggings*, 83.
[60] Lowie, "Sun Dance of the Crow Indians," 16:33.
[61] Curtis, *The Apsaroke, or Crows* 4:70.
[62] Morgan, *Indian Journals*, 183.
[63] Ibid.

were assigned poles. While ten of the bravest generally were honored, four were obligated to stand their ground in the face of the enemy to allow comrades to escape.[64] Undoubtedly the no-retreat honor was assigned to the four foundation poles. Acceptance was conventionalized by indicating that the pole was heavy, while an easy raising probably signaled refusal. However, the pledger assured acceptance by brushing the candidate with the sacred hoop and mannikin. In the context of Crow convention, Two Leggings's statement that riding one of the poles was "some-thing of a disgrace," hardly makes sense.[65]

Those snagging the poles vied to see who would be first to the dance ground. As they dragged the "dead enemy" into camp, small boys attacked to count coup, as happened in real life when an enemy was slain adjacent to camp.[66] After a noon meal, young men and their sweethearts raced to gather willow bundles for thatching the dance lodge. Their honored leader was the first to arrive at the dance site with a lodge-pole.

The reports do not permit determination of how many days elapsed from the initial announcement to the time when the lodge was completed and the dance begun. Meldrum indicated that seven or eight days passed before the Crows arrived at the dance site. Big Shadow entered the Sun Dance lodge at dusk of the third day after arriving at the encampment.[67] The lodge probably was completed on the seventh or eighth day, and the dance was begun at dusk that evening.

The Sun Dance lodge was a large tipi, perhaps as much as three times the diameter of a regular tipi. Young men, with the aid of two poles linked by a short rawhide rope, raised the three-or four-pole foundation until it rested on the

---

[64] Curtis, *The Apsaroke, or Crows* 4:70; Lowie, "Sun Dance of the Crow Indians," 16:33.
[65] Nabokov, *Two Leggings*, 83.
[66] Curtis, *The Apsaroke, or Crows* 4:70.
[67] Ibid.

woodpile that marked the center of the projected lodge.[68] In Meldrum's narrative, the four foundation poles and a center pole, making five in all, were tied and raised together.[69] The woodpile served as a platform to tie the poles together with wrappings of ground-cedar and red birch and to shape the eagle's nest with hides of the two buffalo killed in the special hunt. Ten rawhide ropes were attached to the tops of the foundation poles, "four to be used in raising the [hide] lodge-covering and six by dancers."[70] Meldrum does not mention the eagle's nest or the eagle medicine man.[71]

The drama now shifted to the eagle medicine man as he was raised in the nest along with the foundation poles. Enroute to the lodge, the eagle medicine man undoubtedly followed the ceremonial convention of stopping four times and singing his medicine song for the last time before the west pole.[72] He climbed this west pole and entered the nest, and after three ceremonial feints to the accompaniment of song and whistle, he was raised aloft and the poles set in prepared holes. The eagle medicine man dodged about in a kneeling position, flapped his feather wings, and blew his whistle as the other poles were quickly placed in position.[73] The hide cover, hair side out, now was drawn into position. In summer, a brush thatch was applied.

In a three-pole foundation two poles were aligned on a north-south axis, and the third was positioned to the west.[74] Identification of the west pole climbed by the medicine man is easy in a three-pole foundation, but a four-pole foundation presents another problem, since none of the poles face di-

[68] Nabokov, *Two Leggings*, 83.

[69] Morgan, *Indian Journals*, 183.

[70] Curtis, *The Apsaroke, or Crows* 4:73; Nabokov, *Two Leggings*, 83.

[71] Morgan, *Indian Journals*.

[72] Lowie, "Sun Dance of the Crow Indians," 16:37; Nabokov, *Two Leggings*, 83.

[73] Curtis, *The Apsaroke, or Crows* 4:74.

[74] Nabokov, *Two Leggings*, 83.

rectly west or east. The two poles to the west, usually raised first by the Crows, were positioned toward the northwest and southwest, and the east poles were toward the northeast and southeast.[75] Two poles, one of which carried the hide cover, stood between the northwest and southwest poles; and two poles for the entrance were placed between the northeast and southeast poles. Lowie identified the pole climbed by the eagle medicine man as the one rubbed with the hides used to prepare the eagle's nest.[76] Two renowned warriors rubbed the hides against the underside of the pole and took care not to let the hides touch the ground. This pole probably was the northwest foundation pole, since a northern orientation was important to Crow ceremonials.

Similarities in the construction and plan of the Sun Dance lodge far outweighed differences noted in the descriptions (see Figures 2, 3, and 4). The lodge was a big tipi even in the case of a central support with scalp attached, described by Meldrum. The presence of two pledgers gave a special plan to the lodge. Everything was in twos. There were two pots with consecrated buffalo tongues (although two pots in the lodge were not uncommon). Each pledger had a team of drummer-singers and a cedar tree with two incense fires smoking on either side. Each had a separate bed and danced to a feathered hoop and mannikin hung in a cedar about eight feet high. Beyond the cedars, along the west wall, were mourners, while renowned warriors and spouses took places along the north and south walls. Meldrum made no mention of sham battle areas east and west of the eagle's nest as noted by Lowie, and located west of the nest by Curtis.

The three rows of white sand stretching for about eight feet and located three feet apart, between which the two pledgers danced, according to Meldrum, were unusual.[77]

[75] Campbell, "Tipis of the Crow Indians," 29:28.
[76] Lowie, "Sun Dance of the Crow Indians," 16:37.
[77] Morgan, *Indian Journals*, 183–86.

However, Two Leggings spoke of two piles of white clay between which a pledger stood on first entering the lodge.[78] The absence of buffalo-skull idols in Meldrum's narrative offered another contrast to Lowie and Curtis. Both Lowie and Curtis again located but one incense fire at the foot (east) of the pledger's white earth bed, while Meldrum located two at the head (west) of the bed. Lowie placed small shelters where skewer-fasters rested each evening outside the lodge. In Big Shadow's Sun Dance young men undergoing this sacrifice took positions in small booths within the lodge before beginning their prayer torment, and probably rested there at night.

Big Shadow's dance indicated that ceremonial conventions recorded by Meldrum and Lowie were standard by 1844. These customs included the honoring of a virtuous woman as leader of the firewood party and the assignment of a young man noted for sexual restraint to head a task force to bring white earth for the pledger's bed.[79] During the time the pledger was undergoing a final consecration and rehearsal in his tipi, war leaders, organized as a war party with scouts in front, entered the lodge and circled to the left. Facing east at the back and looking up to the eagle's nest, the pipe holder invoked his power and narrated a prophecy of a dead enemy granted in vision or dream.

The pledger, holding the hoop-mannikin, danced and whistled his entrance of the lodge, making the usual four stops along the way.[80] Meldrum reports that the pledger danced

---

[78] Nabokov, *Two Leggings*, 84. In the Hidatsa *NaxpikE* or Hide-striking, the pledger danced between two mounds of earth, and from the mounds to a central pole and back. A buffalo head with a strip of hide and tail was attached to the fork of the central pole by a berdache. The brush-covered shelter in which the ceremony took place apparently was not a tipi, but was constructed of nine circumference poles and a central pole, for a total of ten. See Bowers, "Hidatsa Social and Ceremonial Organization," 194: 313–22.

[79] Curtis, *The Apsaroke, or Crows* 4:74–75; Morgan, *Indian Journals*, 184.

to the cedar and embraced the tree and kissed it.[81] This was the time for the drummer-singers, bearing tambourine-type drums, to enter and take their places in front of and to the north of the cedar tree. Women singers seated themselves behind, as today.[82] The pledger was followed in his entrance by the bundle owner and his wife or other worthy assistant; and, in Big Shadow's performance, drummer-singers brought up the rear of the procession. Once the pledger stood at the western exterior, the direction in which he circled the lodge is not clear; but inside he circuited to the left, which placed the bundle owner to his right, as occurs today. Once the pledger and bundle owner made their ceremonial entrance, skewer fasters entered their booths, and young warriors, probably with recent victories to dramatize, took up positions on the north and south sides of the lodge, with wives behind.[83]

Dance for Power

The pledger undoubtedly entered the dance lodge at dusk, just as in the present ceremony. Big Shadow's first song-dance was coordinated with sham battles by the young warriors, and in all probability a sham battle at the start of the dancing was an important element of the ceremony.[84] The reward for taking part in the sham battle was a tongue cooked in the pots by women wielding "forks" adorned with scalps of the immediate enemy. This was the time, as during other coup recitations, when warriors pressed their claims for a tongue. According to standard practice, they handed the tongues to sweethearts or spouses.

[80] Morgan, *Indian Journals*, 186; Lowie, "Sun Dance of the Crow Indians," 16:42.

[81] Morgan, *Indian Journals*, 186.

[82] Ibid.; Lowie, "Sun Dance of the Crow Indians," 16:42.

[83] Curtis, *The Apsaroke, or Crows* 4:76; Lowie, "Sun Dance of the Crow Indians," 16:42; Morgan, *Indian Journals*, 186.

[84] Curtis, *The Apsaroke, or Crows* 4:76; Lowie, *Sun Dance of the Crow Indians*," 16:42; Morgan, *Indian Journals*, 186.

Action on the first night ended around midnight, when pledger and skewer fasters bedded down. Only the fire tenders maintained their posts. The pledger rested on a clean buffalo robe, and another covered him as he slept with face ready to catch the first light of Sun.

The major action of the next, or second, day consisted of preparing the skewer fasters and attaching them to lines draped from the lodge poles, poles set up outside and inside the lodge, or to buffalo skulls. Some of them drew fresh buffalo heads, buffalo hides, and bearskins.[85] Those attached to poles had shield and lance raised nearby. A post faster wore a skunk-skin necklace, blew an eagle-bone whistle, and wore an eagle feather in his hair. White was the standard paint for body and for lines to which skewers were attached. Two Leggings was marked with the sign of Morning Star in five places—on both arms and shoulders, and on his breast.[86]

The second day, as in today's performance, was the time of greatest effort and expectation of good things to be given to the suppliants. The drumming-singing and war whooping transformed the dance lodge and all within it into a gigantic exuberant war party. Clan fathers continuously burst out in songs of praise to urge their "children" to brave the ordeal. If skewer fasters obtained a good vision on this day, their personal sacrifices were over, whether they had broken flesh or not.[87] If unsuccessful, they were released near midnight to rest in their booths, or they lay down with relaxed lines near their sacrifice poles and hoped for a sleep-dream.[88] Action continued throughout the day until midnight, except for four breaks.

Meldrum reported that no one drew "bull horns" after the

---

[85] Curtis, *The Absaroke, or Crows*, 78; Morgan, *Indian Journals*, 187.
[86] Nabokov, *Two Leggings*, 46.
[87] Curtis, *The Apsaroke, or Crows* 4:79.
[88] Ibid.; Lowie, "Sun Dance of the Crow Indians," 16:45.

second day, and none began the pole sacrifice after the third.[89] Fulfillment of the power quest in the Sun Dance was expected on the fourth day, just as in the more usual power fast in the mountains. It could go on for five, six, and even seven days, with the bundle owner trying to induce a victory dream on the seventh day.

While war songs filled the lodge in exultation of victory, what went on outside, a short distance from the lodge, was cast in a more lugubrious mold. In the nearby hills the plaintive wails and prayers of mourners and of individual power fasters rose to greet the Sun and his helpers. Here individual suppliants made their fasts and flesh offerings on the second or third days. They often cut off a joint of one or more fingers as an offering to the Sun in the expectation that some of the enemy would be delivered into Crow hands. Meldrum noted that the finger joints were collected in a "willow bowl . . . and left in the lodge tied to the centerpole."[90] The offerings he viewed were never less than forty, and in all probability these were contributed by maternal and paternal relatives of the deceased. There were more offerings for Sun as they left the lodge. The eagle-feathered hoop, painted black, was attached to a pole and leaned against the lodge. Sage was tied to the hoop as a special offering to Sun. Another pole for Sun was draped with a mountain-lion skin, a white buffalo hide, eagle feathers, and the "skin of a silver-tipped fox."[91]

The pledger's prophetic vision was the climax of the ceremony. Old men and women gathered to hear what Big Shadow would relate when his spirit returned to his body. A prophecy of victory brought a great shout from the people, for now they could relax and look forward to good things to come.

Available descriptions of the Crow Sun Dance dating in

---

[89]Morgan, *Indian Journals*, 187.
[90]Ibid.
[91]Curtis, *The Apsaroke, or Crows* 4:80.

memory from 1844, and perhaps earlier, reveal a stable pat-
terning of core features that far outweigh any differences in
the separate performances. There is full agreement on motivation, procedures, objectives, and basic ceremonial instruments
used. Meldrum's account discloses more influences of the Hidatsa *NaxpikE* in presumable River Crow performances, such
as the dancing between rows of sacred earth, a probable dance
movement toward the hoop-effigy and back, and the central
pole. However, the central pole may have been required as a
support for the oversized lodge to accommodate two pledgers.
An absence of elements may be just as useful in tracing connections, providing absence is not a simple omission. The only
significant lack in Meldrum's account relates to the "eagle's
nest" atop the dance lodge, an absence compatible with the
Hidatsa *NaxpikE* or Hide-striking.

CHAPTER 4

Introduction of the Wind River Shoshoni Sun Dance to the Crow Indians

In Search of Power and Meaning: William Big Day

William Big Day and Annie, his wife, had no special purpose in mind when they decided to attend the Sun Dance at Fort Washakie in 1938. They first went to Thermopolis, Wyoming, where William took hot baths for his rheumatism, and then went on to the Wind River Shoshonis. There *was* something else, but its meaning was not clear until William heard the drumming and singing of the Sun Dance. From time to time a dream had come to him in which he heard a song that made all the Crow people happy. Now the drumming and singing of the Shoshoni Sun Dance stirred him inside and he felt happy—so happy that he felt "like crying and laughing at the same time." These were the songs of which he had dreamt—and now he might be able to help his people! He remembered how, at one time, the Crows had been many people. Now when he saw them together, they were few, and getting fewer. They were very fearful about disease and the painful separation from loved ones that it frequently brought.

Big Day was forty-seven years old at the time of his first visit to the Wind River Shoshonis in 1938. He helped out with the singing and also made friends with a Shoshoni dancer, John Truhujo. Truhujo told William and Annie about his adventures with fasting, of the time he used peyote, and when he had danced in the Sun Dance.

Big Day was born about 1891 in Pryor District on the Crow Reservation where he grew up. In its isolation from the mainstream of things, Pryor tended to be more conservative than other districts. Beyond school, church, and country store, there was little opportunity for contact with whites. Even though Crows were beginning to exchange horses and wagons for automobiles in the thirties, the road to Pryor was a long, bumpy, and tire-wearing drive, and people traveled very little until after World War II.

Big Day's outlook reflected far more of his traditional up-bringing than what he learned from schoolteachers, missionaries, and doctors at the hospital. Stories of the old life related by his adoptive grandparents filled his boyish mind, and in imagination he relived the buffalo hunt and war raid. Big Day was frequently sick during childhood, and his schooling ended at fourth grade. Later his health improved, and he wrestled, ran footraces, and raced horses like any other teenager. For a short time he worked as a ranchhand, and at age nineteen he married. For eighteen years Big Day farmed, until rheumatism forced him to give it up. During his active days he entered horses in local races, headed the Pryor rodeo committee for nine years, and served as district councilman and representative to the Tribal Council.

Big Day's contacts with Christianity were as intermittent and casual as with school. Though baptized a Catholic at nine years of age, he never was a staunch church-goer. To Big Day, the white man's religion appeared the "hardest belief [ever] and something that any Indian couldn't possibly fulfill." His forefathers had never worshipped as white men did. Indians and whites were like horses. One was built for racing, the other for drawing heavy loads. "We are just like that—the white man's religion is for the white man and the Indian belief is for the Indian."

Big Day's background and the nature of his contacts during childhood pointed him toward an identity rooted in Indian tradition. But how could one find identity in a world dominated by the white man's books, churches, schools, medicine, and government? Dreams provided Big Day with the clues to his future as an Indian. From the time he was nineteen years of age, spirit beings beckoned to him from a bluff above Pryor, promising wealth and success if he fasted and followed their instruction. But Big Day was afraid and did not answer the call.

Then Peyotism came to Pryor, and Big Day attended an all-night ceremony, about 1916, when he was twenty-five years old. His half-hearted devotion to Catholicism ended some years later when the local priest excommunicated him for attending peyote meetings. Newly excommunicated and thirty-five years of age, Big Day was ready to accept Peyotism in the traditional form of the "Tipi Way." Up to then he was uncertain about peyote as he had come to know it; for in ceremony it did not appear sacred in the Indian way. "I thought that was a man-made way. There was peyote in there; but they were getting other stuff in there like an altar and cross, and no smoking [tobacco prayers] and I thought it was made up by a man," he said. In the Tipi Way he found a traditional identity in the half-moon altar of ashes, the fire, cedar incense, sage, the feathered cane of the leader, the eagle-feather fan for curing, the eagle-bone whistle for calling the spiritual helpers, and the smoking of tobacco in prayer. There was no Christian symbolism of cross and salvation there— it was all Indian.

In the peyote tipi Big Day had the comfortable feeling that he was worshipping with his own people in their own way. Annie, his wife, felt the same way. She resented the superior airs of whites and segregated seating in the churches—as if whites were fearful that some bug would crawl from the Indians to them! Like William, she was convinced that the

Creator had guided her into the Native American Church and into the Sun Dance. Her brother was head of the Pryor district peyotists.

Big Day used peyote in the Tipi Way for five years before he decided to try it out in a traditional fast for power. He wanted the power to cure, since he was fearful the Crows would die out. His first effort was unsuccessful, and after waiting four years, Big Day, in the company of his close friend Caleb Bull Shows, tried again. They took a small tipi to the mountains nearby, and held peyote meetings for three days and nights. A spirit in the form of a bird appeared to Big Day, and as he followed it in his vision, it sang a medicine song for him. At the same time he learned that:

. . . it is natural for people to die, even if little babies, and then on through life they die. That was nature that God had made. I find that out through peyote; nobody was talking to me, but I find that out through his medicine, peyote. Then I did not know what to say or what to do after I found that out. I should have asked for a little power to help people, but I kind of got too excited to ask for anything. I came home the third night and went in the peyote tipi that they put here, and that made four nights.

Big Day's vision quest combined both tradition and novel practice. The search for the power-giving spirits in the seclusion of the Pryor mountains segregated the profane life of the log-cabin encampment from the holy experience. This method was as it used to be. Taking a friend along in a power quest was traditional practice, as was abstention from food and water, the use of smoke-prayers, and the ritual use of the number four. The pitching of a tipi and the use of an hallucinogen added new touches, but Big Day was not the first person to unite peyote with traditional worship. Experimentation with mind-altering agents was congenial to the psychic state sought in Crow power-quests.

His visit to the Shoshoni Sun Dance in 1938 thus was not

without purpose, though momentarily its part in the design of his life was hidden from Big Day. He was increasingly aware and convinced that his dreams were directing him to a life-destiny. Through peyote he was led to seek power, and received a little. Now, with the Sun Dance, he knew the true meaning of his dreams—the spirits had brought him to the Sun Dance. In 1939 he returned to Fort Washakie, thinking that he might dance. Again he talked with John Truhujo and was convinced more than ever that "when they fast in that dance, they always get some gifts or visions for power . . . and that is why I went in." It had been some forty years since a Crow Indian from Lodge Grass, Bill Moore, had participated in the Shoshoni Sun Dance.

The second day of the Sun Dance was critical, for it was then that the gifts of power might be conferred on the dancer. On the second day, Big Day suffered a chest cramp that gave him great pain, and he called Truhujo to doctor him. He had great difficulty making it to the center pole. The image of death gripped Big Day as Truhujo set about his cure. In imagination he saw the cemetery hill at Pryor, covered with melting snow. As Truhujo told him later, this meant that he would have died in the spring had he not taken part in the Shoshoni Sun Dance.

Truhujo's interpretation of his cemetery vision added another sign to the mystic design of his life that Big Day was trying to understand. During and after this first Sun Dance he had several visions, two of which he considered of special importance. In one he saw a Shoshoni and a Crow facing each other, right arms outstretched in salutation. At the time, he did not know that this vision forecast the bringing of the Wind River Shoshoni Sun Dance to the Crows. In another he saw the medicine feathers used by Truhujo passed to him "through the Sun Dance." When Big Day told this to Truhujo, the latter was reluctant to part with the feathers but stated: "If it was given to you through the Sun Dance, that is the only way that I would let go." Later, Big Day was encouraged by Truhujo to take the Sun Dance to the Crows, for then, as he said, "You can pray." It was at the first performance of the Sun Dance at Pryor in 1941 that Truhujo formally presented the medicine feathers to Big Day.

In their timely appearance, critical situations have a way of drawing together the strands of a career that appears to drift between dream and reality. For Big Day, his life-goal of medicine man gradually took shape in a series of events that began with spirit beings urging him to fast in the old way. His experiments with peyote gave him some personal confidence, since he did get a medicine song. The excommunication from the Catholic Church simply reinforced his search for personal meaning in traditional Indian belief and practice. Next, the Sun Dance added confirmation to his mystic dream visitations. Two personal events drew him irresistibly into the Sun Dance. First, in the winter of 1939, his adopted son became deathly ill with double pneumonia. Big Day, worried and suspicious of hospital care, brought the infant home from Billings despite a warning that home treatment meant death. Taking the child outside the log-cabin home, Big Day held him toward the rising sun and vowed: "If this little boy gets well, I will dance." Miraculously the child recovered; and William, together with his brother Henry and his close friend Caleb Bull Shows, fulfilled his vow by dancing at Fort Washakie in the summer of 1940. That winter his brother's child became ill, and nothing could be done to relieve the infant of his pain. Again Big Day addressed himself to the Sun, vowing, with arms extended, to put up a Sun Dance among the Crows if the child recovered. Soon the infant showed signs of getting better, took some beef soup, and within a couple of days was well. "That," said William, "is how the first Shoshoni Sun Dance was put up among the Crow, on account of that baby. I asked John Truhujo and them to come and help me [because] I was going to put up a Sun Dance among the Crow." In 1975, the child, Raymond Big Day, danced in the Sun Dance at Lodge Grass.

Left to right: Henry Big Day and William Big Day. Pryor, 1941.

Reinforcement, Dreams, and Christianity

For Big Day, the telescoping of successes between 1938 and 1940 accelerated confidence that he would wield the medicine feathers in the Sun Dance. Everything reinforced the legitimacy of Indian belief and practice. The Creator gave the Indian people a "way of hardship," a way of "fasting and of dry throats and mouths" in order that they might "look for luck" in this life. Any one who entered the Sun Dance must cleanse himself right down to the dirt under his fingernails and toenails. By smoking himself in cedar incense and sweating, a man made himself clean, just as the animals in the wild. Four days before entering the dance lodge, a dancer should suspend sexual relations.

For Big Day, the Creator was everywhere—in the sun, in the earth, and in the wind. The only way men could know the Creator was through what He had made. The earth was His creation and He put His power into its different parts. The Sun was the owner of the Sun Dance, and inside the lodge they prayed to Old Man Sun. In the churches, away from the Sun Dance, they prayed to God, or the One Who Made All Things; but Old Man Sun and the One Who Made All Things were one and the same. As for the buffalo attached to the center pole, it was just a buffalo, and one never prayed to it, though one could talk to it. Yet the buffalo came "in spirit during the Sun Dance . . . to run over one of the dancers." When this happened, a person began to dream, and the other dancers covered him with cattails where he lay. In dreaming, his spirit "might go to some mountain and might find there what to do—how to doctor some sick person or even he might get a whistle or some feathers to be used in the Sun Dance." A dreamer also heard a song. To be knocked down by the buffalo was a mighty experience, for it brought good luck and wealth, as well as knowledge of ways to cure sickness.

The eagle, or the big bird, as the old men referred to it,

was hardly ever seen. One old man said that he had seen it —a huge bird with a yellow bill and wings. The forked pole of the Sun Dance lodge represented this big bird, the thunder associated with big hailstorms. Once in a while they prayed to the Thunderbird for power to cure, wealth, and good luck. The eagle sometimes appeared in a vision as a person, and Big Day noted that at such times the eagle looked a lot like the late Chief Plenty Coups. The willows tied in a bundle and placed across the center pole, just below the fork, represented a wish for the increase of the Crow tribe and for good luck. One never prayed to the willows. One never prayed to the center pole either, but it was the "lightning rod" for the transmission of power. According to Big Day:

That centerpole was grown by the Creator, so they took and used it. It is full of water. If it were not for that [center pole] some of the dancers might drop in the lodge. When they get the centerpole up it is full of power, and when they doctor, they always touch it. Just before they chop it, when they pray they have the power in that tree. That is the only time power is in there. After it is set up with the buffalo head and willows, by looking at it you know it has power in there.

Once at Pryor they asked Old Man Sun to put some power in the center tree. Big Day lay down and looked up at the tree and noticed something like a heat wave wrapping itself around the pole from top to bottom. He got up and smoked, and thanked Old Man Sun for giving them the power. At another time at Crow Agency he again saw the same shimmering wave, but it went back up and never got to the tree. Whether the Creator sent the power, Big Day did not know. It simply happened that all power came through the center tree.

Big Day's ideas about how the world was organized and how it worked expressed traditional Crow views. The Sun was a mighty spirit, and Big Day equated Old Man Sun with the Creator, or He First Made All Things, of whom the missionaries spoke. The ambiguous association of Sun and Creator echoed traditional theology.[1]

The world view of the Crows bordered on pantheism, and they were more interested in getting protective and career-making power than in a theology of things. Indeed, to them the world was alive with power placed there for men to seek out and use for their own benefit. Indians, unlike whites, deliberately suffered by going without food and water if they hoped to improve their "luck" in life. There was no other way, for that was the Creator's gift to the Indian. The spirit beings who brought good things to the power seeker transformed themselves into buffalos, eagles, and other things of this world. The buffalo and eagle were especially powerful beings who helped Indians cure sickness and brought good luck and wealth. To get lucky and to become wealthy had been solid objectives in the past, but they had equal importance for the present. A seeker after good luck and wealth, as Big Day noted, paid close attention to his dreams, for they were signals sent by spirits, and correct interpretation was essential to success. In his concern for the welfare of the Crows, Big Day also reflected a traditional feeling that one's power should be used to help one's people.

Pathway to the Past: Personal and Cultural Factors

Why did Big Day choose the pathway to a traditional Indian identity rather than the highway to civilization presented in mission and school? There is no simple answer, but personal and cultural factors played important roles.

Big Day's adoption by grandparents followed common Crow practice, and he probably experienced the kind of imagi-

---

[1]Lowie, *The Crow Indians*, 252.

native contacts with the past that other youths of his day shared. The favorite story-tellers during the thirties were old men who recounted the legendary history of the Crows and personal anecdotes of the past.[2] They easily drew a large crowd of good-humored and interested listeners who relished the spice and wonder of those mystic times.

The personal factor of poor health limited Big Day's contacts with American culture in schoolroom and mission church. His youthful dreams, in which spirits beckoned to him and promised wealth in return for fasting, reflected the conservative orientation that led him to reject the Christian-influenced version of Peyotism first introduced by Lone Bear.[3] Only the Tipi Way, with its traditional Plains ceremonial form, symbolism, and procedures was satisfactory to him. Excommunication by the Catholic Church thrust him back to traditional ways. Other personal factors accelerated his efforts to adapt past ideals to the present. There was his prolonged suffering with rheumatism, which forced him to give up farming, and which coincided with his attempt to combine peyote with the power quest. The modest effects of his experiments with peyote finally turned Big Day in the direction of the Sun Dance soon after the government had abandoned its punitive program to eradicate Indian worship. The cure and visions experienced in a first trial of the Sun Dance convinced Big Day there was power to be obtained there. The quick cures of his adopted child and that of his brother brought solid confirmation of the power of old ways.

Big Day illustrated how an individual stood between, and reacted to, the positive influences and pressures of cultural conventions and the "historical" factors of life events and

---

[2] Renowned storytellers no longer attract public audiences, and grandparents do not communicate the life and miracles of the past to their grandchildren. Today the television screen grips and extends the imagination of Crow children.

[3] Robert Kiste, "Crow Peyotism," manuscript.

personal aspirations. It was these "historical" factors, expressed in feelings accompanying interpersonal relations and the challenge of personal crises, that mediated Big Day's relations between American and Crow culture. Admittedly he brought a bias toward Crow culture traceable to "primary" childhood learnings, which Bruner suggested were critical in predisposing biculturated individuals toward a conservative or assimilative posture.[4] However, the choice was not predictable solely on the basis of childhood conditioning, because the bicultural situation confronted the individual with the testing of both traditional and alien cultures in his own experience and in that of others. The moment of truth came when the crisis mounted and the individual became convinced that the cultural procedures then on trial were a failure. This happened to Big Day when the doctors in Billings failed to produce a cure of his adopted child, and yet their dire predictions did not take place. When Big Day vowed to suffer in the Sun Dance in exchange for the cure of his child, he tested American culture as much as traditional culture. From the moment of that critical challenge, his life as a Sun Dance medicine man and traditionalist began more and more to fall into place. The issue of personal choice and actions provoked by crises makes Skinner's behavioral modification model of learning more acceptable in explaining Big Day's experiential choices than a simple stimulus-response model.[5]

Big Day's career is also of interest because it brings out the importance of religion as a primary center of conflict and of choice between American and Crow culture. Here world views met in competition for allegiance to a community of "true" believers. The religious institution came to be the proving ground for retention of an Indian identity versus change to an identity molded by the alien white man. For

---

[4] Edward Bruner, "Primary Group Experience and the Processes of Acculturation," *American Anthropologist* 58 (1956):605–23.

[5] B. F. Skinner, *About Behaviorism.*

Big Day, Indian and white were as different as East and West. Their religions, based on different temperaments, accented differences between the two established by the Creator. Moreover, in the domains of belief and curing, the superiority of American institutions was open to practical challenge. The importance of religion as a base for reorganizing and reaffirming a sense of cultural identity is well documented in studies of American Indians. Time and again prophets arose to revitalize their communities with revelations that legitimated traditional objectives.[6] From the start, Christianity served as a primary instrument for splitting Indian communities and at times segregating Christian converts from traditionalists.[7] Today, religion continues to be an important symbol of personal and ethnic identity, for it is in ceremony that this identity can be lived out. It was this identity and legitimacy of self that Big Day discovered in the Sun Dance. When I last saw him in 1956, he was on his way to the Rocky Boy Crees, where he was invited to lead a Sun Dance.

Dissemination of the Sun Dance Among the Crows

In the old days a pledger of a Sun Dance depended on the chief to mobilize the energies of the people behind his sacrifice of self in order to gain revenge on the enemy. Now there were no chiefs, for the renowned Plenty Coups, their last, had passed away in 1932. A superintendent stood in the place of the chief. A tribal council maintained a semblance

[6]David F. Aberle, *The Peyote Religion Among the Navaho;* Homer G. Barnett, *Indian Shakers: A Messianic Cult of the Pacific Northwest;* George Spindler, *Sociocultural and Psychological Processes in Menomini Acculturation;* Fred W. Voget, "The American Indian in Transition: Reformation and Acculturation," *American Anthropologist* 50 (1956); Anthony F. C. Wallace, "Revitalization Movements," *American Anthropologist* 58 (1956).

[7]Robert Berkhofer, *Salvation and the Savage: An Analysis of Protestant Missions and American Indian Response, 1787–1862.*

of the old political process, though its active members were no longer warriors, but elected representatives from the districts. Clans and dancing fraternities still provided a traditional base for mutual aid.

For the first Sun Dance at Pryor, gaining the superintendent's cooperation was critical for Big Day, since he could supply trucks for hauling poles and brush and approve the killing of buffalo from the tribal herd for the feast following the dance. He also could provide police for the encampment and permit the deputizing of assistants. Moreover, gaining the cooperation of the superintendent was important because John Truhujo had indicated that he would help Big Day if it was "O.K." with the superintendent. Robert Yellowtail, the superintendent, was himself a Crow Indian and a member of the Big-Lodge clan, as was Big Day. Moreover, John Truhujo had successfully doctored Yellowtail's sister Aimee back in 1907, when he visited a Crow half-brother.

At a special meeting in January, 1941, Big Day explained to district representatives the reason for his vow to put up a Sun Dance. He stated his conviction that the Sun Dance would prove to be a powerful medicine and an effective means of prayer were the Crows to take it up. He and his close friend Caleb Bull Shows, dressed in their Sun Dance regalia and demonstrated the dance steps. The several districts pledged help and determined that Big Day should be in full charge, since he was the only one who knew anything about the Sun Dance. Big Day drew upon clansmen and friends, principally from Pryor district, to form a Sun Dance Committee. The committee was charged with organizing and running the Sun Dance, raising funds for the feast, and arranging transportation for the Shoshoni leaders. Local white storekeepers and stockmen were canvassed for contributions. To attract a non-Indian audience they publicized the dance in the *Billings Gazette* and other Montana newspapers. They expected to charge whites twenty-five cents for attending.

The Sun Dance at Pryor drew a large crowd, both Indian

and non-Indian. There were twenty-three dancers, all male: fourteen Crows, eight Shoshonis, and one white, a sheepherder from Shoshoni territory. Four old Crow men also entered the lodge to fast. The majority of Crow dancers were from the two closely linked and most populous clans, the Newly-made-lodge and the Big-lodge. Big Day's main support came from his clansmen and also from his own district. Nine of the dancers were from Pryor, two from Crow Agency, two from Big Horn, and one from Lodge Grass. On the second day, in answer to Big Day's dream, Truhujo presented him with the doctoring feathers.

The Sun Dance at Pryor took place in June. In less than eight weeks the Crows would gather at Crow Agency for their annual fair, established in 1905. The occasion of the fair and rodeo was the high point of social activity when Crows got together for feasting, traditional dancing, giveaways, and ceremonial adoptions. At this time they decked themselves out in handsome traditional dress, decorated their horses lavishly with beaded sashes, and rode around the camp in a colorful parade. In the octagonal dance hall they displayed agricultural products and the classwork and art of Crow students. The rodeo was a prime attraction, which gave Crow riders a chance to show their skill at bulldogging and riding bucking horses in prize competitions. Why not have a Sun Dance every year at the grand tribal encampment? The idea apparently originated with Superintendent Yellowtail, who responded enthusiastically to the Sun Dance at Pryor. He also renewed relations with Shoshoni medicine-man John Truhujo at that time.

When Superintendent Yellowtail approached Big Day about holding a Sun Dance in association with the Crow fair, Big Day opposed it because he thought the dance should be held only once a year, and he felt the festive nature of the fair would turn the Sun Dance into a "show." Big Day considered that he had a preemptive right to the Sun Dance, since he was the one who had brought the ceremony to the Crows and had given gifts to Truhujo in the traditional manner of purchase. However, Crow ceremonial organization was never centralized, since power and authority were distributed among owners of separate medicine bundles. As a tribal ceremony, the Sun Dance was never the property of a single person, nor in the hands of a tribal "priest." Tradition permitted the transfer of mystic power three times through replicas of the original without relinquishing the original. There was no way Big Day could control the Sun Dance or limit the proliferation of power replicas. The key to multiplication of power replicas and the raising up of other medicine men among the Crows was John Truhujo, the Mexican-Shoshoni. The other key figure in the struggles for control was Robert Yellowtail, the superintendent.

The ceremony at Pryor not only kindled enthusiasm for the ceremony but also proved to the Crows that power could be put into the "tree" or center pole. Onlookers witnessed the apparent cures of those who stood barefoot and bareheaded before the tree while being doctored by Truhujo or Big Day. The Tribal Council voted that there should be a Sun Dance at the Crow fair in 1941. Superintendent Yellowtail was charged with heading a delegation to arrange for the Shoshonis to come and direct a dance at Crow Agency. Gus Other-medicine of Crow Agency already had pledged the dance. Confronted with this development, Big Day either had to accept or oppose it behind the scenes. He chose the latter, making a visit to Truhujo in July, ahead of the Crow delegation. According to Truhujo, Big Day tried to dissuade him from letting the people at Crow Agency make a "game" out of the dance. Truhujo in turn indicated that he wished "to give the others a chance, to see what they would do with it." If they made a show of it, he would take action.

The Crow delegation consulted with respected Shoshoni Sun Dance leaders, but the Shoshonis hesitated about giving their ceremony to the Crows. Ambiguities generated by rival conflicts and hesitations made it easy to approach their first choice, John Truhujo, who indicated his willingness to lead the dance at Crow Agency. The Crows offered money for transportation, food, and shelter for the Shoshoni contingent. The second Sun Dance took place from August 21 to 26, 1941, at Crow Agency. The dance was the high point of the annual Crow Fair and Rodeo, which united the tribe in an encampment that included agricultural and educational displays, horse racing, rodeo events, war dancing, modern dancing, and mobile food stands. Performances of the Medicine-pipe Dance of the Hidatsas and of the Crow Tobacco-adoption Dance also took place. The Crows obviously wished to put on a dance that would outshine the Shoshonis, and Superintendent Yellowtail enthusiastically talked of a coast-to-coast radio hookup over which he would speak for half an hour. Publicity was intensive and extensive, with some accounts reaching West Coast papers. Crow Agency cooperated by furnishing trucks for hauling poles and brush. Buffalo meat from the tribal herd was provided for the feast, and portions were distributed to honored guests from other tribes as well as to Crows. Truhujo and his associates, a brother-in-law and a close friend, Tilton West, were each given a buffalo.

The late arrival of Tom Compton, Truhujo's bitter Shoshoni rival, created a flurry of excitement. Compton came to contest Truhujo's leadership, and perhaps to get a buffalo himself. He was angry because Truhujo took the transportation money wired by the Crows and gave him the slip. From the very moment of his arrival, Compton criticized Truhujo and tried to take over direction of the Sun Dance. The contest between the two for the good will of the Crows continued throughout the dance.

In pushing Truhujo into the background and attempting control, Compton acted somewhat abrasively and officiously. While Compton assumed the role of director, Truhujo created the impression that he (Truhujo) was but an adviser working in behalf of the Crows. When Crows questioned whether or not Compton had the right to make all the decisions, Truhujo countered that the pledger was the leader of the dance and not the medicine man. When Compton ruled on the last day of the dance that they must continue until late in the afternoon, Truhujo quietly passed the word that it was all right to quit any time following the sunrise ceremony of the third day. With friendly sabotage and by utilizing the strength of his kin relations with the Crow, Truhujo easily won out over Compton at the seat of secular influence and power, Crow Agency. Compton later supervised dances at Pryor on three separate occasions, but his influence faded rapidly after World War II. According to Truhujo, Compton's medicine really belonged to his wife, who had received it from a former husband. Compton's use of the medicine angered his wife, and she took it away from him. Divorce followed, and the French-Shoshoni medicine man left Fort Washakie and went back to his people, the Lemhi Shoshonis. "They tell me that Tom ain't much good any more. Nothing is right for him any more," reported Truhujo. As things turned out at the Crow Agency Sun Dance, Compton and his followers received no more than the usual ration of buffalo meat and no transportation money except for popular contributions made generally for visitors.

The dance at the Crow fair drew forty-nine dancers, forty of whom were Crows. The climax of the dance came with the apparent cures of Charlie Horse, a rheumatic cripple, and of Herbert Old Bear, a heart patient. Horse fasted along with the dancers and, on both the second and third days, managed to walk to the center pole and to dance backwards a few steps. At the conclusion of the dance, he picked up the stool upon which he sat and walked with difficulty from the lodge—an event that impressed those present. Subsequently, Horse suffered a relapse and became as immobile as before, but the cure of Old Bear was more spectacular. Old Bear was a Crow "cousin" or "brother" of Truhujo and was in the hospital at Crow Agency. Doctors at the Agency hospital warned that he might not survive his first steps, but Old Bear walked barefoot before the tree and was doctored by Truhujo. He then returned home, a living example of the power of the Sun Dance.

Secondary Disseminators of the Sun Dance

Robert Yellowtail: Superintendent and Rancher

Superintendent Yellowtail undoubtedly played a critical role in bringing the Sun Dance to the Crows by throwing the weight of his office and status behind Big Day and contributing resources to make the dance a tribal affair. He also was a leading figure in bringing the ceremony to Crow Agency and in establishing contacts that led Truhujo to centralize authority among relatives and residents in the agency area.

Yellowtail combined a high degree of intellectual sophistication with pride in ethnic ancestry to support Crow traditions. His career also illustrated how the politically ambitious Indian straddled both the old and the new in order to be successful.

Yellowtail's formal education at Riverside, California, was of a junior college level. His practical education came in political maneuverings in Washington, where he fought successfully against those intent on opening Crow lands to further settlement. His political experience, intelligence, and inquiring mind gave him a highly sophisticated knowledge of American society and culture, and of the world at large. When John Collier became Commissioner of Indian Affairs and sought to implement his plan to organize tribes as economic corporations, Yellowtail was the logical choice to carry out this task among the Crows. As superintendent, he was not successful in getting the Crows to accept the Indian Reorganization Act, and when Collier was no longer commissioner, Yellowtail resigned. He was not through with politics, however, and ran for state representative of Big Horn county. Unsuccessful in his bid for a career in state politics, he turned his efforts to economic development and was instrumental in persuading the government to construct Yellowtail Dam in the Big Horn River Canyon above old Fort C. F. Smith.

The Big Horn Canyon area had a sacred quality and was noted as a source for medicine. Dwarf People lived there, and in legend, Big Horn sheep living there adopted a boy later known as Big Iron and saved him from a precipitous death when his stepfather pushed him over the cliff. They named the boy Big Horn Sheep and told him, "This is the name you will give this whole canyon, and the day will come when your people will decide to change the name, and then you will no longer exist as a Crow Nation."

In midstream, Robert Yellowtail withdrew his backing for the dam and came out against the proposed land settlement. At immediate issue was a mountainous game area that supported elk, deer, and bear and where the tribal buffalo herd roamed. The Crows divided on the issue, clustering around Robert Yellowtail, who opposed the land cession, and Bill Wall and Poesy Whiteman, who were in favor of the projected settlement. Yellowtail belonged to the Mountain Crows and Wall and Whiteman to the River Crows. Crow political loyalties still reflect traditional band affiliations.

The River Crows won, and the mountainous area was included in the dam site. Some of the people saw this as a downturn in Crow history and fortune. For a time the lake behind the dam was named the Yellowtail Reservoir, but later the name was changed to Big Horn Lake.

Except for the years spent in Washington, Yellowtail's political ambitions were realized within the reservation community. Kinship reciprocities and respect for tradition remained an important part of his political image. During the twenties he followed custom in accepting horses from the groom's kin for the hand in marriage of a sister. He also honored his "clan uncles" with give-away distributions.

Yellowtail's ambitions for status, wealth, and political influence were quite in line with the objectives of traditional careers. Among themselves the Crows always were very competitive, especially in the wealth exchanges institutionalized in the give-away. In his life, Yellowtail brilliantly combined wealth, respect for tradition, and social status to build a career that made him the top figure in Crow society. He enjoyed a large measure of confidence because he was successful in stemming external political-economic pressures for more Crow land. In line with old and new, he sought to build a bloodline of racing stock. His large barn with milk cows and his fine cattle spread marked him as the most enterprising of the Crows and their wealthiest self-made man.

The "rags-to-riches" mobility demonstrated in Yellowtail's career was characteristic of careers in buffalo-hunting days. However, he lacked the traditional aura of mystical power associated with leadership in former times. After Plenty Coups died, in 1932, the Crows sensed that the link with the past was broken, and that the future shape of political careers and leadership would be different. Some of Yellowtail's critics thought he had ambitions to be a chief and noted with satisfaction that he was not successful in arrogating the chief's song to himself.

There was nothing in Yellowtail's life suggesting that he was governed by deep convictions for any special denomination or belief. He spanned both Christian and Indian belief and practice, but was not deeply involved in either until the introduction of the Sun Dance. He was a member of the Baptist Church at Lodge Grass, but was not dedicated to steady attendance. When he worked with Truhujo, he became a member of the Sun Dance Elk Lodge. He never sought leadership in the Sun Dance and never sponsored a ceremony, and Peyotism never interested him. However, personal crises sometimes catalyze and bring out the depth of conviction, and when he was ill in Washington, Yellowtail sent for an Indian medicine man to treat him. During the war he held Elk Lodge prayer meetings for the safe return of relatives. With regard to the Sun Dance, Yellowtail demonstrated great pride in his Indian ancestry. He felt compelled to make theirs

as legitimate a form of worship as that of the outsiders who
came to look, wonder, and sometimes to scoff. Before the
visitors departed, he informed them that the Great Spirit
worshipped by the Indian was the same as the white man's
God, and that each reached up to the same divinity in his
own way.

There was a dynamism and enthusiasm about Robert Yellowtail that kept him on the go and gave him a flair for
innovation and sensitivity to the public. When Big Day refused to accept the Sun Dance in the setting of the Crow Fair
and Rodeo, Yellowtail was left no alternative but separate
arrangements with the Shoshonis. Direction was needed to
settle the matter favorably, and Yellowtail was not one to
drag things out. The delegation he headed to the Shoshonis
included his brother-in-law, Barney Old Coyote, Al Childs,
a Crow step-brother of Truhujo, and Joseph Hill, a close friend
of Barney Old Coyote. During the first days of the ceremony
at Pryor, Yellowtail made contact with Truhujo and inquired
about his experiences in the Sun Dance, and recalled the time
when Truhujo had doctored his sister. "So for that reason,"
observed Truhujo, "Superintendent Yellowtail had a faith in
my work. So from that time, we kept the Sun Dance going
every summer in the Crow Reservation."

Barney Old Coyote: Excommunicant and Peyotist

Barney Old Coyote was active in the spread of the Sun Dance
to Crow Agency. The fact that Old Coyote was brother-in-
law to Yellowtail probably influenced his relations with Truhujo, which led to acquisition of the rights to the Elk Lodge,
with his wife acting as Beaver Woman and custodian of the
medicines. Along with his friend Jo Hill, Old Coyote was
taught the full-moon ceremony, and much of his activity
stemmed from his duties as head of the Elk Lodge and coor-
dinator of Sun Dances on the reserve. Although Old Coyote
sponsored more Sun Dances and full-moon meetings than

Medicine man Tom Yellowtail offers a smoke-prayer at last outside dance. Lodge Grass, 1975.

any other Crow up to 1948 and ranked third in the number of dances entered, these qualifications did not automatically rank him as first among the medicine men. Upon his death in 1948, the medicines were formally transferred to his eldest son. Subsequently Truhujo withdrew his support and "called back" the power of his medicines, presumably because of irregularities in their use. Later, in 1969, in a ceremonial laying on of hands, Truhujo conferred the power of leadership in the Sun Dance on Thomas Yellowtail, younger brother of Robert Yellowtail.

Like Robert Yellowtail, Old Coyote experienced close contact with whites. He completed his high school education at Gonzaga (Spokane, Washington), and trained to be a school teacher. However, when a white teacher was advanced to a position that Old Coyote desired and thought he deserved, he felt a deep sense of discrimination and decided to give up teaching. For a while he acted in Hollywood movies. He served as tribal delegate to Washington and was general manager of the crow fair and rodeo for a number of years. Old Coyote was fluent in English and had a flair for rhetorical expression. He was an excellent narrator of Crow myths and tales as well. His linguistic skills undoubtedly influenced his selection as interpreter for the Tribal Council and as catechist and assistant to the Catholic priest. At church, Old Coyote interpreted sermons and translated biblical passages and songs.

Old Coyote's intellectual sophistication and sociability opened the door to a wide variety of friendly contacts outside the reservation community. Yet his primary prestige goals were rooted in Crow custom, since negative experiences in the wider society drew him back to his own people. Old Coyote's experience with the Catholic Church also drove a wedge between him and the "American dream" of personal success to which he had been exposed. When his daughter became ill and could not be cured by medical doctors, he vowed he would join the Native American Church if she recovered. She did recover and Old Coyote fulfilled his vow, whereupon the local priest barred him from church. Old Coyote was told that peyote was of the Devil, and that he must choose between true and false belief. In view of his daughter's recovery, the vow could not be withdrawn, and so Old Coyote turned increasingly to native worship and never attended the Catholic Church after excommunication. However, in his heart he never really gave up the Catholic faith and still thought of himself as a member.

Despite negative experiences in the outside world, Old Coyote cultivated relations with non-Indians. He possessed the talents and skills that permitted liaison between the Crows and the white community. For a number of years he organized the Indian camps and dances at the Billings fair and rodeo. During the war he underwrote his Sun Dance activities at times with the sale of a piece of land, savings sent home by sons in the army, and war-time dependency checks.

Curiosity first led Old Coyote, in 1938, to make a trip to Fort Washakie, but he did not participate in the Sun Dance. At the Pryor Sun Dance in 1941, he helped with the singing. In discussions of the Tribal Council he favored bringing the dance to Crow Agency and served as delegate to the Shoshonis. He took part in the dance at Crow Agency in August, 1941, because his two sons danced and because his brother-in-law, Robert Yellowtail, wished to make the dance a success. Old Coyote also hoped for a cure of a persistent stomach ailment.

With the declaration of World War II and with his sons in the army, Old Coyote put more and more of his faith in the Sun Dance. In the summer of 1943 he became so anxious over his sons that he went to Fort Washakie and asked Truhujo to pray for them. While there, he not only danced with the Shoshonis, but also vowed to put up a Sun dance when he returned to the Crows. These actions solidified an already close relationship with Truhujo. In September, 1943, Truhujo put certain medicine bundles inherited from his mother into the care of Old Coyote's wife, since these bundles required a female custodian. At the same time he handed over to Old Coyote a special elk-hide medicine associated with the Elk Lodge. According to Mae Old Coyote, Truhujo's sister no longer wished to care for the medicine bundle, and "they wanted to appoint us." There was opposition to the transfer, but as Mae declared, "Finally I made up my mind that we would get it." As Beaver Woman and custodian of the medicine bundle, Mae was "supposed to approve of everything." This meant that the scheduling of full moon meetings and other matters relating to the planning of Sun Dances were

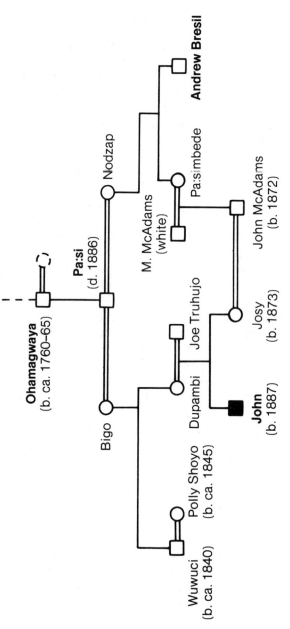

Figure 5. John Truhujo's lineage relation to Ohamagwaya, or Yellow Hand (modified from Shimkin, 1953, 151:412). Sun Dance leaders are in bold. Note that the two wives of Pa:si provided in-marrying descendants for the Yellow Hand line.

brought before her. Validation of the transfer was made with a traditional "payment" to Truhujo.

The elevation of Old Coyote to the "presidency" of the Sun Dance, as Truhujo put it, meant that he played an important part in the building of a Sun Dance organization among the Crows. With Joseph Hill he conducted the first full moon meeting in September or November, 1943. Subsequently either Old Coyote or Hill was present at all prayer meetings held at the homes of real or prospective Elk Lodge members. Old Coyote himself sponsored more than twenty prayer meetings, put on three Sun Dances, and danced thirteen times, three of these at Fort Washakie.

Old Coyote's untimely death in 1948 left a vaccuum in the leadership of the Elk Lodge, even though the medicine bundles were transferred to his eldest son. Old Coyote was a friendly, persuasive, and disarming advocate, and during the war the Elk Lodge prospered as anxious parents and relatives searched for a secure means of prayer in order to bring Crow youths safely home. District chapters were organized, and Jo Hill estimated that there were about two hundred members in 1948. After the war, the Elk Lodge membership declined, and the district organization fell into disrepair. Truhujo withdrew his support from the Old Coyotes, and this move undoubtedly contributed to the breakup of the Elk Lodge organization as then constituted.

Old Coyote's career illustrated how an individual, through his personal experience in bicultural situations, was led to a critical test of cultural procedures and coordinate interpersonal relations. Such personal experiences took on a directional meaning for the individual as they reinforced each other. Thus, Old Coyote's excommunication from the church reinforced his alienation from American society and culture, first experienced in the discrimination episode while he was a teacher on the Blackfoot reservation. In his view, excessive discrimination impaired the value of education for Indians. While he granted the achievements of modern medicine, he felt that some diseases were cured through faith healing, or through the use of herbs such as peyote.

A talented and ambitious man, Old Coyote was frustrated in his youthful attempt to move out into American society as an equal and turned to the Sun Dance for personal achievement. During the war his personal ambition merged with an anxious concern for the safety of his sons far away, fighting the Iron Hats, or Germans.

Joseph Hill: Skeptic

During the war and into the early fifties, Joseph Hill made his mark as the most renowned of Crow Sun Dance medicine men. As other Crow medicine men, he owed much to John Truhujo.

Hill worked actively in the dissemination of the Sun Dance Elk Lodge organization, along with Barney Old Coyote. When the Elk Lodge was established in 1943, Truhujo presented Hill with some feathers and he became "water chief" or head medicine man. Up to 1948, Hill danced but eight times and sponsored no Sun Dances. He cited economic reasons for not taking part in more Sun Dances. In 1948, he and his wife received a combined lease income of around $900 annually, and he worked at odd jobs in order to scrape by.

In comparison with Robert Yellowtail and Barney Old Coyote, Hill's contacts with American culture were limited. He finished fourth grade at the government boarding school at Pryor, and at Crow Agency he worked as an automobile repairman. He cherished no public ambitions, observing that he didn't "like that kinda business." He tried to be friendly to everyone, but admitted a distrust of the white man and his way of life. He considered modern medical practice ridiculous, and he found the ideal of constant work in order to accumulate wealth to be a joke.

Prior to the introduction of the Sun Dance, Hill's interest in religion was characterized by a casual curiosity. He drifted from one church to another, including that of Peyotism. Although he joined the Baptist Church because of a maternal uncle, he never attended regularly. His survey of religion turned Hill into a skeptic. He considered the Bible a product of different people who selected "what was right and what was wrong," and thus the book was not God's word. Moreover, he felt that in the process of translation from the Greek, the biblical text was "all mixed up." From his philosophic reflections, Hill concluded that a person should get all he could out of life, because "after we are gone you don't know where you will go."

In 1938 and again in 1939, Hill visited Fort Washakie because he had "heard so much about the Sun Dance." Each time he helped with the singing and learned quite a few Shoshoni Sun Dance songs. It was Hill's knowledge of Shoshoni songs that attracted Truhujo's attention. In the August dance at Crow Agency, the Shoshoni leader personally asked Hill to help in the construction of the dance lodge.

As a singer, Hill maintained marginal participation in the Sun Dance, but this condition changed when his son departed for the army. Hill danced for his son in 1942, and his earnestness so impressed Truhujo that he asked Hill if he would be interested in taking over leadership among the Crows. When Truhujo returned the following summer, he made Hill drum chief, with power to select others to act in that capacity. The year 1943 was especially critical for Hill's faith in the Sun Dance. He feared for his son in the army, and so went off by himself, where he could be alone with his thoughts. From this fast and meditative prayer, he returned convinced that the worship held promise of help for those who sacrificed their bodies and prayed. Along with David Bad Boy, Arthur Anderson, and Barney Old Coyote, Jo Hill went to see the Shoshoni Sun Dance and John Truhujo. They stayed on after the dance and observed Truhujo doctor a woman who was going blind. They were so impressed with the cure that they requested Truhujo to establish the Elk Lodge among the

Crows, and to set them up with three or four medicine men. Later, at a second dance at Crow Agency held in September, 1943, Truhujo publicly presented Hill with medicine feathers and prayed for him. With the Shoshoni's sponsorship, Hill quickly achieved preeminence as a doctor, and people asked him to pray for them. After the dance, he met with Truhujo, Barney, and Mae Old Coyote, at which time the Shoshoni leader transferred medicine bundles to the Crows and established the Elk Lodge. As head medicine man for the Elk Lodge, Hill performed most of the doctoring. He also selected drum chiefs for each of the districts.

Hill was more traditional in his approach to the Sun Dance than Old Coyote, who was inclined to explain Sun Dance elements using Christian meanings. In 1948, Hill used a short, tubular pipe, following traditional shamanistic practice, to suck the "bad stuff" out of sick people. With the medicine feathers given by Truhujo and the pipe, Hill believed that he had "gotten ahold of something" and possessed the power to cure. He worried over "all these sick Crows" and wished that he could prolong their lives and ease their hardships. He looked upon himself as a doctor, always on call, and he often offered his services unasked. By 1956, arthritis so crippled Hill that he gave up the practice of doctoring.

Crow Sun Dance Leaders: Similarities and Differences

Variations in personal histories and circumstances necessarily conveyed differences in participation and leadership roles. This was the case for the Crows who were deeply involved in the Sun Dance, notably Big Day, Old Coyote, and Hill. There were, however, challenges in the social and cultural context that touched the lives of each and provoked similar attitudes and responses:

1. the ambiguities and challenges to self-identity posed by frustrations and contradictions experienced when living in two cultures at the same time;

2. anxieties over the frequency and deadliness of illnesses that persistently threatened oneself, children, and relatives;
3. anxious fears for the safety of sons and brothers caught up in World War II.

The meaning of each of these challenges was dramatized for the individual in events that greatly influenced careers because of a feeling of alienation from the dominant social and cultural system. Rejection of the dominant culture inevitably reaffirmed the singular value and meaning of traditional beliefs, procedures, and role playing for the individual and the people as a whole.

School and church posed the sharpest and most persistent challenges and threats to Crow culture as practiced in the reservation community. Religion was an incisive and bitter battleground for identity, since the church community visibly signaled out those who accepted the white man's path as against the "pagan" pathway of fathers and grandfathers. Missionaries permitted no middle ground of "fellowship," whether with other Christian denominations, Peyotists, or sun dancers. There was no alternative but to take sides, and, as noted above, for their participation in Peyotism, Big Day and Old Coyote were excommunicated. Never a church-goer, Hill rejected and denigrated Christianity and American culture on his own.

The legitimacy of Indian belief and practice was defended in either of two ways. In one view, God made Indian and white so different that each had his own way and worship, and so it should ever be. That was Big Day's position, and he insisted there could be no mixing of the two. In the other view, differences in belief and practice yielded to an emphasis on the worship of a common godhead. This was Old Coyote's position when he maintained that he remained a Catholic despite excommunication. Old Coyote accommodated the two faiths with dual meanings. Thus, the eagle-down feath-

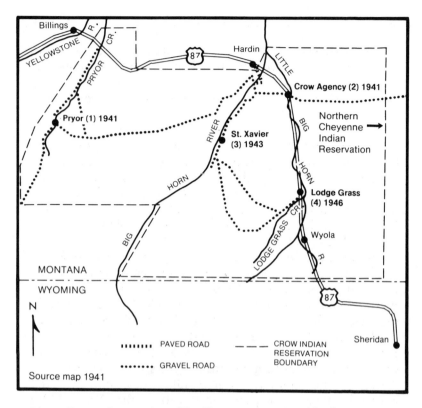

Map 2. District Sponsorship of Sun Dances, 1941–1946. Numbers in parentheses indicate sequence of sponsorship.

ers attached to the little finger of each hand were the wings that held the individual buoyant as he danced to the center pole and back. At the same time, these white feathers stood for "righteousness." In Superintendent Yellowtail's view, Indian belief and practice was just as worthy as Christianity, since each worshipped the Creator in his own way.

An accommodative bicultural and syncretic approach brings the advantage of flexibility and alternatives, leaving choice to vary according to the situation. The disadvantage, of course, is that people may never know precisely where a biculturalist stands on sensitive issues.

The high incidence of sickness in the reservation community provided a special axis for similarities in response. In the cases of Big Day and Old Coyote, both turned to the Indian way of curing when faced with a death-threatening situation. After 1941, fears over the safety of sons in the war merged with anxieties over illness. Although fears over the fate of their sons propelled Hill and Old Coyote into participation in the Shoshoni Sun Dance, it was the miracle cure of the blind woman that stiffened belief and opened the door to full acceptance. At this point personal ambitions were rekindled in competition for Truhujo's favor. A Sun Dance medicine man enjoyed not only a public reputation but also was paid in blankets, money, and sometimes horses for his services. Moreover, as a "clan uncle" with powerful blessings to give to his "children," he was in a very advantageous position to accrue wealth through give-aways, and, in turn, to enhance his own reputation with wealth distributions. Wartime dependence checks provided a relatively constant flow of cash to pay for prayers and distributions to clan uncles for their blessings, and to sun dancers as well.

The three Crow leaders, Big Day, Old Coyote, and Hill, revealed both cultural and individual factors motivated their involvements in the Sun Dance. They were dissatisfied with their experiences in white American society and culture, especially in church and hospital, and these experiences induced a reaffirmation of values found in Crow culture. Forced in their own life-crises to test traditional procedures against modern medical practice, they had successes that progressively reinforced their hopes and expectations. Finally, Big Day, Hill, and Old Coyote shared an average age of fifty-five years. Where the Crow Sun Dance leaders differed most was in the level of education and experience in the wider society. Both Old Coyote and his brother-in-law, Superintendent Yellowtail, illustrated that the degree of participation and achievement in American society and culture were related in some measure to the level of education and skills acquired in that culture.

CHAPTER 5

Pablo Juan Truhujo:
Shoshoni Innovator and Sun Dance Leader

Introduction

Historically, the Wind River Shoshonis served as a central group active in the diffusion of the Sun Dance to Northern Utes in northeastern Utah and to Shoshonis in Idaho.[1] The increase in contacts between the Crows and their Shoshoni neighbors during the 1930s probably would have led to diffusion of the Shoshoni ceremony to the Crows. When the government reversed its repressive policy dealing with native religious practice in 1935, Commissioner John Collier encouraged the revitalization of Indian communities and also stressed the importance of traditional values and customs at the same time. Even in this more favorable situation, however, individuals still were the prime movers and provided initiatives that stemmed from their own personal experiences and ambitions. Thus in 1941, personal factors in the career of John Truhujo made him the natural historical vehicle for transmission of the Sun Dance to the Crows.

[1] E. Adamson Hoebel, "The Sun Dance of the Hekandika Shoshone," *American Anthropologist* 37 (1935): 570–81; J. A. Jones, "The Sun Dance of the Northern Ute," Smithsonian Institution *BAE Bulletin* 157:203–63; Demitri B. Shimkin, "The Wind River Shoshone Sun Dance," Smithsonian Institution *BAE Bulletin* 151:397–484.

Two factors were especially significant for the emergence of Truhujo as an historical figure. First, he had kin among the Crows. His father married a Crow woman, and Truhujo had half-brothers and half-sisters among the Crows. As a young man he had spent upwards of five years on the Crow reservation, and when Crows turned up at the Sun Dance at Fort Washakie, he sought them out. At such times he talked about his Sun Dance experiences and suggested participation. He also offered to sponsor Crow dancers and helped in getting dance outfits together. Second, Truhujo was at a stage in life when he was ambitious and confident of his own powers, but had not yet gained acceptance among his own people as a Sun Dance leader.[2] Although he was a descendant of the historic founder of the Sun Dance, Truhujo was excluded from the inner circle of leadership.[3] Kinship with the Crows and frustrated ambition converged to make Truhujo the logical person to show the Crows how to pray in the Sun Dance lodge.

After his initial appearance in the Sun Dance at Pryor in 1941, Truhujo maintained constant and intimate contacts with the Crows. Out of nineteen Sun Dances performed between 1941 and 1946, Truhujo served as the ceremonial leader of twelve. Tom Compton, Truhujo's arch rival from Fort Washakie, directed three; and Charlie Bell, a Fort Hall Shoshoni related to Big Day, two. William Big Day directed two Sun Dances at Pryor, one of these when Truhujo failed to arrive on time.

[2]Fred Voget, "A Shoshone Innovator," *American Anthropologist* 52 (1950):53–63.

[3]In adapting the Wind River Shoshoni Sun Dance to their changed conditions on the reservation, medicine men challenged and wrested leadership from the Yellow Hand line. Truhujo noted that a maternal uncle, undoubtedly Andrew Bresil, danced but never sponsored a ceremony. Shamanic rivalry transformed the Sun Dance into a stage for display of mystic power and created the usual in-group and out-group. A shamanic reputation was a prerequisite for acceptance as a pledger and leader of the Sun Dance.

Denied fulfillment among his own people, Truhujo realized his Sun Dance ambitions among the Crows. He not only played a critical role in the transfer of the Sun Dance to the Crows, but also set up the organizational machinery by which he maintained control. In 1975, John Truhujo was eighty-eight and still active in the Sun Dance. At Lodge Grass he assisted his new choice for Sun Dance leader, Thomas Yellowtail, in directing a ceremony sponsored by Thomas Lion Shows, whose father, the initial pledger, had suffered a stroke. Truhujo painted and doctored dancers, but did not dance himself. After traveling home to Fort Washakie by bus, Truhujo was called back to Lodge Grass, where he doctored the ailing John Cummins, a leader in the Sun Dance during the war years. Today, Truhujo's reputation as a medicine man remains high among the Crows, and he still exerts some control from the wings, despite turning over leadership and medicines to Thomas Yellowtail in 1969.

Early Life and Education

Pablo Juan Truhujo, sometimes referred to as Treeo, Trehero, Rainbow, and Middle of the Belly (Crow name), was born in 1887. His father, Joe Truhujo, "was from Spain . . . and he lived in old Mexico, and he came out into the northern country here." Joe Truhujo worked for cattlemen and did some freighting. He lived for a time among the Crows, married, and had one son, known as Finger Inside the Mouth. Following the death of his Crow wife, Joe Truhujo went to Fort Washakie, where he married a full-blooded Shoshoni, Mary Morton, and settled near Milford. Mary Morton came from a family "which did not have very much." She was married three times, once to a full-blooded Shoshoni, then to Truhujo's father, and finally to a white man, Ruben Reynolds. John Truhujo was next to the youngest of eight children from his mother's marriages. His first name was Pablo, and

he indicated that he didn't know "wherever I got this John."
He was very close to Juanita and Maria, the two sisters
nearest to him in age. At one point, as he reviewed his life,
Truhujo saw himself as a

. . . poor boy [who] always rustled for [my]self. [I] never get anybody to help me, and I'm a kind of orphan. Had a mother, but
she didn't care for me. My uncles wouldn't help me but a little bit
in a few places when I was a little boy.

The self-reliance forced upon him during childhood was reinforced by work in the company of adults.

I don't believe that I was a boy that was much about making any
toys [or playing]. I was always around where there was grown
people, . . . hunting horses in the hills, maybe working . . . in the
fields. For that reason I haven't any little boys' way about me when
I was young. And after a while, I got in where they have meetings,
prayer meetings, and I got thinking I ought to join this prayer
meeting—that be better for me so I wouldn't get into trouble. I'll
stay out of trouble if I live up to what the meetings mean to me.

These prayer meetings were connected to peyote.

Truhujo was about six years old when his father died, and
he was sent to a government school in White Rock, Utah.
Within two years he was back at Fort Washakie attending a
government-supported mission school run by an Episcopal
Minister, the Reverend John Roberts. Vocational on-the-job-
training was an important part of the program, and Truhujo
spent his afternoons either building wagons, smithing, or
working in the flour mill. He was about nineteen when he
completed the eighth grade.

Marriage and Work Career

In 1905 Truhujo married for the first time, but had no children by his Shoshoni wife, who died in 1915. A year later

he married Deborah Kagawoh, sister of Cyrus Shongutsi. Deborah had three children by a previous marriage. Truhujo never had any children of his own, but in 1948 was proud of his fourteen grandchildren, two of whom lived with him. He spoke very highly of his two wives, referring to them as good women, and noted that he was never one for playing around.

As a young man, Truhujo hauled coal and wood for the government, served as an interpreter, and was a member of the police force for about eight years. Police work made him more enemies than friends, and so he gave it up at the age of thirty-two. He considered himself "too good[hearted] a man to be on the police force" and prided himself on never making any arrests. Off and on Truhujo ran cattle (25 to 40 head), but became disgusted because he thought the wealthy men were favored by the superintendent and always got more than their share of the range. Because inadequate range limited the size of his herd, most of the time he ran sheep. Truhujo's last herd of sheep (some 290 head) were sold by his wife while he was away, sun dancing at Crow Agency. In 1948 he indicated jokingly that he was "working for a handout" —that is, doctoring.

Religious Background and Sun Dance Career

At age fourteen or fifteen Truhujo was baptized an Episcopalian by the Reverend John Roberts. However, Truhujo considered himself nothing more than a "church member, that's all." He was "still with it," attending church when he felt like it, usually on special occasions like Christmas and Easter. His primary religious interest, however, early centered in the Sun Dance. His mother's brother, with whom he was close in his youth, taught him that the Sun Dance was the only true belief. His uncle never sponsored a Sun Dance, but he did dance. He also was a member of the Elk Lodge, which served as a kind of mutual aid and curing society associated with the Sun Dance.

Truhujo grew up with the Sun Dance as a living family tradition. Through his mother he was related to Chief Yellow Hand, who had introduced the Sun Dance to the Shoshonis (see Figure 5). Great grandfather Yellow Hand had brought the Sun Dance from the Crows, and the Sun Dance medicines were passed down through the family.[4] Two years before she died in 1922, Truhujo's mother gave him the Sun Dance medicine bundles.

When he was about eighteen, Truhujo decided it was time to enter the dance. His sister considered him too young, and suggested that he wait a while. However, Truhujo sneaked an outfit from his maternal uncle and went into the dance. After the dance his uncle looked at him in a funny way and remonstrated, "I believe you're the boy that got away with my necklace, otter hides, armbands, bracelets, and my eagle feathers." Truhujo denied it outright, but later regretted his deviousness. His mother was pleased that he took part in the

---

[4] In comparing form elements of the Wind River Shoshoni Sun Dance with the Kiowa, Comanche, Arapaho, Oglala Sioux, Crow, Blackfoot, Plains Cree, and Kutenai ceremonies, Shimkin in "The Wind River Shoshone Sun Dance," 151:414, concluded that the Shoshoni and Kiowa ceremonies were more alike. In Shimkin's view, Yellow Hand probably derived his Sun Dance from the Kiowas, close associates of the Comanches.

Truhujo maintained that Yellow Hand was a Crow who originated the Shoshoni Sun Dance from the Crow Beaver Dance, indicating a connection to the sacred tobacco. According to Lowie, "The Tobacco Society of the Crow Indians," 21:197 & n. 4; also, pp. 178–79, the Beaver Dance "chapter" possessed no medicine bundle that gave an exclusive right to plant tobacco as was the case for the Blackfeet and Sarsis. The sacred tobacco originated with the stars. In one account Morning Star was the tobacco and claimed cactus, berry, onion, and beaver as his servants. Dirt from these objects was part of a mix when planting tobacco. Beaver was especially active in adopting visionaries who were orphans and had no one to give them mystic power and support against those intent on doing them harm.

dance, because she wanted him to believe in the Sun Dance and be a good member of the Elk Lodge.

When he first took up the Sun Dance, Truhujo, because of his youth, did not expect to get any power at that time. One year later, in 1907, he visited his Crow half-brother, Alfred Blackbird, who was related to the elder Yellowtail, and together they visited the Yellowtails near Lodge Grass. At this time he met Arthur Bravo, a nephew of Blackbird's wife, who came to Truhujo and asked if he could help a girl who was very sick. The girl was Aimee Yellowtail, sister to Robert, who later became superintendent. Truhujo's doctoring proved effective, and Aimee recovered in two days. Truhujo spent some five years on the Crow reservation, making a last visit in 1922.

Truhujo held back from his search for power until he was invited to go along with three honored Shoshonis, White Colt, Tree Sap, and Eagle. They fasted in the hills by the medicine drawings located in Dinwoodie Canyon. Although he was thirty-three years of age, Truhujo described himself as a boy with a good reputation in the Sun Dance and prayer meetings. During this fast, power came to him "just like in a . . . dream; but whatever you do, obeying your dream, it comes true." White Colt encouraged him to get a stronger power by doing what was right. Truhujo at this time was experimenting with peyote; but his dream experiences, in which a "being" spoke to him, led to a rejection of the herb. Peyote made one feel and act as if he were drunk, and Truhujo felt there was no power in it.

There was something came between me and the peyote. "Thou shalt have but one way." So I took this [Sun Dance] lodge way because I thought it was the best. I thought that . . . the Creator made . . . [the rule about] not using the herb—that you would pray to the Creator not taking dope. That is what the dream told me. This [being in the dream said], "You meet without dope, you pray to the Maker without dope. That [way] your prayers will come true." I don't know why it said that to me.

Among the Shoshonis, membership in one of the quasi-hereditary lodges associated with the Sun Dance was a must for anyone ambitious for leadership. According to Truhujo, the traditional societies were the Antlers or Pack-antlers, Elks, and Nose-pokes.[5] During the post-reservation period, these societies foundered and then were revitalized—the Antlers in 1902 or 1903, the Elks in 1923 or 1924, and the Nose-pokes in 1930. Membership in the societies was by adoption, and when a member died, a close relative usually replaced him. Truhujo claimed membership in both the Antlers and Nose-pokes, and left the Antlers about 1940.

The societies provided a base for rivalries over Sun Dance leadership, although ostensibly they assisted a pledger in putting on a dance. None had a large membership, and each remained viable with difficulty. In 1939, financial transactions of the dance committee selected by the pledger came under scrutiny of the Shoshone Business Council. Also in 1939, the Shoshone Dance Committee was organized under the tribal constitution, bringing both ceremonial and secular dances under direction of the Shoshone Business Council.[6] By 1945 the traditional societies were inoperative. At this time a pledger organized his own committee, which worked with the Shoshone Dance Committee. However, older men of reputation, active in the Sun Dance, ran the ceremony.

In former times, according to Truhujo, members of the Elk Lodge prayed for warriors and hunters and put up Sun Dances. His mother's grandfather, Yellow Hand, was the original Elk

[5] Shimkin, in "Wind River Shoshone Sun Dance," 151:437–38 reported that the "Horn Packers" was a "vaguely hereditary group" which organized Sun Dance performances, and through their support, commonly selected pledgers. Truhujo and associates probably created the Elk Lodge as a counterfoil to the established lodges, whose members dominated the Shoshoni Sun Dance. (See Appendix A for a description of an Elk Lodge prayer meeting or "sing" among the Crows).

[6] Fred W. Voget, "Current Trends in the Wind River Shoshone Sun Dance," Smithsonian Institution *BAE Bulletin* 151 (1953):485–99.

Lodge leader. After the death of Truhujo's mother, John Mc-Adams, a brother-in-law and first cousin, called a meeting to get the Elk Lodge started again, but only six people appeared. They followed a casual nominating and election procedure, and Truhujo emerged as the "president," with another brother-in-law "like a vice-president." They set up a dance committee of six, with three elected from the tribe. In Truhujo's view, this was the beginning of a formal Sun Dance Committee. Those present at the initial meeting were John McAdams, Cyrus Shongutsi, Tilton West, Leslie Isis, Matthew Newship, and John Truhujo. McAdams, Shongutsi, and Truhujo were brothers-in-law.

The reconstituted Elk Lodge purportedly served as a mutual-aid society as well as a Sun Dance committee. As Truhujo put it,

We're hoping that we could help a man or a woman that weren't able to take care of himself. We got this group to what they call a helper for the people—to help them out either in the money or whatever they need. A man's down sick; we go there and help him out. In case of a man lost his home by fire or get destroyed somehow—that's what I meant. Was that a good plan? That's what we got this lodge for. And we also combine it in a way of the white man's Christian way. So that's our main point by getting up this Elk Lodge plan.

The Elk Lodge provided a base from which Truhujo projected his quest for leadership. Although he possessed Sun Dance medicines passed to him by his mother, Truhujo admitted that, at the time, he had no standing as a medicine man. He received some good publicity by standing up to Superintendent Haas in 1920, when performances of the Sun Dance were banned. Truhujo offered himself as spokesman and found himself in the agent's office under threat of five years in Leavenworth for his defiance. However, a supervisor from Washington arrived, witnessed the dance and took pictures. On the second day, Truhujo predicted they were "in the clear," and there would be no further prohibitions of the ceremony. Tom Compton wasn't so sure; he expected everyone to be "slapped into jail." At the end of the dance, the special supervisor told the agent in Truhujo's presence that there was no regulation in Washington that gave the superintendent power to prohibit such a ceremony. Moreover, he himself saw nothing wrong with it.[7]

Truhujo had some success in curing people, and developed some faith in his medicine. In 1935, when he was forty-eight, he dreamt about the medicine bundle inherited from his mother. Soon afterward he dreamt of a Sun Dance in which he used a staff and a gourd rattle. In this dream the lodge was made entirely of pine—center pole, rafters, and support poles. Only the brush was from the cottonwood tree. It seemed as if the dream "was drawing [him] to this medicine." He counseled with an old man, and was told that the dream meant that he was to put on a Sun Dance. This he did in 1938, the same year that William Big Day, Barney Old Coyote, and Jo Hill visited Fort Washakie to see the Sun Dance.

In 1938 Truhujo's career as a medicine man began to unfold. He had completed the dream cycle that validated his leadership through the medicine bundle received from his mother. In the Elk Lodge he had a coterie of brothers-in-law and close friends who were disaffected with current leadership of the Sun Dance. Proud of his family connections with the Sun Dance, Truhujo considered leaders then in charge to be ignorant of proper ceremonial form and quite content with the "meaning." Moreover, they were not properly responsive to the dreams of a Sun Dance pledger, for they rejected Morgan Moon's dreams of a one-, two-, and finally a four-day ceremony. Moon was forced to accommodate

---

[7]Shimkin credits Morgan Moon with reviving the Sun Dance openly in 1920. Like Truhujo, Moon "had experimented with the Peyote cult at one time. . . ." See Shimkin, "Wind River Shoshone Sun Dance," 151: 435.

his dreams by walking out of one dance on the second day and fasting for one day before the ceremony to make up the four days.

Truhujo's Views of the Sun Dance and of Christianity

Truhujo began his personal narrative by stating, "My uncle taught me to be a friend with everybody."[8] He also stressed that he was brought up in the Sun Dance and was committed to it. The Sun Dance was like a "church. . . . [and] That was something I had to believe in."

In the context of reservation life, the challenge of Bible and Christian truth versus Indian truth was not easily put aside. Truhujo personally resolved the issue by insisting that the Sun Dance was a church and was just as valid as any attended by white people. Parallels between Indian beliefs and white man's beliefs guaranteed legitimacy to both Indian revelation and Christian teaching. In Truhujo's view,

We got our messages through the medicine-man, and that's how we got to learn of our Indian Church. 'Course we live up to that, to those words that was told to us. We got so we understand what our white brother says when he's reading the Maker's Book, because . . . us Indians, we don't have any writing at all, and we get quite a bit out of the white man's Bible. Today we stand about even with the white man in this church, only we don't yet fully understand in places about what our Savior's words [meant] that has been written in this book. In places the Indians hits these words that He said to the people when He was on earth here, without any books, so the words must be true. . . .

---

[8] Rev. John Roberts, Episcopal missionary, in 1948 observed that John Truhujo was a "good-hearted man," and that his desire to be well-thought-of by his people was a very important influence in his life. Shoshonis in heated arguments might call him a "Mexican," but generally speaking he was well-thought-of and accepted as a "full-blooded Shoshone" because of his cultural orientation.

The conflict between the two ways, in which the Indian Way was denigrated, made Indians defensive; and they sometimes mixed elements from both cultures and also attached Christian meanings to Indian forms. The arrival of Episcopalian and Catholic missionaries stimulated a process that led Sun Dance leaders between 1800 and 1905 to integrate "Christian elements" into their own ceremony.[9] In 1948, a Shoshoni, Lynn St. Clair, was staunchly committed to uncovering and publicizing positive correlations between Christianity and the Sun Dance. As for Truhujo, William Big Day reported that he considered Christian interpretations were made to "fool the whites." In the Shoshoni view, Truhujo's contradictory public and private convictions created ambiguities about his true position, especially when they noted how he mixed peyote ceremonial forms with the Sun Dance, while at the same time rejecting Peyotism. A sensitivity to good public relations apparently led Truhujo to tailor his interpretations to the expectations of his audience.

In his interpretation of the Sun Dance, Truhujo offered an interesting and curious intermingling of Christian and Indian form and meaning. In literal translation the Shoshoni term for the Sun Dance meant "Stand in Thirst."[10] Truhujo referred to the Sun Dance as "Our Father's Dance" or the "Creator's Prayer Meeting," and noted that it should be held but once a year.[11] The Creator laid down "Twelve Commandments in the Indian Way" to be followed when in His Lodge.

Here is what the Indian says [that God told him]. "Thou shalt not worship images. Worship me." He says, "That is the Indian custom." And He goes on about [it] and He says, "Ye men, ye

[9] Shimkin, "Wind River Shoshone Sun Dance," 151:436, 472.
[10] Ibid., 418.
[11] Truhujo's names for the Sun Dance are derived from traditional Shoshoni references to the Creator, who dwells in the sun. See A. G. Brackett, "The Shoshones or Snake Indians, Their Religion, Superstitions and Manners," 330, cited by Shimkin, Ibid. 463.

men shall fast three days. . . . In your lodge there is Twelve Commandments:

1. Ye should do no lie against your neighbor.
2. Ye should not bother any property which he has got, without his permission.
3. Ye should not steal from your neighbor.
4. Ye should not bear no witness against your neighbor.
5. Don't pray for no evil.
6. I am the only Maker and Creator of life.
7. You're to live up to the Lord's call.
8. You must use my song. There is four songs.
9. You are to use my long-lived tree, [the] cedar. [Cedar is used for incense].
10. You must use my pines for the number of my disciples. There is twelve poles. The thirteenth one [center pole] is my crucify tree. They have to pray for that separate.
11. Forgiven [the] people who were of my betraying.
12. My resurrection is three days.

That is the Commandments in the Indian Way.

There were other correlations between Sun Dance and Christian worship. The "Creator's Lodge" built for the Sun Dance represented the hill on which Christ was crucified. The center pole was the "crucify tree," with the willows signifying the cross proper. The three black bands painted on the center pole "meant the Lord laid in the tomb three days and the third day they opened up his tomb—the resurrection." Truhujo observed, "That compares with the Bible in all ways." The charcoal rings also indicated that the dance would last three days. When a child was brought forward to complete the charcoal ring begun by a respected elder, the wish was for a long life for the child. The two pennants attached to the forks of the center pole represented "the Savior's garments which are white today. We had blue during the war time, and we are clear [of war] and come back to the old-fashioned white garment."[12]

[12] Blue probably was coordinate with black, the traditional victory color.

The buffalo was created especially for the "Red race to live on." White clay and yellow paint were applied to the buffalo head and snout because they were the "proper Indian paints." The "sweet sage" placed in the buffalo's nostrils "was to be our tea or coffee, whichever we take that." Just before sunrise the buffalo "comes in the spirit. He is the first animal we see before the sunrise, then the otter, then the eagle. . . ." At the time when the buffalo was created by the Maker, "There are two persons only created on earth at that time. . . . We are supposed to have been animals at that time when He created this [buffalo]."

As the "daylight messenger of God," the eagle was painted yellow. The medicine man was the special recipient of messages carried by the eagle. The eagle also was the "Indians' flag . . . to bind the American government to the U. S. rights . . . ," for the eagle also represented "the Americans."

The twelve rafter poles of pine signified the Twelve Apostles. The aligned support pole to the west, by which the medicine-man took position, represented the "truth of the lodge." The north and south uprights supporting the rafter poles represented the "two thieves."

We are not perfect. The two thieves were not in the right. They was forgiven. The same as the two on each side of Him—the two north and south poles stand for them. They was the first ones they had to put up—them are their trees.

The fire built in the lodge around midnight symbolized "Hell," where the "bad men . . . unbelieving the Creator" go.

The cane used by the drum chief to mark the beat of a song was like the "shepherd's hook" carried by Christ. The Lord also "had the gourd to call his sheep with. . . . It is something like a church bell." This was the meaning of the rattle. Like the eagle, the Sun Dance mannikin was also a messenger of God. While a medicine man received messages from the mannikin, the owner of the "little man" alone received and interpreted messages with exactness.

The whistle used by the dancers represented the birds, and was made from either the right or left humerus of the eagle. One prayed to the Creator through the whistle, regulated in sets of four. The long shrill blasts in combinations of four echoed the cry of the eagle when it swooped down to earth. The feather plumes worn by the dancer brought to mind the "picture of Christ when he is standing on the clouds." Christ said, "You must wear the plumes to be a believer in my lodge."

During the three days in the lodge, dancers prayed for their personal desires—"that the Maker would take pity on us" and grant a long life. Truhujo emphasized that during the war he led Sun Dances "for my people so the Americans [could] be free as they ever was." He always prayed for the government and for the general welfare of the people. In his opinion, the Crows did not pray enough for the government and the president.

Truhujo prayed solely to the Creator or to God. He considered God to be

beyond Jesus. He is the man we don't understand how he came to be the Creator. He must be spirit and the Son was sent here to be attraction to go in [to heaven]. . . . You see, God sent his Son down here on earth to teach us—not what is going on, or what is going to go on, but to teach us His Word, and he left word that he was coming later. The white man had it written down, and it is true. You cannot say it is not true, because it is written down. Now the things that He said, I don't know how the Indian got it; but that was [handed down] from generation to generation.

When speaking of Jesus, Truhujo referred to him as "our great brother."

Truhujo combined both prayer and physical manipulation to expunge disease, but he restricted sucking out the "bad stuff" to private practice. In public, he cured by prayer and fanning of the patient with medicine feathers. The actual cure he attributed to the Maker.

Do you know the people that come to the tree? They rather to live on the Maker's earth longer than they would call for, and I beg for them to receive their wish. Just like Susie Childs. She called me from Fort Washakie for her help, and I took her for three days and three nights. And I prayed for her, and the third day she received her wish.

When doctoring, Truhujo positioned himself behind the patient, facing the tree. He waved his feathers four times to the south and north, followed by west and east. He then fanned the patient four times on the chest (east), right side (south), back (west), and left side (north). For failing eyesight, he placed his feathers over the eyes and prayed, at the same time blowing a long shrill blast on his whistle, followed by a staccato. Tuberculosis was especially resistant, and treating these cases Truhujo fanned a patient six times. When he concluded treatment of a serious case, he frequently placed both hands on the center pole and prayed. At the same time he looked up at the buffalo head and blew a long shrill blast, followed by a staccato. As he danced back to position, he struck himself four times with his feathers, alternately on each shoulder. In this way he protected himself from the disease and "receive[d] the truth" about the patient. Truhujo knew when people had lung trouble and claimed that on the second day of the dance he could even predict who would step forward for treatment. The "bad stuff" he collected at the patient's feet and then brushed it away, to be carried out of the lodge somehow. The songs were integral to any cure, and Truhujo asserted that "There is one if they sing, I can do almost anything."

A sponsor and drummer-singers prayed together in order to work together without tiring the dancers. The sponsor offered a pipe to the drum chief and the other drummers, who used the occasion to pray especially for the people. When prayers were being said, cedar incense was cast on the fire

Truhujo doctoring Horse. Crow Agency, 1941.

because cedar "puri[fied] the evil so there will be no evil among the people."

A man entered the ceremony of his own free will. Power came to a person through the Sun Dance, but the Maker was the ultimate source of power. The individual was a vehicle for power, and the feathers were his instruments for wielding the gift of power. The center pole, with its attached buffalo head, willows, and eagle, was the immediate source of power. When he was "run over by the buffalo," a suppliant received a gift of power and instructions for its use. Truhujo apparently never was knocked down by the buffalo, but he had many dreams, and he stressed his skill in interpreting the dreams of others.

Dancers never knew when power would come, whether on

Truhujo doctoring group of old men. Revered Fred Bird, in left background, carries an eagle-feather fan. Dancer is William Big Day.
Pryor, 1941.

a first or a twentieth try. A dancer never stopped with one
dance, but danced two or more, and always ended on an even
number or pair. A second dance often was an act of giving
thanks for good things received.

Power to predict was received through the Sun Dance, and
it was the responsibility of the medicine man to bring out
the real meanings of dreams to their owners. When a man
sponsored a Sun Dance, he expected important dreams. The
eagel feathers Truhujo used were like a radio that received
messages, and he claimed that everything he told the Crows
came true. He reported in confidence that he saw "another
war coming, with the Rooshans this time." However, he predicted a short war from which the United States would emerge

victorious. Truhujo also used his mystic powers to check up on Crow Sun Dance leaders, and he wrote to them from Fort Washakie that his spirit helpers brought news that the prayer meetings were not being held on schedule.

Possession of a medicine was not required in order to dance, but without it a dancer suffered unduly. Truhujo's personal medicine included an ermine pelt with feathers ornamented with dark blue, green, and orange zigzags to depict lightning. "I left the feathers with the lightning drawing to a few [Crows] so they could learn the ways for themselves through the dreams." As with other Shoshonis, Truhujo painted himself with white clay upon first entering the lodge, then changed to yellow on the critical second day.

Christian "Reinterpretation" of the Shoshoni Sun Dance

John Truhujo's wording of the "Twelve Commandments," his quick references to the shepherd's crook, Christ on the mountain, and the two thieves disclosed more than a passing knowledge of the Bible. This indoctrination probably came during his early education under Rev. John Roberts, who used Truhujo as a monitor.

Legitimation of his Sun Dance worship through correspondences with Christianity was vital to Truhujo, for he frequently asserted, "That story compares with the Bible in all ways." He was also sensitive to any sign of skepticism, as he observed, "That sounds foolish to you." In this aim for legitimacy Truhujo drew upon a public tradition of accommodating Shoshoni belief and practice to Christianity while individually maintaining multiple participations in Peyotism, the Sun Dance, and the Episcopal and Catholic churches. The addition of Christian interpretations and forms to the Sun Dance was well along by 1905, and elements symbolic of war and use of the Sun Dance doll were abandoned gradually.[13]

[13] Shimkin, "Wind River Shoshone Sun Dance," 151:472.

The center pole as the tree on which white people hung "our Brother until he died," the twelve rafters as "our Brother's brothers," Christ's fasting, and the three days in the tomb constituted the core of well-known parallels. Individuals introduced special interpretations, sometimes seeing the forked rafter as symbolizing the righteous path of life to the right, and the evil to the left. Willows with their leafy branches might suggest "Holy water that Christ made in the mountains."

The main reason for believing in the truth of the Sun Dance did not rest on correlations with Christianity. People were cured in the lodge, and those who ridiculed the Sun Dance often met with misfortune. A Shoshoni who showed disrespect by cutting off the leafy tips of the forked center pole was later paralyzed. Those who lied about dreams in order to sponsor a Sun Dance could expect to be brought down with a disease. Anyone who sponsored a Sun Dance right after a death in his family courted death himself, as well as those associated with him. Those who disregarded the mandates of their power dreams reaped nothing but bad luck and an early death. As with any religion, the Sun Dance contained positive and negative sanctions for its worshippers.

Some Shoshoni Views of Truhujo in 1948

Considering the stage of Truhujo's career in 1941, the invitation to introduce the Sun Dance to the Crows was well timed. He possessed not only the necessary career assets and mature confidence essential to success but also important connections among the Crows. His friendly demeanor was a distinct asset, which Truhujo himself recognized.

In pursuing the career of medicine man, Truhujo had not pushed himself brashly forward. He had followed the typical career pattern and worked for public acceptance through a gradual buildup of reputation. However, Truhujo seemed an opportunist to conservative leaders who had renovated the

Sun Dance and taken over leadership from Yellow Hand's descendants. The Elk Lodge, which Truhujo claimed to head, was a concoction. According to Tom Compton, it was "some of John's work . . . connected with peyote." There was no full moon meeting associated with the traditional Sun Dance; and here too, Truhujo modeled his meeting after the full moon meetings of Peyotists. Actually, Compton pointed out, there were no lodges associated with the Sun Dance. Coming in 1948, after the Shoshoni Dance Committee took over, this denial of lodge association with the Sun Dance undoubtedly was true.

Another informant with a deep interest in the Sun Dance also denied that there was an Elk Lodge. Truhujo's Elk Lodge probably referred to the Pack-antlers, whose name came from their practice of packing antlers on their backs to trade. Although the informant held nothing against Truhujo, and indeed liked him, "You could never trust what he was saying." For example, in a July performance of the Sun Dance in 1948, it was rumored that Truhujo and not Toorey Roberts was the real sponsor.[14] Many felt that Truhujo should not be allowed to stay in the Sun Dance. When the feelings of the people were communicated to Truhujo, he offered to withdraw. However, the committee did not demand withdrawal, and Truhujo stayed on.

Signs indicated that "one of these days Johnnie will fall." In the 1948 Sun Dance, Truhujo had not used a stuffed eagle on the pledger's rafter pole. Instead he tied six eagle feathers to each of the twin tufts of needles left at the tip of the pine pole. During the dance, six of the feathers fell to the ground, an evil omen. Shoshonis usually will not pick up such feathers, but St. Clair gathered them up and returned them to Truhujo. Five or six people died after this Sun Dance. It was said that

[14] Truhujo claimed that Toorey Roberts asked him to help, and after entering the lodge, Roberts told Truhujo to "take the lead." Voget, "A Shoshone Innovator," 52:61, n. 21.

Truhujo was too casual about the Sun Dance, as was a brother-in-law, who later died as a result of his "sins" against the Sun Dance.

Truhujo's friendliness and willingness to help in the Sun Dance were appreciated, but doubts remained about his qualifications. He was suspected of breaking Sun Dance rules by taking water during one performance. His associates also were questionable concerning their dedication to the Sun Dance. When Truhujo took the ceremony to the Crows, there was resentment that a group of three gave away the Shoshoni Sun Dance without consulting the tribal body. Some even went so far as to say that the Shoshonis had no Sun Dance, since Truhujo gave it to the Crows. Shoshonis who saw performances among the Crows disapproved of what they saw, and thought that Truhujo and his associates were motivated by financial gain—by the money, blankets, and other gifts they received.

Truhujo's attempts to introduce variant elements of his own ceremony into the Sun Dance at Fort Washakie also were resented. Tom Wesaw, who sponsored a ceremony in August, 1948, accused Truhujo of making all kinds of changes to suit his fancy. He denied there was an Elk Lodge headed by Truhujo. During Wesaw's Sun Dance, Truhujo slipped his "little man" into the ceremony without consulting Wesaw, and when Wesaw got up to dance on the morning of the second day, he saw the little man tied to the centerpole. Although Wesaw ordered the mannikin removed, it remained tied to the tree. At the end of the dance, Truhujo hung the little man around the neck of a dancer.[15] On first telling about the little man episode, Truhujo indicated that Wesaw requested its use; but then he changed his story and pointed to Tilton West, a close friend, and to Cyrus Shongutsi, brother-in-law, as the ones who had made the request.

Once established among the Crows, Truhujo imported

[15] Dr. Ake Hultkrantz, personal communication.

Crow leaders to introduce into the Shoshoni ceremony special elements which he had made a part of the Crow Sun Dance. Thus, for a Sun Dance he sponsored, Truhujo brought in Joe Hill, drum chief of the Crows, and insisted that his drummer's cane be used to start the singing. During this performance someone leaned against the cane and broke it.[16] However, Truhujo had no success in his efforts to turn back the ceremonial clock of the Shoshoni Sun Dance.

Among his Shoshoni peers, Truhujo was something of a prophet scorned. People doubted his veracity and ridiculed his pretensions to leadership in the Sun Dance and his claims as a doctor. According to Hultkrantz, some older Indians perceived Truhujo as walking the left road that did not lead to God.

Establishing the Sun Dance Among the Crows

Persons rejected by their peers sometimes have built reputations abroad and then returned in triumph. To some extent this was true of Truhujo, who gained acceptance but never was accorded preeminent status by the Shoshonis. However, he did score a triumph in 1967, when sponsoring a Sun Dance with heavy Crow participation.

Truhujo had the ability to attract and retain many friends and followers. At the same time, he was a consummate social strategist, adapting to situations, and appealing to individual ambition. He made timely use of the dramatic to create a favorable effect. As a social tactician, he made his moves only after obtaining the approval of power figures among the Crows. He maintained close relationships with the prominent families, and when he took up the wish for a Sun Dance at Crow Agency, he broke with his protégé, Big Day.

[16] Thomas H. Johnson, "Structure and Function in the Wind River Shoshone Sun Dance, 1966 & 1967," manuscript.

In August, 1941, Truhujo laid the groundwork for the Elk Lodge organization and put on a full moon prayer meeting.[17] Among those present were Barney Old Coyote, Mae Old Coyote, Joe Hill, David Bad Boy and Herbert Old Bear. Truhujo remembered, "I started off that same summer that I started the Sun Dance. That same summer I gave the feather to Mrs. Old-Coyote to be a Beaver Woman." The Sun Dance originated from the Crow Beaver Lodge. Hence the title, Beaver Woman. At first the Crows referred to the Beaver Woman as Water Woman (as in Peyotism), but that was a mistake. Yet Truhujo himself made reference to a Water Woman:

We give them all—the staff, the cane, the feathers, the drum chief, water woman [sic], the leader of the staff, and the vice-president, [and] fire chief. And those were the things which came with the Sun Dance Lodge. They got them all there among the Crows. The water woman is the woman that looks after carrying the water the last day. And the fire chief, he tends to business [from] the first night to the quitting time. The drum chief takes care of the drum while the Sun Dance is going. The man with the gourd and with the cane [is] supposed to be at the drum every day and every night. If anything else is needed, the Sun Dance leader and his assistant will give orders.

In 1942, Truhujo formally introduced the full moon meeting as an element of the Sun Dance. Some time after the performance at Crow Agency, Old Coyote informed Truhujo that they wished to "adopt this way of having a meeting." Old Coyote talked matters over with Robert Yellowtail and obtained his consent. Then Truhujo, with expenses paid, was brought to Crow Agency to teach his followers how to run these meetings. While Big Day earlier had learned about the prayer meetings, in Truhujo's judgment he did not know how to run such a meeting.

[17] By coincidence, there was an Elk Lodge chapter in the Tobacco Society. See Lowie, "The Tobacco Society of the Crow Indians," 21:115.

He [Big Day] just doesn't understand how to run it. He never put out any prayers . . . and he never brought no water into it . . . and no smoke. He just went into it as if he [were] putting on a party. I never been to his meeting. If I'm around, I don't think he put it on.

Big Day also was remiss in not allowing members to offer their own prayer smokes.

By 1942 the break with Big Day was complete and Big Day turned to Tom Compton and to a Fort Hall Shoshoni, Charlie Bell, to supervise Sun Dances at Pryor. Bell was related to Big Day. According to Annie Big Day, Joe Hill and Barney Old Coyote wished to be celebrated and remembered as the ones who brought the Sun Dance to the Crows. She confronted John Truhujo at the time, saying "You gave these feathers to William and William was the first to bring the Sun Dance to the Crow, and now they say that you took the power away from these feathers." Truhujo denied that he took back the power, but advised both William and Annie that if William didn't want the medicine feathers he could throw them in the river.[18] In this way Truhujo indicated that he would never take the power away. Yet, the possibility that he would change his mind and take back the power was an important element in Truhujo's control over the Sun Dance among the Crows and of the careers of Crow medicine men.

At the request of the Crows, the Elk Lodge was organized in 1943. Present were Al Childs, Joe Hill, Barney Old Coyote, Mrs. Old Coyote, Robert and Mrs. Yellowtail, Mark Real Bird, David Bad Boy, and Jim Buffalo. Truhujo was "to fix up three or four men for them so they could doctor for them." He then noted,

[18] A river carries things away, and hence anything connected with mystical power is best disposed of in a river. If evil threatens, as an automobile or other accident foreseen in a dream," a person can rid himself of the threat by offering a prayer smoke to the water spirit, cutting off a lock of hair, and throwing it into the water.

I gave them some feathers, and I also gave them otter hides, beaver hide, [and a] bear tooth. See what else I gave them—sparrow hawk feathers. [I] told them, "Now friends, if these things don't work for you, there's nothing that I could do for you. If these things work for you, you have [a] chance to learn these things by your own experience, by working with them."

As to the appointment of officers,

Barney was supposed to be their president; then Jo, the vice-president, then Dave [Bad Boy], he was a scout. That's it. And they have pretty good results to the medicine, so they thought they'd keep it. I told them, if it wasn't satisfactory to them, I'd like to have the stuff back to me. So they said they [were] going to keep it.

Truhujo did not request any payment, but "just what they give me of their own will."

As a mentor and critic, Truhujo insisted that the Crow learn the proper form of the Sun Dance one step at a time.

Those steps that I put in for them was for them to understand, for them to know what comes this time, and what comes in another time. . . . For instance, we have those morning ceremonies; then we didn't have any cedar [prayer] at the Pryor meeting. Then we didn't have any fire tenders at Pryor the first year. During that summer we didn't have any at Crow [Agency]. [Then] . . . at Pryor, the next summer [1942] . . . we have the cedar [prayer]. We have the Cedar Chief there. . . . I didn't establish any gourd and cane until '42, that was the second year we have [a] Sun Dance at Crow [Agency]. Then they say, "We like to adopt the Sun Dance the way you run it" (Jo Hill, Barney Old-coyote, and David Bad-boy). Then I think it's in that '42 again, I says, "Friends, we're going to have a medicine meeting up in my tipi tonight before you boys leave." Then we have that meeting up there, [a] prayer meeting [full-moon].

By proceeding in stages, Truhujo always added something extra to strengthen the effectiveness and authenticity of the ceremony. This was especially important to sponsors of Sun

Dances and served to assure the return of loved ones from the war. In 1943, Truhujo introduced a special prayer to the Sun because Barney Old Coyote wanted the ceremony to be as authentic as possible. Old Coyote sponsored the Sun Dance for his sons overseas. The pledger, his assistant, the medicine-man (Truhujo), cedar man, and other respected sun dancers gathered at dawn to reaffirm the pledger's intention to complete the dance. However, in order for this prayer to the Sun to be introduced into the ceremony, the medicine man directing the ceremony was required to take part in the practice dances preceding the Sun Dance. Truhujo indicated that this prayer to the Sun was to be used all during the war.

As World War II drew to a close, the Old Coyotes inquired as to their rights to transfer the medicine bundles received from Truhujo to their sons. To this Truhujo replied, "You're the President and you're the Beaver Woman. You have privileges to do [with] them what you want. But if you do [transfer the medicines] you're standing outside the ring now. That is the whole thing in a nutshell." In 1948 during a Sun Dance at Crow agency, the transfer of the Elk Lodge medicines was made.

Postwar Disenchantment with Crow Leaders: A Second Laying on of Hands

Following World War II, Truhujo became disillusioned with leaders at Crow Agency. At a dance in Pryor, he reportedly decided to borrow medicine feathers from those he had raised up as medicine men. If the feathers stood upright, the power was still there; but in most cases the feathers drooped. Truhujo reported to a Crow friend that one by one the medicine helpers had passed by his place in Fort Washakie and announced: "John, I'm going home." From that time on, the feathers earlier dispensed were nothing more than meaningless objects, and Truhujo was unable to restore the powers to the original owners because they had used them for "wrong ends." Allegedly, the medicine helpers abandoned owners because the medicine feathers were used to attract women, to make owners wealthy, to harm others, and also were used in conjunction with peyote and alcohol. This disenchantment with original leaders apparently peaked in the sixties. In 1969, Truhujo made a new transfer of power to Thomas Yellowtail of Wyola. In effect this was an internal transfer, since the Yellowtails and the Old-Coyotes were in-laws. Tom Yellowtail and eight other Crows danced at Fort Washakie in 1967. Truhujo was the sponsor and head medicine-man of the dance, and he issued strong invitations to the Crows to attend. According to Johnson, Truhujo's assistants were Crows, and the "ceremony might more accurately be called a joint Crow-Shoshoni venture."[19]

As he grew old, Truhujo considered the matters of retirement and who should succeed to the power among the Crows. The 1967 Sun Dance provided the stage to determine who was favored to receive the mystic power. In this final laying on of hands, Truhujo was guided by the Spirit of the Sun Dance, Seven Arrows. In the 1967 Sun Dance, Tom Yellowtail was the fourth man away from Truhujo.

On the second day . . . John was up there dancing. I laid down to rest. John was doctoring. As he went to the pole, I heard him cry out, "Tom, tomorrow (that would be the third day), tomorrow these little feathers are going to be yours. I'm giving these to you."

Some of them [other Crow dancers] spoke up, "Why don't you give them to me, John?" John said that Seven Arrows spoke to him and said, "That man, the fourth man from you—give these feathers to him."[20]

In referring to the order received from Seven Arrows, Truhujo joked that he thought he was being fired. However, there were

---

[19] Johnson, "Shoshone Sun Dance, 1966 & 1967."

[20] As fourth man, Yellowtail's selection was in agreement with the ritual number four.

other clues. That winter Truhujo, as usual, came up to a celebration among the Crows. Neither Tom nor his wife, Suzie, expected to see John at the dance hall. They arrived early, went over to John, shook hands, and visited. Prior to their arrival, according to Tom Yellowtail, "John . . . was told by Seven Arrows, whispering in his ear, to pay attention to the next couple which came through the door." That couple was Tom and Suzie Yellowtail.

The next spring (1969), Truhujo visited Tom Yellowtail for about a month and indicated that he had something important to do.

I'm supposed to turn all my medicine powers over to you. I received this order from Seven Arrows. He has picked you, . . . and you are the man to carry on. Seven Arrows has picked you among the Shoshones, Crow, Bannocks. There's a lot of Crows asking me, "John, you're getting old, give your medicines to me." (But Seven Arrows told him not to give in, "We'll pick a man for you.")

I refused everybody until that time you came into the dance [winter holiday dance]. There came a whisper in my ear. He said, "John, you watch the door and see the couple that comes in. That's the man to receive your medicine. That's the man we pick among the tribes, the Shoshone, Bannocks, some Utes." Seven Arrows has been at every Sun Dance and he has picked you.

Such were the words of Truhujo as remembered by Tom Yellowtail.

In setting about the transfer, they got a tape recorder and Truhujo sang three songs. The first or opening song was dedicated to the "medicine fathers," to the little people (dwarfs), the elk, the otter, and the white goose. The second was connected with all the birds, since these were the ones who communicated with the dancers on the second day. The third song referred to the white goose from which power to cure was derived. This was the power that Tom should use at all times when doctoring.

After singing the songs, Truhujo instructed Tom in their use. He then faced Tom to the east and, standing behind, prayed with his hand raised over Tom. Next Truhujo doubled his right fist, placed it between Tom's shoulderblades and blew heavily, emitting the shrill bugle of the elk. In this way Truhujo blew the power of the Elk Person into Tom and thereby made him head and owner of the Elk Lodge and recipient of his medicines. The transfer of power was not a purchase from Truhujo, but a gift, and Yellowtail was not obligated to give four things of value as in the case of a "purchase." This was the first time that the power of the elk was given to a Crow by Truhujo. Henry Old Coyote had some medicine feathers transferred to him earlier by his parents, but Truhujo maintained that the power had returned to its owner.

In 1975, the careers of Crow medicine men, such as Thomas Yellowtail, Arthur Anderson, and Hugh Little Owl, were as dependent on Truhujo's blessing as were those he raised up in the forties. By 1975, Truhujo's career as the maker and unmaker of Crow Sun Dance medicine men spanned thirty-four years.[21] In 1941 he gave his half-brother, Herbert Old Bear, a looking glass to assist him in curing. At the same time he warned Old Bear, who was "cured" of heart trouble in the Sun Dance, never to dance. He gave whistles for drawing water from the center pole to Jim Buffalo and David Bad Boy. He gave Joe Hill a replica of the "little man." All the medicine-men, including William Big Day and Barney Old Coyote, received medicine feathers for doctoring.

In Truhujo's judgment and experience, mixing doctoring and liquor was bad for a cure. There was the time when he improved the vision of Holds the Enemy, who, in appreciation, vowed a "giving thanks" meeting the following week. Unfortunately, before Truhujo completed the cure, two Crow youths returned from Billings and stumbled intoxicated into

[21] Truhujo, because of arthritis, is now in a home in Thermopolis, Wyoming. Personal communication from Professor Rodney Frey.

the meeting. Subsequently, Holds the Enemy lost the sight he had partially regained. This angered his granddaughter, who had warned the youths never to appear at a meeting when drunk. The true mark of a medicine man was demonstrated by his unerring perception of the meaning of dreams. David Bad Boy was not always sure of what he saw. Once during the war, Bad Boy wished to know whether he would soon receive a letter from a son in the army. At a prayer-meeting Bad Boy sat within the altar circle and got a good look at the mirror which Truhujo had given to Old Bear. Something white appeared in the mirror, which Bad Boy took to be clouds. Truhujo told him to look again and suggested that the white represented snow. He then informed Bad Boy that his son was overseas and that he would soon receive a letter. Within two days a letter came which told that the youth was in Japan and had gone skiing.

Avoiding peyote and intoxicating liquors in the Sun Dance, Truhujo maintained the image of a devoted and sincere worshipper and leader, always friendly and helpful to those who wished to learn how to pray.[22] At the same time he was a big success at doctoring. As one informant put it, "The things that man has done!" Friendliness and good will toward others were intrinsic to use of power in the Sun Dance. In Truhujo's view, it was anger that stood in the way of Charlie Ten-bear when he tried unsuccessfully to get power through the Sun

---

[22] Truhujo's spontaneous gift of his eagle-bone whistle to Jo Hill following a Sun Dance is a good illustration of his sensitivity to personal need and of how he added psychological strength to his relationships. Having learned that Hill's son was in the fighting overseas, Truhujo removed the whistle from his neck and stated, "Here's the whistle that I have used all through the dance and several before. I suffered a lot with that whistle, and we used it a lot in doctoring in the Sun Dances. You take this and keep it for your boy." Elmer Hill returned safely from the war and recounted a war blessing at the Sun Dance of his father-in-law, John Cummins, in 1946 at Lodge Grass.

Dance. The Creator apparently wanted no one to get too much power because of the damage he might do with it. As for Big Day, his trouble was that he insisted on a certain payment when he doctored, and when he used Charlie Bell and Tom Compton as leaders he brought undesirable changes into the Sun Dance.

John Truhujo as an Historical Person

Truhujo possessed many assets that made him more willing than his Shoshoni peers to transmit the Sun Dance to the Crow Indians. These resources included a determined, but frustrated, ambition kindled by the historical preeminence of his family in the Sun Dance; a family Sun Dance bundle validated by personal medicine dreams; medicine power to cure; a friendly and persuasive personality; and adaptive social skills and creativity. In addition, he had family connections with the Crows and was familiar with their important ceremonials, notably the Tobacco Society, which he acquired during periodic visits from about 1907 to 1922.

These resources, however, were insufficient to propel Truhujo into the ranks of historic innovators. For the ceremonial transfer to take place, two conditions were essential in setting the time. First, interest in Indian worship and custom needed to be heightened. In this way Indians would travel and exchange ideas and feelings about Indian ways and come away with the feeling that what they had seen possessed utility for the present, whether for immediate personal needs or as a basis for a career. The first condition was fulfilled by the lifting of government restrictions on Indian worship in 1935 and by encouragement from Commissioner Collier that Indian values should be used to revitalize Indian communities and adapt them to changing conditions. Thus, curiosity, intermingled with a search for personal meaning linked to Indian ways eventually led Big Day, Old Coyote, and Hill to meet at the Shoshoni Sun Dance in 1938.

To get the transmission process going at the right moment in Truhujo's career, his ambitions and resources also had to merge with the ambitions, career objectives, and needs of individual Crow Indians. With his conservative orientation, his aspirations to become a medicine man, and the psychological reinforcements of his own dream experiences, Big Day satisfied the second condition by seeking Truhujo's assistance just as the latter's career among the Shoshonis was getting under way.

Accidental events also played a part in the timing. When Big Day's adopted child and then his brother's child became ill, Big Day, in the course of his experimentation with the Sun Dance, eventually vowed to sacrifice himself in the Big Lodge in his home district, Pryor, in 1941, provided his brother's child recovered.

General cultural developments and individual ambitions and needs also combined to spread the Sun Dance. While personal cures and the acquisition of wealth convinced many Crows that there was power in the Sun Dance, it took the ambitions of Yellowtail and Old Coyote to organize the immediate spread of the ceremony. Furthermore, the coincidental outbreak of World War II stimulated the enthusiastic acceptance of Truhujo's leadeship in directing the Crow people to victory, good health, and greater wealth and population through the power of his Sun Dance way. As of old, war transformed the Sun Dance into an exuberant war party, with four ceremonies pledged each year. Petitioned by anxious parents, Truhujo prepared eagle feathers with his rainbow emblem and blessed them with his power. Quite a few Crow youths carried these medicine feathers during the war, and at war's end, following tradition, returned them to Truhujo with a gift.

CHAPTER 6

The Shoshoni-Crow Sun Dance: Ceremony and Symbolism

Introduction

Crow attitudes toward religious ceremony did not require that every performance of the Sun Dance should be just alike. Although they were sensitive to ceremony, the Crows were not strict ritualists, and historically speaking, no ceremony was without variations. Instructions from different spirit helpers prompted individuals to introduce special elements according to their own revelations. However, the public measured changes in accordance with traditional expectations regarding belief and practice. Among the Shoshonis, public consensus mediated by shamanic peers ruled against John Truhujo and others who sought to introduce variations based on personal revelations. On the other hand, Truhujo was not so restrained by the Crows, since he was the instructor and they were the pupils. This was the usual relationship between mentor and apprentice when sacred power was transferred along with appropriate procedures for evoking and controlling medicine. Crow petitioners asked Truhujo to teach them his way, and in response, he introduced the peyote-inspired full moon prayer meeting and other special elements, such as the pledger's cane, drummer's cane, rattle, and traditional coup-striking on the lodge poles.

Special elements that Truhujo introduced are often absent

in the present Sun Dance, and the ceremony now appears closer to the simplified Shoshoni form. The Elk Lodge and full moon meetings are still elements of the Sun Dance organization, but the Elk Lodge is hardly functional and does not unify a select group of worshippers as it did during the war years. Moreover, when Truhujo selected a new leader for the inheritance of his medicine bundle and ceremonial rights, he intensified an existing estrangement and reopened competition for leadership. The Old Coyotes at Crow Agency continued a separate ceremonial control.

Sponsoring a Sun Dance: Dream and Vow

The Crows referred to the present Sun Dance with their traditional term, "making a little tipi" or more exactly, making a tipi replica.[1] More often, they spoke of the Sun Dance as the Big Lodge.

Today, any male of reputation may vow to put up a Sun Dance or follow a directive to do so received in a dream. In the past confirmation of a directive usually was sought by consulting a medicine man. Campbell Big Hail once illustrated the way in which vow, dream, and interpretive advice of a medicine man converged and led to sponsorship of a Sun Dance. In 1941, Big Hail's granddaughter and an adopted girl were seriously ill. At that time "I said that if they got well, I would dance." This he did at Pryor in June, 1941. The continued illness of his daughter and his own rheumatism, next led Big Hail to Fort Hall, where three Sun Dances were taking place simultaneously. A "doctor" at Gibson told him that if his daughter got well, he should put up a Sun Dance. She recovered, and he prepared to go ahead with his vow. In the meantime he had a dream about the Sun Dance. Big Hail remembered that "Before I put up that Sun Dance, I saw that Sun Dance . . . that they put up that center pole.

[1] Lowie, "Sun Dance of the Crow Indians," 16:8.

I seen that—a lot of people in there." Big Hail consulted with William Big Day, who told him that he had to put up a Sun Dance and there was no getting out of it. Campbell Big Hail also dreamt of horses and cattle. After the Sun Dance he received some horses and expected some cattle within a month. "I think this Sun Dance is power for that [getting wealth] too." However, bad luck sometimes followed the Sun Dance, for as he danced, Big Hail saw that the ridge pole under which he, as sponsor, danced, was white with snow. In January his son died.

When war broke out and Crow youths left for the army, brothers and fathers vowed Sun Dances if brothers and sons returned home safely. As Al Childs saw it,

About the boys going to war. I thought we would try and make a prayer and oath in the Indian Way and take charge over these boys being saved and come back alive. And if they did I would go and put up a Sun Dance. That is how I got that Sun Dance up. Alongside with that I took [the] religion that I believe [Catholic], I took that up, too, and prayed. Now I don't know which of these made the results.

Francis Rock vowed a Sun Dance at the time when his classificatory brothers (one of whom was adopted by Rock's father) returned from the war. Bringing the Crow soldiers safely home was an overriding motive for dancing in the Sun Dance. Jim Buffalo, a medicine man, vowed to dance every

Sun Dance they put up til the war was over. I'm praying for all the boys that the war will be over and the boys will come back safe. So I'm keeping up my prayers this year [1946]. This will be the last one unless they have one next summer and the sponsor comes over and asks me to dance.

Robert Howe stayed out for awhile, but then asked himself what he could do to bring the boys back safely. Suddenly he determined to dance, and after dancing he had no fear for the safety of the Crow soldiers. He figured that the "Lord told him to dance." In between and in addition to the sacrifice for the soldiers a man danced for relatives who were sick. When Francis Rock's "mother" was in the hospital, he danced for her recovery. The solicitations of friends and relatives also precipitated decisions to take part, as happened to Charlie Ten Bear when he attended the first Sun Dance at Pryor in 1941. There he saw his old friend Johnny Trehero (Truhujo) at the ceremony when the center pole was raised. John spoke to him and said,

"Charlie, you ought to go in with us tonight." I said, I'm not prepared to take part in this Sun Dance, as this is the first one I have seen. I would not know what I have to do. But John said, "Go in with me tonight, and sit beside me, and I will assist you in the ceremony."

That evening when the ceremony was to be taken over by the sponsor, we were advised to go to the creek, wash up, and eat a good supper, and we did this. So I went up to John and asked him how to dress and he told me, "Get a whistle, get a white plume and attach it to your little fingers. Get a shawl and put it around your waist, and get a blanket and something to lay on. Come in barefoot." So I did.

The Sun Dance was especially appealing to those with chronic and threatening illnesses. David Bad Boy first entered the Sun Dance in 1941 at Crow Agency after he inquired about its meaning and why they danced. He was told that you went in as an individual and that it was a "main help" for the sick. If you went in and put all your faith in the Sun Dance, "you will be cured." While working for the WPA, Bad Boy caught a cold that developed into bronchitis. Agency doctors examined him but seemed unable to help and expressed fear that Bad Boy was becoming tubercular. This downturn in his health worried him because he had a wife and small child to take care of. He never told his wife about going into the Sun Dance. She knew he was ill, and he figured she might try to stop him. When she found out, she asked the doctors to stop him, but they said they could not, and that it might cure him. Bad Boy got through the Sun Dance pretty well, but felt "kinda funny" when he came out of the lodge. At home his wife made a bed for him on the floor, but suddenly everything started spinning and he got up and went out. At the door he threw up thick blood, a large bowlful. It was some time before Bad Boy recovered from the cough that developed three days later. However, he knew the Sun Dance had cured him. "I asked God that I be cured, and it seems that my prayers were answered that time."

At Crow Agency in 1942, Bad Boy danced to "give thanks that I was well." He prayed for the safe return of all the soldier boys, both Crow and others. Bad Boy also danced once to pray for a sick "aunt," and again for a sick "uncle." In 1944 he felt obligated to dance at Big Horn (St. Xavier) because the sponsor, Al Childs, was his classificatory brother-in-law. In 1946 John Half asked Bad Boy to dance at Big Horn to help him fulfill his "promise to God that his boy will come back to where he was born and will live here afterwards." During the battle for Okinawa, Bernard Tobacco's brother, a marine, was under constant threat of death and vowed that if he got home safely he would take part in the first available Sun Dance. The Sun Dance thus reached out to the distant battlefield and inspired vows of thanks for a safe return.

Organizing a Sun Dance

A pledger of a Sun Dance encountered extensive organizational problems. He not only made arrangements to build the dance lodge and conduct a proper ceremony, but he also maintained an orderly encampment and provided food for the feast at the end of the ceremony. Also, some payment had to be made to the medicine man and his associates invited to direct the ceremony, including transportation and food.

To coordinate matters, a sponsor relied on a Sun Dance Committee of relatives and close friends. For basic arrangements at the first Sun Dance at Pryor, William Big Day depended on Caleb Bull Shows, his assistant; Bill Wall, secretary; and Jo Turns Back Plenty, treasurer. As he put it, "they look upon me as a chief, and I did not have to bother." All three were clan mates of Big Day, and Bull Shows and Wall were close peyote associates. Turns Back Plenty was a Baptist, but he was not antagonistic to the Sun Dance. He indicated that at one time he intended to dance, but was unable in practice to handle the dance step, so decided against it. The "gatekeepers" were Stanley Rides the Horse, (Sore-lip clan), and Claude Milligan of the Newly-made-lodge clan. Six policemen were selected by Wall. Big Day turned to a Catholic and Peyotist, Austin Lion Shows, to canvass his white friends for donations. Lion Shows raised $200 for the feast.[2] Altogether

---

[2] Austin Lion Shows was a brother-in-law to Big Day. In 1946, he indicated no interest in the Sun Dance other than as an observer. He did think the Sun Dance was a "good thing for the Indians, for we Indians in our history . . . always have the Sun before then as a God." He thought the Indians worshipped the Sun as God until the white man came and told them that God was behind the Sun. However, Indians became confused by the "many preachings; now we don't know where we are today." The dancers, using medicines and sufferings received in return "good luck, horses, and good health, and they can cure sickness. . . ." They asked for help from the Sun or God, [for] nobody knows where God is. . . ."

Lion Shows revealed a common tendency to turn to traditional practices when confronted with a crisis-illness. Thus, when doctors at the hospital recommended that he go to a sanatorium to convalesce because of a lung infection, he went home and sought doctoring with peyote. He continued to go to peyote meetings and to use the herb for doctoring. A brother, Oliver, a leader of Peyotists at Pryor, induced Austin to try peyote. His approach to worship echoed a common eclectic and pragmatic orientation. "My relationship," he noted, "is Catholic, and besides that, I go to most any place [church]." In 1975 at Lodge Grass, Austin Lion Shows pledged a Sun Dance, but then he suffered a stroke that left him paralyzed. He continued sponsorship, but a son, Thomas, carried out the role of sponsor.

some $400 was turned over to treasurer Turns Back Plenty
for the purchase of food in Billings.

The pledging of a Sun Dance created pressures on district
residents to help and to put up a tipi at the encampment.
Appeals for dancers, singers, and tipis were sent out to other
districts, especially to the one with which a district maintained the closest social and mutual aid relations. William Big
Day especially invited older men from Big Horn district to
take part in the first Sun Dance. Because of district pride
and competition, however, the production of a Sun Dance
remained a local affair. For his special needs, a sponsor first
sought aid from brothers and brothers-in-law, real and classificatory. Social pressure was such that when a brother called
for assistance, refusal was hardly possible. A sponsor asked
for the loan of a team or of a truck, the donation of labor,
or even the early termination of mourning to allow the relatives to help out with the singing. In the latter case, the sponsor made a public request of his brother-in-law to shorten
his mourning and announced the gift he would receive for
doing so, usually a horse. Kinship ties were stronger than
religious differences, and close relatives of Christian faith
helped as much as non-Christians.

A sponsor organized the work and obtained all the materials
for the lodge. He depended heavily on brothers-in-law, dancers, clan mates, and district volunteers to assemble the poles
and construct the lodge. He could count on volunteers to supply one or more of the pine poles in the hope of sharing in
the blessings of the Sun Dance. Older men were especially
active in erecting the lodge. A sponsor and the director of the
Sun Dance supervised but seldom took a hand in the heavy
work unless necessary.

The sponsor laid down the rules guiding the dance. He
reminded dancers of the solemnity of the occasion, cautioned
against bringing wet towels into the lodge, and warned that
only those who could complete the ceremony should enter the
lodge. It was his duty to watch the condition of dancers, and

he terminated the dance early if necessary. The appointed policemen patrolled the lodge and accompanied dancers to the outside toilet. A pledger usually appointed a trusted friend or relative to take charge of the profane part of the lodge, to keep spectators in check, and to keep track of shifts of singers. The sponsor selected a veteran to recite his war deed and to ring the center pole with black charcoal. He also selected veterans to maintain the fire and to provide willow shoots that the women's chorus moved up and down in time to the music.

Appointments were made informally, and the execution of office was not rigid. At every dance, participants usually complained about small boys who burrowed their way into the lodge and pilfered cigarettes. On occasion, too, a dancer entered the lodge intoxicated, but as long as he was not a nuisance, he was tolerated and quietly laughed at by dancers and spectators alike.

Consecrating the Sun Dance

From the time that he determined to put up a Sun Dance, Big Day was obligated to rise before sunup and pray to the Creator, He Made All Things, and to Old Man Sun. In his prayer to the Creator and the Sun he reported his intention to put up His lodge in the summer. He asked the Creator to send power to help with the Sun Dance to enable him to get along well with his people, the Crows. Big Day also prayed that the Crow children would grow up and that all kinds of food that grew on earth would be plentiful. He petitioned the Maker not to send diseases or sickness among the people. In praying, Big Day offered a smoke, for "It is the Indian law that if I offer a smoke to the Maker, He cannot say 'No.' Because I'm giving it in the Indian Way to answer my prayers. When I look into the sun, it doesn't hurt my eyes, just like the times when I pray."

Messenger eagle resting on cottonwood foliage frame pointed to the sun. The stick marks location of the center pole. Crow Agency, 1941.

Usually in February, the sponsor invited everyone to a "sing" and feast that signaled the start of the Sun Dance. At this time he announced the days when he intended to put up the lodge. From now on, there was no turning back. Ears listened for the first roll of thunder in the spring, for the Sun Dance was linked to thunder and lightning. The eagle on the forked rafter pole under which the director took his position was supposed to be "crooked like lightning," i.e., Thunderbird. A first thunder was a "good sign" and marked the time for the first of four "outside dances." The first outside dance was held after the first, second, or third thunder in the spring. The next two were held at any time, and the fourth on the night before the dancers entered the lodge.

Consecrated and painted buffalo head with sage in nostrils. The tripod frame with cottonwood foliage is placed east of the cottonwood center pole. Pryor, 1941.

Usually the third and fourth outside dances were scheduled consecutively. At Lodge Grass in 1946, John Cummins scheduled his outside dances May 3, June 10, 28, and 29, and began the main dance on June 30. One week before the last outside dance, the sponsor pitched his tipi directly west of the projected Sun Dance lodge and aligned it with the sun and stake set for the center pole.

John Cummins's Outside Dance, Lodge Grass, 1946

The May 3 date for Cummins's first outside dance was set by John Truhujo at a prayer meeting held in February. Truhujo gave the message to Joe Hill, brother-in-law to Cummins and medicine man of the Elk Lodge, of which Cummins was a member. With Hill's assistance Cummins placed four poles

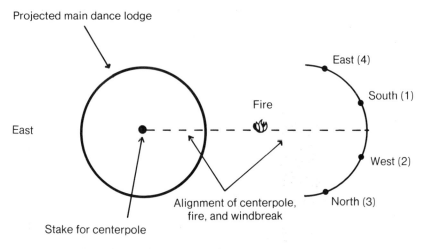

Figure 6. Plan of "Outside Dance," Lodge Grass, 1946.

in a gradual curve just west of the projected boundaries for the main lodge. They worked in the afternoon of the day on which the dance was scheduled. Cummins furnished the pine poles from his corral stock. They were spaced at four paces in a north to south direction and represented the four cardinal points (see Figure 6). He was assisted by brother-in-law Hill and John Whiteman, a "father-in-law," because Whiteman's wife had brought up Cummins's spouse.

The dance ground was viewed as a tipi, and the canvas attached to the poles represented the outside of the imaginary tipi. The tipi faced east, with fire and stake centering the main lodge on an east-west axis. Cummins furnished the wood and made the fire ready. It was placed some twelve paces from the windbreak, just far enough away so the dancers would not feel it too much, "for . . . a fire gets pretty hot."

The Crows traditionally exited a tipi by going to the left of the fire. This practice accounted for the order in which the poles were erected. At the end of the outside dance, the dancers departed by going to the left of the fire. The tent canvas, furnished by the sponsor, was attached to the poles just before the sun went down, indicating the start of the dance. By the time the sun dipped behind the western hills, a crowd of about two hundred had gathered, including some twenty young men on horses. It was a chilly evening in May, and some twenty cars and pickups were arranged in an oblong on either side of the windscreen to dull the bite of the cold wind. Men clustered in a group east of the fire, while a number of women gathered behind the drum, where they made up a chorus. They wore ordinary clothes, topped by the usual blankets, and some of them carried babies. As the dance warmed up, so did the children, who played and ran around without interference, clambering up on the cars and tapping their feet on car bumpers and running boards in time with the drumming. The sky glittered with a great arch of stars, and the moon, in its first quarter, was flanked by Saturn. It was a spectacular and auspicious night to begin the Sun Dance cycle.

The band-type drum was furnished, at Cummins's request, by the Lodge Grass committee in charge of dances and recreation. Cummins sent his truck to pick up the drum and singers from the district. No one was asked to dance or to help with the singing. It was purely voluntary, and pledger Cummins learned who his dancers were just before the start of the dance. However, the day before, he had spoken with two veterans of World War II, Elmer Hill, his son-in-law, and Joseph Medicine Crow, his brother-in-law, saying to the latter, "Brother-in-law, at the occasion of the first practice dance of the Sun Dance, I want you to build our fire for us." The two veterans told their war deeds and wished the same good luck with which they had been blessed for the dancers and all present. They also served as "fire men." Normally only one veteran was called upon to recite a deed blessing, but pledger Cummins wished to honor all soldiers and thus called upon veterans from both the Pacific and European Theaters.

The sponsor and three other dancers completed dressing for the dance behind the wind screen. Cummins delayed the start of the ceremony until he had a dance team of four, since combinations of two and four were ritually prescribed. Rounding the north side of the screen, Cummins met medicine man Hill on the sacred ground between fire and screen and told him that he was ready to start. The two veterans, Hill, and Bird Horse, the announcer, gathered east of the unlit fire and faced to the west. Medicine Crow reported the following to the announcer, who repeated it aloud for all to hear.

I was in the infantry and fought as a foot soldier for 188 consecutive days. During these 188 days of front line duty, I seen some very hard days, and suffered a lot physically as well as mentally, and there were days that were almost too difficult to endure. I recall particularly two occasions when my company was surrounded by the German soldiers, and it seemed like annihilation was imminent. But I was fortunate to have got out on both occasions, and particularly on the last. . . . I was left behind as a rearguard, like a Crazy-dog. My company left me, and I was there until I thought it was about time to pull out. For that night and part of the day I was exposed to blizzard, imminent capture, and deep snow. I finally rejoined my outfit two days later. Having gone through that hard experience I eventually reached the comparative safety and happiness and rejoicing of my fellow soldiers and comrades. These young men [dancers] who have dedicated themselves to four [sic] days and nights of hardship, it is my wish and hope that they shall come through their ordeal feeling well repaid for their efforts, and their suffering, and whatever they have prayed for and wished and held sacred in their hearts shall be fulfilled at the end. This is my wish for the sundancers.

During this recital, Medicine Crow's mother, grandmother, and mother's sister brought up a comforter and five dollars for him to give away. His mother and stepfather told him how to distribute the goods and money, for many Crows were not aware of important or distant kin relations who should be honored with gifts in a public give-away. The comforter and one dollar went to honor an old Hidatsa who was visiting his mother's sister's husband, a Newly-made-lodge, paternal clansman and "father" to Medicine Crow. One dollar went to Cummins because he was a "brother-in-law and because Cummins's wife was brought up by Medicine Crow's clan mother. The dollar also honored Cummins as the sponsor of the Sun Dance. Hill and Bird Horse received one dollar apiece because they were paternal clansmen and because they were "active in the Sun Dance organization." Finally, one dollar went to Jim Blaine, a Whistling-water clan mate of Medicine Crow, because Blaine had a "tribal license to sing praise songs." All these, including the Hidatsa visitor, and especially his social "father," reciprocated with prayers for Medicine Crow, and Blaine sang a praise-song in his honor.

After this distribution of goods, Medicine Crow simply lit the fire with a match. The other veteran, Elmer Hill, completed his narrative blessing and made a small distribution also. At this point, medicine man Hill took an ordinary shovel and cleared a bed for coals to purify the ritual paraphernalia. Half-kneeling west of the fire, Hill threw incense on coals taken from the fire and drew the drummer's cane and rattle through the incense, moving from east to west. He rotated his hand with palm down and moved the cane and rattle from north to south through the incense. He next sanctified the cane and the rattle separately, following the same progression. At this ceremonial moment the pledger came forward and passed his leader's cane through the incense, progressing from west to east. Then, rotating his hand to the left, he drew the cane from north to south. Again turning the cane with his palm upright, Cummins raised and lowered it twice for a count of four, the Crow ritual number. A palm upturned was symbolic of a request, and when moved toward the body, it signified the drawing of the thing requested to that spot or person.

After the pledger returned to his place in the center of the screen, Hill took up his former position in front of the coals, with cane in right hand and rattle in left. With head bowed, he prayed that the "sweet-smelling cedar" would purify the air, so that no one might get sick from any bad air that might be around. He prayed there would be no accidents in the coming Sun Dance; that the children would grow up to manhood and womanhood; that the Crows would have good luck throughout the tribe; that the sick would get well; that the dancers would not suffer severely during the three days they were to dance; and that whatever wishes the dancers might have would come true. He also asked for the safe return of soldiers still overseas, and, in particular, he prayed for Bernard Cummins and Thomas Tobacco. Bernard, son of Cummins, was convalescing in a hospital in California, and Hill prayed the Sun Dance would bring about his cure. Thomas Tobacco, step-son of Robert Yellowtail and "brother-in-law" of Cummins, arrived home three days after the prayer.

Hill prayed in a voice inaudible most of the time, and during part of the prayer the singers drummed and sang softly in practice. He gave the drummer's cane and rattle to Guy Bulltail and selected him as drum chief "because he's a fellow that catches songs easily." While all singers knew the songs for the most part, at times only certain songs were sung, and so "we get one leader who knows just when to sing these songs so the rest will follow up—might as well say he's the bandleader." The "Drum Chief" sat east of the drum and faced west, where he had an unobstructed view of the sponsor of the dance, prepared to take his cue on signal. He did not drum, but began the songs and indicated their start and end with the rattle. The rattle also was used to beat out the time of the drumming. Occasionally the rattle was passed around among the drummer-singers, but not the drummer's cane. The drummer's cane and rattle were made by Hill at John Truhujo's request in 1943.[3]

When ceremonial paraphernalia were put into use, the cane always was smoked first. As Hill explained,

[3] See Appendix B for description of the drummer's cane.

It is a rule that you got to smoke the cane first because that is the lodge cane. If you see an old man or an old woman trying to get up, you will always see the cane work out first, and again it represent[s] a kind of staff like the Almighty have—like a shepherd's staff. At these dances we don't have shoes on and I pray that they won't blister their feet. . . . And if there's anybody get hurt on the feet . . . that cane will come in handy so they can support themselves on that cane, and we also pray that after they handle that cane and use it that they will get well quick so that they can go without that cane.[4]

When he gave the drummer's cane and rattle to Guy Bull Tail, Hill told him to start with the "water song" and to follow with three other songs. The water song was so named because, on a fast with three other Shoshonis, John Truhujo saw a "person" (spirit-being) come out of a lake. This person "taught him to use this song in all the leading ceremonies as well as the Sun Dance."

The area between the fire and windscreen was the sacred ground of the dancers, and no spectator was allowed to walk upon it. Shoes were prohibited in the sacred area. It also was forbidden to pass in front of a person offering a prayer, because this movement interrupted communication with the divine.

At the beginning of the first song, or water song, the dancers blew a long sighing blast on their eagle-bone whistles, followed by a series of four staccato notes. They danced in place and bent their knees in rhythm to the drumming and singing of the eight drummers and a women's chorus of twelve. The dancers ended each song with a long blast and staccato, at which time the women came in with a stylized ending. With the exception of one Crow Sun Dance song, all the songs used in the first outside dance were Shoshoni, and without words.

[4] Pledgers of the traditional Crow Sun Dance sometimes were so exhausted that they used "canes" to support themselves on leaving the lodge.

As the first song ended, Bird Horse, the aged and respected announcer, encouraged the dancers. "You are here to dance. Come forward and dance as though you were in the main dance."

In the chorus of the fourth song Cummins found his cue and half-ran, half-danced forward to within five or six feet of the fire. He blew his whistle in staccato to the beat of the drum and carried his leader's cane in his right hand. He then retreated in half-step back to his starting position. At the next song, all the dancers joined in. Some twenty minutes after the start, the four dancers were joined by two others.

The dancers used a "Spanish" fringed shawl or a fringed light-weight Navaho blanket as a wrap-around kilt. It was held in place by a broad beaded belt to which a beaded bag was attached, or by a beaded sash that draped along the right leg. From the little finger of each hand hung an eagle-down feather tied with a string of buckskin to the finger or to a ring. The eagle-bone whistles were tipped with from one to three down feathers of the eagle.

With one exception, all the dancers were members of the Elk Lodge. To show their affiliation, each drew a small ring of red paint around each wrist and a pencil-line of red from the corner of each eye extending for about an inch. Fred Bird, a non-member, painted himself red from the bridge of his nose upwards to the hairline. All carried Pendleton blankets to throw over their shoulders when not dancing.

Such were the essentials of ceremonial dress, to which each dancer added his own touch of individuality. Three wore colorful kerchiefs over the chest attached to a necklace, rolled and tucked at the belt line, and tied at the back. Earrings, bracelets, rings, and armbands also were worn. Cummins wore false braids wrapped with strips of otter skin, and from his beaded headband hung two metal tubes about five inches long with a shell attached. Bob Howe and Hugh Little Owl also wore false braids, while Dan Old Bull wore dark glasses to shield his eyes from the glare of the fire.

All of the dancers carried full medicines, but Cummins, as sponsor, wore an Elk Lodge medicine given to Hill by Truhujo. It consisted of a seashell to which a piece of elk-hide, blue muslin, and six eagle feathers taken from the wing were attached. The elk-hide measured about one foot nine inches in length and five inches in width. Two stone settings, one consisting of crossed arrows, adorned the front, while the back carried a six-peaked zigzag lightning design in green. The muslin carried a spangled, many-starred piece that represented the sun. The necklace was of two strands of beads, and the shell was decorated with rainbow and lightning marks.

All dancers wanted to take part, because the Sun Dance was designed to thank the Creator for the safe return of the soldiers and the end of the war. Cummins and Old Bull fulfilled their vows for the safe return of "brothers," and Cummins especially felt concern for his son, recovering in California. Howe, brother-in-law and close friend, joined in to help Cummins in his vow. In addition, there were personal concerns. Fred Bird vowed to dance if his wife was safely delivered of a child. In general, dancers hoped to get some "blessing" for themselves and their families. They prayed as they danced, for "when you are dancing, that is the time that you are praying, and your only thought is a prayer."

The act of blowing the whistle, according to Old Coyote,

. . . stands for prayer. The whistle signifies that the eagle knows no evil on this earth, and the Indian uses the right eagle bone and passes his prayer through that while he is blowing to the Almighty; and there isn't supposed to be any evil in that while he is blowing his whistle.

When the dance first began, Jack Covers Up, 75 years old, got up and stated:

Since the boys, our brothers, sons and relatives returned from the war, it has ended well. They are almost all home safe, and we are putting this dance on purposely for them. Stay by your agreements and go through your ceremonies like you always have. We are mighty proud the boys are back with us. We see some of them with us here now. There are some who have not returned as yet, but we hope they will be returned in time to see this dance in July.

He followed this speech with his praise song, "The boys come back from the war-party. Come along, and thank you!"

What Covers Up said about the "soldier boys" prompted Jim Blaine to borrow a cigarette, which he gave to Hill to pray for his son still in service. Standing south of the fire, Hill used a brand from the fire to light the prayer smoke. Bird Horse and Blaine knelt behind him. Bird Horse uncovered his head, but Blaine did not, because he was wearing a cap tied up with a blue handkerchief to protect his ears. Hill puffed on the cigarette just long enough to get it started, and then extended it toward the fire, burning end down, and prayed in a voice not audible. From time to time he motioned with the smoke almost imperceptibly to the heavens and earth, and sidewise. He explained, "These motions in the sign of the cross are in there. A sideways motion is to take away sickness, and when it goes up we pray to the Almighty to bring a soldier boy here to this place, when you draw towards you.

Hill had six prayer smokes during the dance—for soldier boys, sick people, and to assure the easy birth and life of the newborn. At times he lit one prayer smoke from another. The spent cigarette was tossed into the fire, because the fire burned up the sickness. For soldiers, casting the prayer smoke into the fire symbolized their turning away from war and coming home. Burning the cigarettes also prevented a scattering and trampling of prayer smokes. Each cigarette represented a separate prayer and lasted from six to eight minutes.

Dancers added touches of individuality to their prayers. In his prayer, Howe took a few puffs and extended the cigarette toward the fire with a vigorous motion in order to make the prayer strong. He looked intently at the smoke offering and prayed silently. Twice he took two or three puffs on the cigarette, and then blew the smoke in the direction of the fire and over the burning end of the cigarette. In this way he blew the sickness away from Bernard Cummins. He offered the cigarette to the fire again and withdrew it quickly, letting his arm rest across his middle. With this act he asked that Bernard return home safely and soon. Fred Bird simply puffed on his cigarette and then held it at his side during prayer. Both were given prayer smokes by the sponsor to pray for the quick recovery and return of his son, so that he might take his place among the dancers in the "big lodge" in June. David Bad Boy, a medicine man from Crow Agency, prayed and then moved the prayer smoke to the south. Facing the prayer smoke again to the east, he prayed, and once more moved it to the south. In ending his prayer he offered the smoke to the Four Winds, first to the south, west, north, and then to the east, and then he tossed the butt into the coals. Bad Boy prayed especially for Bernard Cummins with a cigarette given by Mrs. Cummins. Medicine men Hill and Old Coyote thought that Bad Boy's sweep from east to south and back to east and again south would not succeed in removing sickness because he failed to complete the movement. However, Bad Boy indicated that with such movement he offered the smoke to the Maker wherever He might be.

The cigarette was an excellent prayer smoke, since it burned long enough for the drummer-singers to get into the fourth rendition of a song sequence. Dancers were able to complete prayers and dance back into position during the fourth refrain. Each song included a twenty-five-second refrain, when the drummer-singers repeated the theme twice to get used to it. This was followed by a heavy thunder imitating drumming and chorus for about two minutes and twenty seconds. The women added a five-second refrain at the end.

The Crows recognized two speeds in dancing, a slow and a fast step. The dancer ran to the fire, then in slow step shuffled backwards, knees dipping and wrists flipping the feather plumes held between thumb and forefinger, while he blew the eagle-bone whistle in drum tempo. Body movements in the fast step were vigorous, but the progression backwards was no more rapid than with the slow step. Youths often preferred the fast step, while older dancers paced themselves.

Because of the chill of the night, two five-minute halts were needed to heat up the drum for tone and resonance. Shortly after one of these pauses, around nine o'clock, the announcer, Bird Horse, spoke out.

> We have six men here tonight to start the dance. They have their medicines tied on themselves. This is no plaything you are doing! It is in thanks that our boys returned from overseas as well as they left us. We are very proud of them. Anyone who wishes to have a prayer offered, do not hesitate to ask. Tobacco must be offered and you can ask them to pray for any member of your family.

Just before the final reheating of the drum around 9:30 P.M., Bird Horse called out,

> There will be another outside dance June 10th. If there are any boys who want to dance next time, come up earlier; because there were a lot of boys who wanted to dance, but they got left out this time.

This announcement was the cue for women to request prayer smokes. By custom, women deferred to men in food lines as well as in ceremony. Awaiting her time, Mrs. Pretty on Top borrowed two cigarettes from her husband at the drum and offered them to Bird Horse to pray for two sons who were still in service. At this time Bad Boy, at the request of Mrs. Cummins, offered a prayer smoke for her convalescing son. This was the last prayer of the dance, which ended unceremoniously as Bird Horse announced, "This is all." The last stick had been placed on the fire, the signal of the end. Dancers, drummer-singers, and spectators climbed into cars and departed, and the sponsor and close associates removed the canvas screen from the posts. The fire was left to burn itself out. The dance had lasted approximately two hours, ending around 10 o'clock.

The remaining outside dances followed the style of the first performance, except that attendance and participation fell off. Cummins announced that he wanted as many dancers as possible at the last practice dance, but only seven showed up. John Truhujo was present and smoked the ceremonial paraphernalia. The dance lasted but an hour, from around 9:15 to 10:15 P.M.

Cummins announced that the next day, when they went into the main lodge, they intended to do it in the right way. He did not want any wet towels brought into the lodge. The dancers all knew that his son, Bernard, was well, but they planned to go ahead anyway, in order to get an answer to their prayers. Wives were instructed not to distract their husbands while they were dancing, nor were the people to do so. Policemen were on hand to keep order. The dance would last for three days, and at the end of the third day, wives should have ice cream and watermelon ready for their dancer-husbands. People were not to bring food or drink near the lodge.

Blake Whiteman, Cummins's brother-in-law, announced his intention to wake the camp up early, about 5:30 A.M., and he encouraged people to start work early on the lodge. He reported that he was offering a team of horses to help with construction of the lodge. He also had five houses in town that were available for any visitors who had no place to stay. Visitors could turn their horses into his pasture, just below the Sun Dance site.

Building the Big Lodge

The Big Lodge required a center pole that was forked and towered some forty feet into the air. Twelve long pine poles that interlocked at the crotch of the center pole also were needed. As with the centerpole, the tips of these pines bore natural growth, and the pledger's pole was forked.[5] Twelve forked uprights of cottonwood, pine, or other wood without foliage were needed to mark the circumference of the lodge, as well as twelve connecting stringers upon which the pine rafters rested. Finally, cottonwood brush was used to enclose the lodge, providing shade and a degree of privacy for the dancers. They attached a bundle of willows to the center pole, or "tree," just below the fork; and below that, a buffalo head. An eagle was tied to the forked pine rafter. In lieu of a stuffed eagle, twelve eagle feathers sometimes were used. A blue and

---

[5]When Truhujo first introduced the Sun Dance, Crow pledgers, following Crow tradition, commonly positioned themselves under the forked rafter pole with eagle attached, placing the medicine man to their right. Sometimes, however, the medicine man located himself under the forked rafter, following Shoshoni practice. After World War II, medicine men supervisors apparently began to position themselves regularly under the "chief pole." According to Rodney Frey, in "Sacred Symbols of the Apsaalooke Sun Dance Religion," manuscript:

The "chief pole" runs from a forked post standing directly behind the stall of the . . . [medicine man] "running" the dance to the center pole. This . . . [medicine man] sits at the western point of the lodge. Unlike the other eleven overhead poles, prayer and a pipe of tobacco and fire are offered just before the cutting of the "chief pole." The ceremony is similar to that given the "forked tree" with the exception of not "counting coup" on it. As the center pole opens to the sky, the "chief pole" is also forked at its tip some six to eight feet, and opens to the Morning Sun. From it, the Eagle is suspended and faces the Sunrise.

In accordance with Shoshoni and present practice, in the text that follows, I have assigned the forked rafter to the medicine man. There is, however, a close connection between the chief pole and both the sponsor and the medicine man. In a prayer just before cutting the forked pine rafter, Tom Yellowtail reported to Seven Arrows, owner of the Sun Dance, that this pole was the "chief." This was the pole on which the eagle would sit and under which both the pledger and medicine man would take position. In his prayer he also addressed the Chief Pole as if it were a person, noting that "we are giving you a smoke before bringing you down . . . without breaking [for] we want to use you in our lodge. . . ."

a white pennant fluttered atop the forks of the center pole, to each of which a sack of Bull Durham tobacco was dedicated, tied to the limb just below the pennant.

The Sun Dance was the pledger's responsibility, and he organized the collection of building materials well in advance. Only the center pole, brush, and willows were left for the day when the lodge was built. At the third outside dance, at Cummins's request, Henry Pretty on Top, his brother-in-law, snaked the pine poles out of the Wolf Mountains and trucked them to the bluff above the Little Big Horn River, where the Sun Dance was to be held. In former times this spot was a favorite for horse racing.

Cummins wished to use pine for the center pole of his lodge, but when the tree was felled, it cracked and skinned one of the axe men. This was not an auspicious beginning, and led to the selection of a cottonwood, which grew nearby along the Little Big Horn bottoms.

Ceremony called for a "scouting" of the pine poles and of the center pole by a "war party." At the first Sun Dance at Pryor, when John Sarres, the Shoshoni brother-in-law of Truhujo, found a center pole, he simply called for Big Day and his party of ten to come and see what he had found. Two old men were then sent to scout the tree, while the others sang a Shoshoni war song used when sighting the enemy. They sang until the old men returned. One of them said, "There is that tree standing over there. From now on the Crow tribe will be increasing, all the new children will be born, and everything will grow."

When Big Day approached the center pole tree, he smoked and prayed. With left hand holding the smoke, he faced the sun and raised his right hand, palm toward the sun.

Creator, You made this tree to grow here, and now I'm going to take it and use it. We want it for a centerpole. While we have it for a center tree, we want Your medicine. We have it for the center post because You made the tree grow. We want to live in peace

and on this land. We want everything nice and growing, and no
sickness. We want You to dodge the sickness from the Crow tribe.
I thank You because I call on You today.

At the Sun Dance at Crow Agency in July, 1946, Truhujo
introduced a special sunrise prayer for success of the ceremony before going for the center tree. The ceremonial party
of Elk Lodge leaders included the sponsor, his assistant, the
medicine man, cedar man, drum-chief, and local water woman.
Facing east beside the stirred-up fire of the outside dance of
the night before, the cedar man threw incense on the coals
and then prayed. Next the medicine man took the pipe, Sun
Dance doll, drummer's cane, rattle, and leader's cane and
smoked them four times as a bundle. He also prayed for success of the venture, and was followed by the sponsor and his
assistant. Sponsor and assistant took positions just west of
the stake set for the center pole. With the sponsor on the
right, both now offered individual prayers. The sponsor held
the pipe in his right hand the remainder of the paraphernalia
in his left. After the assistant's prayer, the sponsor took a
coal from the fire and lit the pipe, pointed it to heaven, earth,
and the four winds, smoked, and then passed it to the rest.
The entrance and sponsor's tipi were aligned with the rising
sun, and this concluded the ceremony.

Construction of the lodge with its center pole and brush
was an all-day affair, and Blake Whiteman roused the camp
at Lodge Grass at 5:00 A.M. He encouraged his brother-in-
law, Cummins, to "Get up and start the day right and get all
the help you can. I am going to go and get my team."

By 8:45 A.M., Cummins headed off in his truck with Truhujo after the chosen tree, followed by a brother-in-law with
team and wagon, and several cars. Brothers-in-law and paternal clansmen ("clan uncles") were prominent in the twenty-
man party. The tree was close by and near the road, and Truhujo asked Cummins if he wished a coup struck at this time,
or just a prayer. They decided on prayer, and all removed

Ceremonial raising of center tree with tobacco and cloth offerings to Sun. Crow Agency, 1941.

their hats as Truhujo took his position west of the tree, bowed his head and prayed in Shoshoni. As he ended his prayer, Truhujo handed some sage to the respected Bird Horse, signifying that he would be the one to paint the buffalo head. Tilton West, another Shoshoni, now took an axe and cut the cottonwood to the point where sap oozed out. Cummins, Truhujo, and West rubbed the sap on their faces, chests, and hair, followed by others in no special order. They joked about the water in the tree and commented that it would come in handy on the second day—how they would wish for some of that water when they were "dry"! As West cut farther into the tree, it sprayed a fountain of sap, and again Cummins, Truhujo, and West drank of it, followed by others. Several men pushed against the tree as it leaned, felling it toward the east. Just before it crashed, Truhujo exclaimed, "The war is over

Getting ready to attach the buffalo head. The pickup serves as a working counterpart to the woodpile raised at traditional Sun Dances. Lodge Grass, 1975.

Manner of interlocking of rafter poles, with willow bundle and buffalo head. Note the black rings on pole. Crow Agency, 1941.

now boys, so cut off all the limbs. We don't want any more wars."

The tree was hardly on the ground when most of the party rushed upon it and broke or chopped off the branches. Brother-in-law Howe carted the tree to the dance ground on his wagon. Cummins and Truhujo measured the tree, which was six and a half axe-handle lengths from the fork. Then they gathered some willows and departed. Cleo Medicine Horse and Henry Big Day, "brothers" to Cummins, remained to shape the tree to size. Many of the party continued to drink and to rub themselves with sap from the stump, since sap from the holy tree was considered an excellent therapeutic for aches and pains.

By 9:30 A.M. the tree was at the dance ground, and soon a wounded veteran, Harford White Hip, a "son" to Mrs. Cummins, was brought forward. He took the leader's cane with its two eagle feathers tied to the top and struck coup on the sacred tree.[6] Bird Horse, the herald, announced the war deed and blessing:

The time I was in the service in Germany, one time I was in battle for three months. The second time I made a surrender of the Germans at the Falaise Gap. At the time some of the boys got killed, but I came back safe. I was about the only Crow boy there and I was pretty lucky. I hope you will not have any trouble in this Sun Dance.

As White Hip ended his recital, his father walked to him and gave him fifty cents, which he immediately handed to Cummins, his classificatory clan father.

While the pole was unloaded from the wagon, Hartford ringed the area where the hole was to be dug for the center pole. Jo Blaine proceeded to dig the hole, since he had requested this task, as a prayer sacrifice. Others set to work digging post-holes for the exterior of the lodge. The twelve forked uprights were furnished by five men, two "brothers-in-law," a "father-in-law," and two clan brothers. Jim White Hip, "brother-in-law," furnished six. A team led by Jim Real Bird, Cummins's assistant, completed work on the support poles and raised the stringers into position. "Brothers-in-law," clan brothers, "fathers-in-law," and close friends were basic to team membership. John Truhujo and his associate, Tilton West, worked with sponsor Cummins and Charlie Ten Bear when decisions were required. Truhujo was inclined to rest and was disturbed only for hard decisions.

An hour before the sun reached its zenith, West brought a tripod of three pine saplings, under which he placed the buffalo head, facing west. The willow bundle was set in the crotch and the eagle placed on top, also facing west. The leader's cane was set atop this altar.

[6]In 1941 at Crow Agency, Ten Bear used a traditional coup-stick to strike the pole.

At this time Yellow Brow announced it was forbidden to shoot off firecrackers in the vicinity of the dance lodge. Anyone who did so would be fined $5.00 or five days in jail. In the days ahead, young boys did not always heed this injunction as they popped crackers in a Pre-Fourth of July celebration. Yellow Brow followed his announcement with a praise song and a statement that honored Blake Whiteman and Jim White Hip.

That man there, Blake Whiteman, is helping the Lodge Grass bunch in everything that comes up, and so is Jim Whitehip. Right after this dance, Jim Whitehip is going to give a dance through the camp.

During this public announcement, Bird Horse mixed some white clay in a basin of water and painted the buffalo with a spray of silver sage. He worked from back to front and down to the snout. He painted the nostrils yellow and also the eagle's beak and head. He added silver sage to the sprig given him by Truhujo at the cutting of the tree and placed this in the nostrils of the buffalo. When he finished, he rolled a cigarette and offered a smoke-prayer. The sage was linked to medicine and protected the dancers and their medicines. Old men enlivened the work with encouraging remarks and praise songs for the workers. Jack Covers Up, the Lodge Grass announcer, sang a praise song and told them to do everything right, to fast and to pray for the people. Fox stated, "All these young people come home from the war because of our prayers. We are going to thank the Sun and Creator, for all of you come home alive I thank the Creator for all that has happened in the last two years. That shows that the Creator is with us." Yellow Brow extolled the Lodge Grass district, "Whatever district puts up a Sun Dance, it is always bumming [stuff], but we Lodge Grass bunch are not going to bum off our white neighbors, but are going to put up everything ourselves." As 11:30 passed, the Lodge Grass herald told the women to get dinner ready so the men could come back right afterwards and get to work. A few minutes later, Cummins, through his herald, gave the official word: "We will dig the other postholes after dinner. We will try and get all done by three o'clock. Some of the boys are still down at the river cutting brush. Go ahead and get your dinner." All departed with the exception of Bob Howe, who continued skinning the west upright post until he had it up. Elmer Hill, Cummins's son-in-law, dug the hole. Howe dedicated this pole as a sacrifice to the Sun for his little boy. This was the chief pole on which the forked rafter and eagle would rest. It was the first pole to be put up and was required to be in the ground before the sun reached its zenith.

By one o'clock the Lodge Grass herald called for the workers, but they arrived forty-five minutes later. The center pole lay with the butt end facing east, close to the hole into which it would be placed. Cummins took his position along the right side of the butt end and was followed by Truhujo and West. The assistant stood to the left. Pledger and assistant now offered smoke-prayers. Cummins prayed for the success of the Sun Dance and asked that his wishes be granted. He prayed for the welfare of the Crow tribe and the United States. He also prayed that the "white people and Indian would work together so that they don't have this prejudice—that we be one people." He asked for peace among the peoples of the world and requested that the Creator grant any of the prayer wishes of the dancers. There was no ceremonial dress for this prayer, in contrast to Big Day's Sun Dance at Pryor, although Cummins carried his leader's cane. Bird Horse announced the war-blessings of three veterans. Joe Wallace reported, "I have been to Germany and helped beat the Germans. I was there when this was all over, and I had good luck all the way through. Nothing serious happened to me, so I hope that this Sun Dance will come out without any trouble. This is the truth, so we will all have good luck during the Sun Dance." Hartford White Hip and Joseph Ten Bear, who had been in the army in Germany and had the good luck to return safely, also wished for the success of the coming Sun Dance.

Each of the three warriors now started a ring of charcoal paint around the butt end of the center pole and spaced each about eighteen inches apart. Four children between the ages of two and six years completed the marking of the tree. They were supervised by Charlie Ten Bear and Jim Buffalo, who were older men prominent in the Sun Dance, and who had received special power. The ringing of the tree expressed the wish that the children would live to old age and that the boys would live to take part in the Sun Dance. For the dancers, the charcoal rings meant they would be in the lodge three nights. Black was prophetic of success, for black was the traditional color of victory. As the charcoal ceremony came to an end, White Arm, a respected old man from Lodge Grass, advised, "Dance hard and feed all who come around. Don't send anybody home with bad feelings, but send them home happy, and give them a little stuff."

Twenty young and middle-aged men worked hard to get the support poles and stringers in place, while Cummins, Real Bird, Truhujo, West and Buffalo prepared the tree. They tied two bundles of willows, stiffened with short poles, to both sides at the crotch. As they worked, Yellow Brow reminded one and all of the war dance they planned to have right after the Sun Dance. "We ain't going to have this Sun Dance alone. We are going to have a parade dance given by Hartford White Hip and his brother. This is a big day, too."

As the heat increased, the pace of work slowed and the number of workers fell off. The ceremonial leader, Truhujo, dozed off under some shade. Old men sat around and told stories, from time to time encouraging the workers and those who had pledged to dance. The assistant, Jim Real Bird, along with Guy Bull Tail, Lester Jefferson, and Henry Pretty on Top, formed a team to complete the post work. Truhujo was awakened by Cummins's call and helped tie the buffalo head just below the fork. At Jim Blaine's request, Buffalo tied two white pennants to each arm of the center pole along with two bags of Bull Durham. Blaine put up the "flags" as a sacrifice to the Sun and Creator for the good of his family. He chose Buffalo because he had acquired power through the Sun Dance, and his prayers were known to be effective. Normally a white and a blue pennant of dress goods, approximately five yards in length, were attached, but in 1946 at Lodge Grass and at Crow Agency only white pennants were used, at Truhujo's recommendation. During the war, according to Truhujo, they had used blue, but now, with the war over, "we are in the clear and come back to the old-fashioned white garment." The flags, he noted, were the "Savior's garments," and hence should be white.[7]

Women and workers drifted back as the time approached for setting the tree. Four two-man teams held two tipi poles linked with rope. The task of elevating the tree was assigned to these young men, although upwards of fifty men took part. To help raise and support the tree, a rope was slipped through the fork.

For the tree-raising, Truhujo positioned himself at the head on the left side of the pole. Cummins was directly behind Truhujo, and his assistant, Real bird, stationed himself at the fork.

---

[7] At Pryor, in 1946, two blue pennants were used because the donor was unable to get white cloth.

A blue flag properly was attached to the south fork and white to the north. Blue represented a cloudless sky, which they wished for the Sun Dance, or darkness. White symbolized daylight, water, snow, and earth. Blue to some represented evil, while white was "everything that is pure," including light and truth.

White in tradition evoked the idea of ceremonial cleanliness, and albino buffalo hides were prized as offerings to the Sun. This traditional view may have supplied the context for Truhujo's call for the "old-fashioned white garment."

West stood opposite Truhujo on the right, and helpers arranged themselves along both sides.[8]

Truhujo and West now led in the singing of four Shoshoni songs to the Four Winds. They sang each song four times, while all clapped rhythmically. As the fourth rendition ended, all gave a war whoop and raised the pole a short distance off the ground, and then set it down. This was repeated twice more, with the pole raised higher each time. People were in a joyful, joking mood, because this was a time of happiness, and they wished it to continue. When they were ready to begin the last song sequence, the news was passed along that now the pole must go up. As the sixteenth chorus ended, war whoops sounded and the tree was swung upward with the aid of the pole teams. At one point they faltered, drawing exclamations of alarm from the crowd, because it was very bad luck for the tree to fall back to the ground. At the raising, the buffalo head faced the east. The tree was not put in place until the buffalo head, facing west, and the sponsor's position were aligned with the entrance, sighted through the middle of the tree fork. The alignment was left up to the sponsor, although others gave advice. The height of the buffalo head from the ground was important, since dancers experienced early fatigue if they were forced to tilt their heads too much.

The erection of uprights, rafters, and stringers followed an order, but, except for special core alignments, variation was possible and made each lodge construction a bit different. Key uprights were the medicine man's pole at the western periphery, and the left and right entrance poles. After these had been posted in order, the two poles on either side of the entrance posts were erected, followed by a clockwise circuit in setting the remaining posts. The forked chief pole with eagle

---

[8] At Pryor, in 1941, Big Day and his assistant stood on the left side of the tree, while the Shoshonis, West, Sarres, and Truhujo lined up on the right side, in that order.

attached was the most important rafter, followed by the right entrance, and then the cardinal south and north rafters. The remaining pine rafters were placed to achieve a solid interlocking. Rafters were seated in the forks of the uprights and stringers were used to lock them in. At Lodge Grass in 1946, workers interlocked the stringers in a counterclockwise direction, beginning at the left (NE) entrance pole. This counterclockwise movement reversed the direction of positioning the uprights.

Truhujo's longtime Sun Dance associate, Tilton West, tied the eagle to the chief's pole without ceremony. In the meantime, Cummins got together a special team composed of six "brothers-in-law," two clan brothers, his assistant, a close friend, and two respected dancers from Pryor district. This team raised the chief pole with dispatch and then followed a sequence indicated by Truhujo, who relaxed in the shade. Under Cummins's informal supervision the rafters and stringers were in place within an hour. The time was near five o'clock, and Bird Horse announced. "It is ready for the brush now, and all help out. Then get ready. Take a good bath with soap. We are being watched by the creatures in the Wolf and the Big Horn mountains. We are right in-between them now, so we look upon their medicines."

As the cottonwood foliage was placed around the base of the lodge for a screen, Cummins came to Jack Covers Up, the Lodge Grass herald, and asked him to make an announcement.

Look here, I was afraid I was going to be without an announcer. Jack Covers Up lost his nephew just a few days ago and I knew I was going to be without an announcer, and I went over to Arthur Bravo and he said that Jack could go ahead and be the announcer, and be around as much as he can; so that is how it comes that Jack is announcing for me, in which he never figured in doing this early. I am going to be short of singers, and now I am going to ask you, my brother-in-law, Henry Pretty on Top, to join in the singing for me. I know you lost your boy last winter and you was

Dancers in front of the Sun Dance Lodge. *Left to right:* Robert Howe, John Cummins (pledger), Henry Big Day, and Fred Bird. Lodge Grass, 1946.

feeling bad about it, and I was feeling bad about it too; but it has been quite a while now, and we are in another season, so sing for me and take part in the Sun Dance. I'm asking you, brother-in-law, Henry.

Through this public announcement Cummins protected those in mourning from criticism because of seeming irreverence for the dead. A short time later, Covers Up sang a praise song for Cummins: "The war party is coming back. Join them." Then he stated, "Johnny, your Sun Dance is coming up. Everything is finished. You cannot back out now. It is up to you."

Sun Dance lodge at Lodge Grass, 1975.

Brother-in-law Henry Pretty on Top indeed would be among the singers.

Building the lodge was the responsibility of the medicine man. At night-fall, when the dancers entered the lodge to worship, the pledger took full responsibility and direction, consulting with the medicine leader at all times.

Ceremonial Entry of the Lodge

Consecration of the lodge was just as important as in the days when buffalo roamed. To Ralph Saco the lodge was filled with stars. The medicine man's pole represented the moon and the center tree the sun. Facing east, the left entrance pole stood for the Morning Star and the right for the Dipper, the Seven Bulls or Brothers. The remaining poles

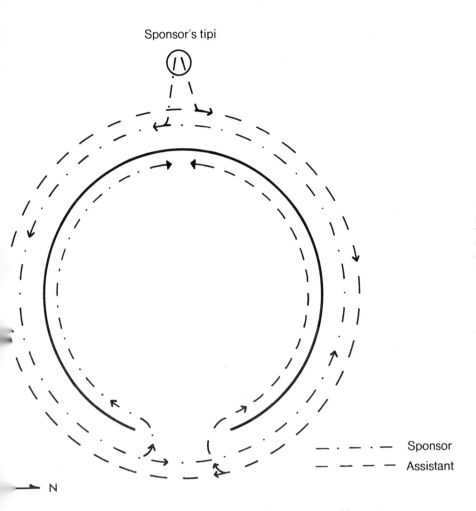

Sponsor's tipi

— . — . — Sponsor
— — — — — Assistant

N

Figure 7. Ceremonial Entry of the Big Lodge. The sponsor and his assistant encircle the lodge one and a half times, proceeding in opposite directions. When they meet for the first time at the entrance, the sponsor takes the inside track. Upon meeting for the second time they enter the lodge and take their places at the rear.

were stars. To some persons, the twelve poles represented the "moons" or months of the year, while the Christian-oriented identified with the Twelve Apostles. The Christian-oriented also considered the three charcoal bands around the base of the tree to be the three days Christ spent in the tomb. Whatever meanings individuals found in the poles, buffalo head, eagle, and other elements, they were not important enough for doctrinal division or abstention. Above all, the Big Lodge raised to the Sun was a place for prayer, where the Creator answered wishes and sent power to cure disease. The ordeal of body and the promise of prayer wishes lay before them as the dancers went without food and water for two and a half days.

The dancers assembled west of the lodge in two files at sunset. To the east, the moon rose above the Wolf Mountains, and its radiance was accented by the golden red luminescence of the disappearing sun. In preparation, dancers bathed or sweated and ate a good meal, which traditionally included a beef soup. They came in full regalia, painted, and with their individual medicines, many borrowed from paternal or maternal kin, or from Truhujo. Cummins headed the right file of dances, and Real Bird the left. Cummins chose Real Bird as his assistant because he was a clan brother and was a truly "honest" person.

The pledger and his assistant sometimes offered prayers before circling the lodge and blowing long shrill blasts of the eagle-bone whistle at each of the cardinal points (see Figure 7). Cummins went right and Real Bird left. They circled the lodge once and on the second turn entered the lodge on opposite sides and filed into position.[9] Midnight marked the last mo-

---

[9] Crow Peyotists make a clockwise ceremonial circuit of the tipi and file clockwise to places inside. See Kiste, "Crow Peyotism."

A clockwise circuit was ceremonial convention among the Crows (as among Northern Plains tribes generally), and the Crow pledger of a traditional Sun Dance probably took a clockwise circuit when entering the lodge. In the present Sun Dance, the pledger starts on a counter-clockwise

ment that dancers were permitted to enter the ceremony, but latecomers were rare.

In 1946 at Lodge Grass there were forty-two dancers, plus several old men and women fasters (see Figures 8 and 9 for plans of Shoshoni-Crow and Shoshoni Sun Dance lodges).[10] Dancers usually had buddies, and they tried to dance side-by-side; but only established and older dancers reserved a preferred location, usually where some relief from the hot sun was possible. A distribution of bedding brought by relatives of the dancers halted the ceremony momentarily as the heralds called out the names of recipients. After the dancers accepted their bedding, they formed a circle, seated, around the center pole. Under Shoshoni guidance the four wind songs were sung four times. Cummins now arose, and with the leader's cane in his right hand, prayed in a subdued voice with prayer smoke held aloft in his left hand. "Creator, look down upon us! I

(right) circuit and enters clockwise, while the assistant begins clockwise and ends counterclockwise. In a vision Plenty Coups saw a spirit person approach the back, or west, side of a tipi and go to the right to reach the entrance. See Linderman, *American*, 38.

[10] In the post-reservation period the Sun Dance among the Shoshonis gradually was transformed into a curing ceremony and became a primary arena for medicine men in competition to display their powers. Prominent medicine men were the most acceptable pledgers of Sun Dances. As pledger *and* medicine man, a Shoshoni sponsor took up position under the forked pole, to which eagle feathers were attached. The pledger–medicine man customarily appointed an assistant, who took a place to his left, although in an August, 1966, performance, the assistant was located to the right of the sponsor–medicine man. See Johnson, "Shoshone Sun Dance." In a July, 1966, Sun Dance, Johnson observed that the pledger–medicine man had two assistants, one to his left, and one to his right, a visiting (?) "mixed-blood Ute." In 1967, John Truhujo, as pledger–medicine man, had two Crow assistants flanking him on either side.

Northern Utes, who took over the Wind River Shoshoni Sun Dance about 1890 and adapted it to their curing complex, in which individual shamans displayed their excellence and competed for status, as among the Shoshonis today. Sometimes two or three medicine men holding dream sanctions shared sponsorship. See J. A. Jones, "The Sun Dance of the Northern Ute," Smithsonian Institution *BAE Bulletin* 157:244.

thank You for the Sun Dance. We wished and prayed for it for the whole year. Now that we are in here, and You were kind enough to let us have the Sun Dance, I want all our wishes to come true." The Creator knew what was in their minds, and they wanted to help out by putting up the Big Lodge. Cummins also prayed that any sick person who entered the lodge would be cured. "I wanted Him to help us live like white people, and think like white people, because I thought that was the only way the Crow could better themselves. I wanted my son home and my other relatives in the armed services. I wanted Him to give us good luck in everything we do."

When the prayer ended, Cummins took the drummer's cane and rattle from Truhujo and carried it to Guy Bull Tail, the drum chief. Four loud beats on the drum signaled the beginning of the singing, and the dancers stood in place and removed their Pendleton blankets, whistling and rhythmically moving their bodies up and down in time to the music. A female chorus, composed largely of women from Lodge Grass district, trailed the ending of each song. Elk Lodge members

---

The mentor-apprentice relationship between Truhujo and the Crow pledger introduced positioning contrasts in relation to the Shoshone ceremony. Amongst themselves, the Crows have preserved this traditional mentor-apprentice relationship, and hence no Crow sponsor has operated both as pledger and as a medicine man–director. Crow Sun Dance personnel today includes the medicine man, the pledger, and an assistant, with the medicine man positioning himself under the forked rafter with eagle attached. However, in the beginning, Crow pledgers sometimes positioned themselves under the forked rafter, with the medicine man to the right, as in traditional Crow ceremonial convention.

In the Wind River Shoshoni ceremony, the incense fire outside the sacred area near the entrance (NE) noted by Johnson in "Shoshone Sun Dance" in the 1966 and 1967 performances probably was added after World War II and may have been a temporary addition prompted by a dream. Dancers used it after the sunrise ceremony, apparently to purify and strengthen themselves. Although a flag-raising ceremony was introduced during World War II, it may not always be included.

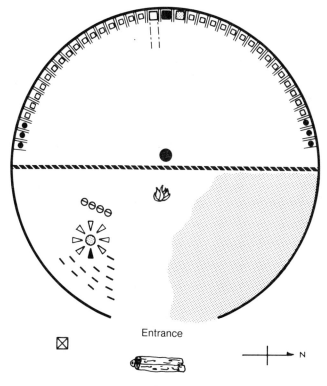

Entrance

N

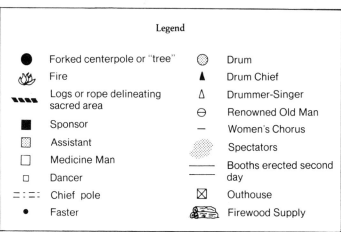

Legend

●	Forked centerpole or "tree"	◉	Drum
🔥	Fire	▲	Drum Chief
▰▰▰	Logs or rope delineating sacred area	△	Drummer-Singer
■	Sponsor	⊖	Renowned Old Man
▨	Assistant	—	Women's Chorus
☐	Medicine Man	⠿	Spectators
□	Dancer	──	Booths erected second day
⁼ ⦂ ⁼	Chief pole	⊠	Outhouse
•	Faster	🪵	Firewood Supply

Figure 8. Plan of Shoshoni-Crow Sun Dance Lodge, 1946.

were prominent in the chorus. Susie Childs sang because she had been cured by Truhujo, and he had told her, "Now Susie, you can sing your praise [to the Creator] during the dance."

The sponsor and his assistant, or the medicine man and the sponsor, initiated the dancing to the tree, operating as a ceremonial pair. Their cue was the "water song," which followed the singing of three warm-up songs.[11] As the drummer-singers accented the water song refrain with accelerated loud beats, the dancers blew a shrill staccato invocation and then settled into the rhythm of the drum beat. At this point Cummins and Real Bird ran to the center pole and began a dance retreat to their stalls. Once the two leaders began their backward movement, other dancers advanced, while the rest whistled in the wings. At this time, all the dancers usually began their own dancing and filled the Big Lodge with the tonal prayers of their eagle-bone whistles. Occasionally, as was the case this night, a dancer showed up under the influence of liquor. Uncoordinated whistling and faltering steps drew titters and comments from the crowd as they considered the travail of the dancer when he began to dry out, especially on the second day.

While moralistic issues were not a part of Sun Dance philosophy, some persons sought help in the elimination of "bad habits," just as they did in cases of "bad" sickness. Cummins noted that the "Almighty taught you to fast and to do penance [so] that your prayers may be granted and your sins forgiven. You can try to get rid of bad habits." "Wishes" sought touched every personal need, and those of relatives. A dancer sacrificed himself for a school loan, an ailing relative, a brother in the army, or a brother in politics. The careers of those in public office were vulnerable to envious

[11] A "water song" is central to Peyotist ceremonial on three occasions, namely, at midnight, dawn, and just before members leave the tipi to end the meeting. The "water woman" first brings water at dawn and is said to represent all mothers on earth. See Kiste, "Crow Peyotism."

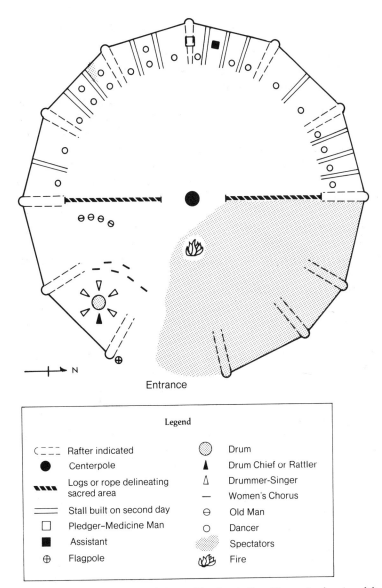

Entrance

Legend

⊂⎯⎯⎯	Rafter indicated	⊙ Drum	
●	Centerpole	▲ Drum Chief or Rattler	
▰▰▰	Logs or rope delineating sacred area	△ Drummer-Singer	
═══	Stall built on second day	— Women's Chorus	
☐	Pledger–Medicine Man	⊖ Old Man	
■	Assistant	○ Dancer	
⊕	Flagpole	⣿ Spectators	
		🔥 Fire	

Figure 9. Plan of the Wind River Shoshonis Sun Dance Lodge (modified after Shimkin, 1953).

sorcery, and power obtained through prayer in the Sun Dance turned aside such hateful uses of power.

The first evening was not the preferred time for curing, because the power was not yet present in strength. Only the wife of Tilton West, Shoshoni assistant to Truhujo, stepped forward to be doctored. Barefoot and with head bowed, she stood west of the center pole, facing east. West, who was not dancing, knelt east of the tree. Truhujo advanced and stood back of the patient, holding a smoking cigarette in his left hand, whistling and fanning himself as he looked up at the buffalo. Moving to the right, he touched the medicine feathers to the base of the pole, and then fanned the patient in front, on the right side, at back, and on the left side. At the end of the doctoring he held the feathers to her bosom, rested his left hand on her back, then quickly withdrew the feathers and shook them out four times.

Doctoring required alerting the power beings associated with the four winds and the spirit owner of the lodge, as well as the Sun, Buffalo, and Creator. The medicine feathers in prayer were raised and shaken to the cardinal points, accompanied by a long blast and staccato at each direction, and ending on a sighing note as the breath played out. This call to the helpers or spirit beings was repeated at least twice, and usually four times. It preceded the actual doctoring during the prayer smoke. Feathers were held directly aloft to alert the Creator and bird message bearers, especially the eagle. The order in which the Four Winds were called varied individually, but Truhujo usually pointed first to the south, then north, west, and east. These motions simulated a plus-type cross, a common representation of Morning Star. Fanning of the patient proceeded from the upper body to the feet. In this way the "bad stuff" was withdrawn and whipped away, to disappear into the air. The eagle feathers transmitted power from the center pole to the patient. Power in the consecrated tree was sent by the Creator in response to prayer smokes.

However, more power was needed for severe illnesses, and Truhujo touched tuberculosis patients six times. He ended by placing his hands on the tree while he blew a long blast on his whistle, with his eyes fastened on the buffalo. Before he danced back into position, the medicine man placed his prayer smoke at the foot of the center pole, and this practice was followed by all who came to pray. Dancers with reputations were often called forth during a doctoring, to dance and add their power to the prayers.

The Ceremonial Fire

The ceremonial building of the fire in the lodge was timed with a change of singers about 11:00 P.M. Cummins requested Frank Medicine Horse and Harold Carpenter to be fire tenders. While Medicine Horse readied the firewood, Bird Horse announced Carpenter's blessing-narrative. Each statement was punctuated with four heavy beats of the drum, each a note of respect. "Come, listen! I have been to the South Pacific fighting Japs, and I rode up in a car. My crew got killed, but I came out alone. I must be lucky, because I'm still living and I'm back to my people. So I'm wishing this luck towards this Sun Dance, that you get through all right." Carpenter now distributed a small amount of money and cloth goods to honor important guests and relatives in the Sun Dance. Truhujo received dress goods donated by Carpenter's sister, while West received money. Jim Blaine, "chief" of the Lodge Grass district in charge of the lodge and the fire-tender, Medicine Horse, also received gifts. The fire was lit before midnight, according to ceremonial convention, but the actual time was determined by convenience or the cold of night.

After the fire was lighted, action dwindled to a handful

Relatives on the second day bring cattails and sage to cool and sustain the dancers. In this way they show respect for the sacrifice undertaken. Lodge Grass, 1975.

of dancers. The focus during this first night was on the leader's cane, for once set "in motion," it had to be carried for a twelve-hour stretch.[12] Although it was not required to be used the first day, the leader's cane had to be kept in motion on the second and third days. Usually the sponsor or his assistant carried the cane for a good part of the night, but others sometimes volunteered to do so. On this first night, Real Bird, the assistant, and Howe, brother-in-law of the sponsor, alternated dancing with the cane. By 2:30 A.M.,

[12] See Appendix B for a description of the sponsor's cane, its meaning and care.

Interior of the Big Lodge, with dancers grasping poles erected by relatives on the second day. Pryor, 1941.

however, all dancing halted, because the singers were exhausted, and there were no others to take their places.

Greeting the Sun Person

As the thin, pale light in the eastern sky ushered in the dawn of a new day, the dancers were aroused from sleep by the excited arrival and stirring of people who gathered for the greeting to the sun. As the sky took on a brilliant pink glow, the drum chief struck up a special "sunrise song." At this point the medicine man, sponsor, and assistant moved to the center pole and took their places along with other important sundancers in the front row. While waiting for the sunrise, the dancers stood in place, blankets draped over their shoulders. They whistled their prayers and moved up and down in

Running at the buffalo. William Big Day and Plain Feather to the right, two Shoshoni youths to the left. Pryor, 1941.

unison with the music. The medicine men carried their doctoring feathers and the sponsor held his cane in his right hand. As the light spread over the horizon, the dancers threw off their blankets, and then, as the golden red ring of the sun appeared, they blew a long sighing blast on the whistle, followed by a staccato. They repeated the whistling four times as they stretched out their arms to the Sun Person and then touched their chests with the feather plumes attached to their little fingers.

This was a critical and personal moment for prayer as dancers drew attention to their own "wishes" for health and luck, for at this time, the Sun was near and could be easily reached in prayer. The path to the sun was kept clear, and no one was permitted to step across the entrance and block the prayers

Dancers at Crow Agency, 1941.

as the sun's rays touched the dancers. Persons wishing to get to the other side of the entrance went around the lodge.[13] Spectators at this time reached out to the sun in prayerful attitude and patted parts of their bodies to drive out lingering aches and pains.

When the sun had fully risen, the medicine man signaled the drum chief, who stopped the singing, and all gathered around the fire. The medicine man and the sponsor faced to the west. The former carried his doctoring feathers, the latter had his cane in his right hand. Women fasters, who had lined up at the back to greet the sun, now returned to their places; for they were not permitted to take part in the special purifi-

---

[13] Occasionally someone may drive a car past the entrance at this time and draw angry glances and mutterings.

Women dancers at Lodge Grass, 1975.

cation and prayer to the Sun Person and Maker of All Things.[14]

The seated male dancers, draped in their blankets, were led in song by the Shoshonis. The songs were the same as those used to begin the Sun Dance and were without drum accompaniment. Each song was repeated four times, when all blew their whistles in four long, tapering blasts, without staccato. At Cummins's dance, Bird Horse, the respected old man who had been selected to offer the "cedar prayer," now moved to the fire and faced east. He removed a good pinch of cedar

---

[14] In the 1950s, when women began to dance with eagle-bone whistles and medicines in the fashion of men, they still were excluded from this ceremonial prayer, as they are today. In 1975, after the male prayer and purification, the medicine man brought coals outside the lodge, to the east of the entrance. There, at four separate fires, women dancers purified themselves in the precious cedar incense traditionally obtained from Spokane Indians living near the Cascade Mountains.

from a soft buckskin pouch and sprinkled it on the fire, moving his hand from south to north and then from west to east, the sign of Morning Star. As all bowed their heads, he prayed:

Listen to me, Father, Creator of All Things! Look at me this morning at the beginning of day! I'm going to pray for Bernard Cummins especially this morning, wherever he is. This is his Big Lodge, so bless him wherever he is this morning. Bring him home pretty soon. See that he has good things sent him, and shake hands with him. Bless the fireman and help him all You can in his work toward this lodge—not him alone but with all his family, wife and kids, and the whole Crow tribe—and the ones that move up here and make everything good.

We want You to help the ones that take part in this, and the dancers, too, like myself, I danced all the Sun Dances on the reserve except one; but . . . I ought to be answered—like what I have been asking You all the time.

I pray, too, about Your looking down upon us and on the ground to all the little creatures. I pray to You, and now I'm pretty thankful for all [the] returning soldiers, and I say, "Thank You! Thank You!" And I'm satisfied even if I miss two boys [two Crow youths lost in the war, unrelated to Bird Horse]. Look on the sick! Everyone that came into the lodge to be cured, I would like to have them all cured. I want new luck and better life for the many poor children and the little children that don't know about You, that they will come to lean on You someday.

If there is anything I might not have prayed for, I like to have it looked over, and make a good answer for my prayers. I'm repeating this prayer past the time, so listen to me this pretty morning! I thank You for what You have done for many thus far, and we want to keep it that way—to eat together and shake hands together, and to receive good answers to our different prayers.

Bird Horse's "aho!" (thank you) was followed by a chorus of "ahos!" from the dancers and spectators. Sponsor Cummins now moved to the fire, and, with cane in his right hand, prayed:

Almighty Creator, last year I promised that I would put up this lodge today. It has been done exactly as I wanted to put it on, and here I am. I ask that all the people that take part in this affair be blessed. I further ask that my son be returned home very soon, so that he can come and visit me, his mother, my wife, and his little boy, whom I kept during the war while he was gone.

I further ask that I still have some relations in the army and some overseas, that they come home safely and be among their parents. I further ask that anyone that has pains in their bodies and have come before this lodge, be cured. I want to be assured that they will be cured. I ask You to make these Crow Indians willing to raise stock, and that their stock increase and that they live better. I ask that my Crow people be wealthy.

I further ask that whatever their wishes are, they come true and that each family be provided with the necessary food in the future. I ask that their wishes and prayers be answered. We have some . . . Indians among the tribe that are very old in age. I ask that they have more years so that they can be with us for some more years to come.

I thank You that what I ask You shall come true and be answered.

It was now time for visiting, and the dancers exited to talk with relatives and friends, to arrange for necessities overlooked, and to relieve themselves. For several hours the camp was at rest. People breakfasted, visited, and the dancers relaxed and painted up for the first hot day of their ordeal.

Sacrificing for Power: The Second Day

The first night was a warm-up for the second day, when power was most likely to enter the center tree, and when dancers anticipated the granting of their wishes.[15] The second day of the power quest was marked by the fullest cooperation

---

[15]With rare exception, the daily routine of the dance was the same, and hence, the critical second day can be used to describe the general order of events.

Greeting Grandfather Sun. Note coupstick carried by the pledger (behind tree) next to Truhujo. Old men at right front are fasters Yellow Face and Holds the Enemy. Crow Agency, 1941.

between relatives and dances and between singers and dancers. Solicitous relatives and friends gathered cattails, erected stalls, and brought sage, mint, and mentholated cigarettes to refresh the dancers.

Immediately after the sunrise ceremony, barefoot male relatives, observing respect for the sacred lodge, wielded shovel and crowbar to set the peeled cottonwood saplings that the dancers used for support. The cottonwood poles were rubbed with yellow ochre and firmed with a bundle of willows tied below the top. The willows helped the dancer when he was thirsty, for they symbolized cool, moist, and growing things. Yellow ochre was the paint associated with the eagle, the "messenger of God" or Sun and helped in getting power. Once the stalls were completed, dancers hung up white sheets to give

Praying to Sun. Note women in front row; drummers in foreground.
Lodge Grass, 1975.

themselves privacy for resting and painting up for their hardest day of suffering. The day proved to be a busy one for
medicine men and sun dancers of reputation, because more
people than usual brought smoke-prayers and stood west of
the tree to be cured.

To mobilize all sources of power on this second day, the
medicine man tied a "little man" (literally, "offering a person") to the tree, several feet below the buffalo head. He
sometimes did this right after the greeting of the morning sun,

Tobacco prayer by Thomas Lion Shows, pledger for his ailing father. Observe how Sun touches the fire during prayer. Before the pledger prays, a respected elder offers a cedar prayer to clear the way to Sun in order that nothing will block the path of the prayer. Lodge Grass, 1975.

but usually it was during the evening of the second night. The mannikin was distinctive of the Elk Lodge and was given to Hill by Truhujo in 1943. Hill reported that it represented "the Indian" and conveyed messages, especially to its owner and to the medicine man. To David Bad Boy, there was a "god" in the figure. As with other ceremonial forms, the effigy was smoked before it was tied to the tree.[16]

Veterans added a further blessing to the day with a war recitation, and they raised the American flag on a pole set at the south side of the entrance. As they raised the flag, they

[16] See Appendix B for a description of the "little man" effigy.

drummed a song that was dreamt by Henry Old Coyote when he was overseas. The flag-raising sometimes took place shortly after the sunrise greeting, but more often it occurred just before the dance resumed. At sundown the flag was lowered to the same accompaniment, and it was raised again on the third day. Since 1942, no Sun Dance has been without the flag raising. The war also prompted the introduction of flag raising among the Wind River Shoshonis.

Paints and Medicines

Some three hours after the sunrise ceremony, Bird Horse, the announcer for ceremonial affairs, told the dancers to get up and get ready to dance. A few minutes later, the herald for the Sun Dance lodge, Covers Up, called to the singers to eat breakfast and get right over to the lodge. An hour later, sponsor Cummins brought the drummer's cane and rattle to John Whiteman, his father-in-law and drum chief, and signalled they were ready to begin. Shortly after 9:00 A.M. the dance was under way.

In preparation for this day of power, dancers wore their strongest medicines and generally changed from a white clay body covering to eagle-yellow. Bob Howe, though, danced with the same paint design of the first day—a red forehead with red streaks dropped diagonally from the corner of each eye, and red earlobes. To his red forehead, Fred Bird added a yellow face with two blue lines under each eye. As on the first day, Henry Big Day covered his entire body and face with yellow ochre, leaving two red splotches on his temples. Sponsor Cummins added yellow ochre to the lower half of his face and a blue line that crossed his nose at midpoint. He painted his upper face and forehead red, as on the first day. He also substituted a black lightning streak down each arm in place of a red design used the first day. At the start, Truhujo painted both Cummins and his assistant, Real Bird. He drew the same red lightning design on their arms and red lines horizontal to their eyes, because they belonged to the Elk Lodge. Truhujo added yellow splotches to his own torso and arms. Several dancers on the first day were not painted, while others changed paint after the sun reached its zenith on the second day.

"Medicines" varied in construction and in interpretation. Eagle feathers were basic to most medicines, along with weasel and otter hide, for they were "tough little animals," and, like the eagle, were linked to the Sun Dance.[17] Truhujo distributed eagle feathers marked with dots or zigzags or purple, yellow, green, and blue to represent the rainbow and lightning. Occasionally streamers of muslin in different colors were used to represent the rainbow and lightning. Four purplish dots on a feather symbolized the four seasons. Seashells with blue beadwork indicated the water of a lake, notably the one from which Truhujo saw the elk emerge during his vision. An elk tooth signified the Elk Lodge, and an old bear tusk represented old age. Small down feathers from the eagle recalled that bird and especially the eagle perched in the dance lodge. The reflecting properties of a mirror suggested lightning, and a multistarred glass piece, the sun. A glass-studded cross stood for the cross of crucifixion.

Traditionally the elements of an original medicine bundle were assembled in answer to a medicine dream or vision during a sacred fast. Elk Lodge medicines, however, were wholly products of Truhujo's inherited medicine bundle and his own mystic experiences. They included medicines worn by the sponsor and his assistant during an Elk Lodge Sun Dance.

A dancer without a medicine lacked the means to get power and so turned to medicine men or to relatives, especially "clan uncles" for medicine. Truhujo and his Shoshoni asso-

---

[17] Weasel and otter provided prime war medicines in former times, and the purpose of the Crow Sun Dance was to mobilize medicine for revenge against the enemy.

ciates were the primary extra-tribal suppliers, but the Crows also used kinship and friendship with Bannocks and Northern Utes to obtain medicines. Truhujo either gave an applicant a medicine of his own manufacture or told him how to make it. In return for the medicine and its blessing, Truhujo could expect four different gifts, in accordance with Crow tradition. A man gave whatever he could get together, sometimes with the aid of kin. Control of the power came to the "purchaser" through a dream or what he saw in the Sun Dance. Al Childs obtained a medicine from Truhujo, but the following summer was told by the Shoshoni medicine man that the power had returned to him. This was the first that Childs knew of the flight of the power helpers, although he knew that it had not worked well for him. The improper handling of medicines not only led to flight of the power-person but also caused disturbing dreams.[18]

Paternal clansmen, the medicine brokers in the Crow system, functioned as sources for Sun Dance medicines. The ceremony stimulated dreaming and fasting, and Truhujo himself suggested that the Crows make up their own medicines according to their mystic communications. In painting a "child" the "clan uncle" usually taught him the song and gave him a replica of the medicine, which included feathers and animal hide. An old man sometimes painted himself and sang the medicine song to help his "child" get something good out of the Sun Dance. The strongest medicines were reserved for the

---

[18] Sun Dance medicines were carefully safeguarded against menstrual blood. To prevent accidental contamination, owners stored their medicine objects in places where women normally did not go. A husband expected his wife to inform him of her condition, and he then removed his medicines to a safe location outside. Women custodians of medicines must have passed the time of menopause. When medicine men noted that their medicine feathers were not working, they warned menstruating women to leave the lodge. However, they were not able to control non-Indian women, and, on query, indicated that the rule applied only to Indian women.

second and third days, at which time the buffalo might run over the dancer and give him power. A medicine was carefully guarded against falling to the ground, and if this mishap occurred during a dance, a warrior retrieved the medicine and recited a war deed and blessing. Then he returned it to the dancer.

When a dancer in Cummins's Sun Dance lost an eagle plume, Bird Horse, the announcer, picked it up and placed it at the foot of the center tree. When a warrior was ready to eliminate the threat of bad luck occasioned by dropping the consecrated feather, Bird Horse retrieved the plume and waved it back and forth. The warrior then reported his power-deed filled with good luck.

I'm going to tell you some of my luck. I went out on a warparty once with a bunch of men and on that warparty I took one of the enemy horses. I brought it back to my people and gave it to my relative.

I will make it two stories. I was out on another warparty and I captured a white-looking horse with another good-looking gelding. On the way home I got on the white horse thinking I might try it, and chased a buffalo. I killed the buffalo and I had a feast with the warparty. So that horse must have been good, and I brought it back to my people and gave it to my relative. So that is some good luck I had, and I wish everybody good luck in this Sun Dance.

And now I will tell you a little about my dreams. I dreamt and I saw a deep snow with a road through the deep snow. So I'm wishing all of you to go through that deep road with me.

To these good wishes of Bird Above, the Crows responded with "aho!" (thanks).

Praise and Encouragement

Old men and relatives played a vital role in keeping dancers going during the difficult second and third days. They offered words of encouragement and "praise songs" in honor of their "children" to strengthen their resolve to dance. Praise songs periodically rose above the throbbing of the drums as "clan uncles" drew attention to "children" who were sacrificing themselves.

At times there was a play upon district competition, drawing invidious distinctions, as Bear Ground did at Lodge Grass.

I heard last week when they had the Sun Dance [at Crow Agency] a woman came and stood in the doorway a while and then said, "I came here to watch a dance, not to see everybody lying down like a bunch of fresh meat."

A call to make a good showing for the visitors stimulated pride, and twenty-nine dancers took up the challenge.

You take the visitors that are here from other reservations. They stand out there and look on you boys and wonder, "How many pretty young bucks!" So when they go back, they will talk about this Sun Dance all the time. You dancers, get up and dance! That is what you are here for! In jocular vein, male vanity was piqued.

The women are here to see, but there is more to it than that. They are here to see you dance. If you have any girl friend, you should dance well. They will be telling their chums, "Look at that boy, he dances well!"

"Clan uncles" encouraged their "children" to have a sense of pride in clan.

Look here! Look here! My "son" and all the Tied-in-a-knot clan! Keep with the dance. I'm your "father." I'm a tough man [meaning, don't shame me by being weak]. Keep it up, my children, keep it up!

A maternal clansman stiffened his "nephew" who had a drinking problem since returning from the war.

We know you have been over there and that you came back [before the war ended]; but don't be ashamed of coming back. Go ahead and dance! If you dance every dance, there will be nobody who will say anything against you. Go ahead! Don't be bashful, my clan son. Some on, my clan son, and dance!

Bird Above pointed out that he never had been very sick and always was able to get around. He was up to his old age and going strong, except that his eyes were weak. His health indicated that he was favored, and he continued, ". . . You fellows are young now. Dance, and look upon that buffalo as much as possible. You might find something good up there!" He also urged them to pray. "Blow your whistles hard. That is what the onlookers like. Make every song worth something." Those awake were advised to throw off their blankets and dance, while those asleep were told to continue in expectation that they "might get a good dream." At other times the appeal was more direct. "More of you get up and dance. Don't die out! Don't let down! Get up and dance!"

White Arm empathized their suffering. "It is going to be pretty tough in this dance, but do the best you can and try hard. It is pretty hot now. I did it before, and I know what it means [to fast]."

In a praise song composed for the occasion, Black Bird Well Known held the dancers to their objective. "I came myself [of my own volition]. I'm going to be there until the end of the dance."

Such encouragement, interspersed with warwhoops, praise songs, and jokes heartened the spirits of the dancers and often got them back on their feet.

In a more serious mood, White Arm reminded all that the present Sun Dance had begun at Pryor, and next was taken up at Crow Agency and St. Xavier. Now it had come to Lodge Grass, and he had been doctored because of failing sight.

We don't want to be laughed at in what we are putting on here. We are taking the Sun Dance as a "medicine," so help me out, Lodge Grass people. Help me out in all the prayers that you can offer to the Creator. He is watching us, so we get through this thing without trouble.

Mrs. Little Owl sang a special song in praise of the young warriors and thanked them for protecting their country.

In the morning of the second day, Black Bird Well Known extended an invitation to a Sun Dance, using the Lodge Grass announcer, Covers Up.

I am glad I am here to take in this Sun Dance which is given by the Lodge Grass people. I came here with my Big Horn people to take part in it. You have ten of our dancers in this lodge from Big Horn, and we are going to have our Sun Dance about the middle of this month [July]. So you Lodge Grass people, come to my Sun Dance and dance and help me out and camp there, like we do here.

I always feel like Lodge Grass is my partner. So come on over and have a good time with me, like I am doing now. I call upon John Cummins, Jim White Hip, Matthew Good Luck, Jim Blaine, and yourself, Jack Covers Up, my announcer, all to come over with your people to take in my Sun Dance—to make it good for me.

I'm very glad I have been here today. So, I'm putting this out [announcement] so you can come over and have a good time with me like I am doing for you Lodge Grass people. So listen this day and take hold of my words, please. I love you all. Come over when the time comes. Aho!

Anticipation of the feast and good times that followed the dance added another incentive to keep going. In the late afternoon, through the Lodge Grass herald, Robert Yellowtail announced that they were short on beef, therefore he would butcher one of his own. Since the last of nine clan brothers had returned from the army, he also would hold a give-away at the time of the feast.

Drummer-Singers and Dancers

Words of praise, encouragement, and thanks did not always arouse dancers during their ordeal. However, one thing always

Shoshoni dancers praying to Sun at sunrise. Fort Washakie, Wyoming, August, 1948.

got them on their feet—the singing of a favorite power song. For most Crows, the "water song" dreamed by Truhujo was the favorite when doctoring and when dancing for power.

The relationship between the drummer-singers and those sacrificing themselves required the fullest sensitivity and cooperation. It was not just a matter of irregular drumming that threw the dancers off their rhythm and tired them. When there was a full synchronization between the two, the dancers could maintain an easy rhythm and concentrate better on their prayers. The drum chief sensed when power was about to strike one of the dancers. With his selection of songs and steady drumming, he in effect directed the Buffalo Person, who ran over the suppliant and bestowed a gift of power. A drum chief also urged his team of singers to maintain a strong beat and voice when the power traveled down the pole during curing.

A Shoshoni pledger, Tom Wesaw, praying after greeting Sun. Dancers are gathered in prayerful attitude around consecrated fire. Fort Washakie, Wyoming, August, 1948.

Singers and dancers worked together, yet they were like "two teams fighting each other." The smoking of a pipe unified these two teams, and gave them an opportunity to work together in prayer. On the second day, the sponsor presented a calumet to the drum chief before high noon, and his assistant repeated this gesture late in the afternoon or evening. The lighted pipe was taken directly to the drum chief by the sponsor or sent via a herald of reputation.[19] The drum chief stood

[19] Only those with a good reputation linked to their mystic power could pass or receive a pipe that was used to pray for the public welfare. Strong power implied approval by the spirit helpers and quieted anxious public criticism. A sponsor without a secure reputation, or one whose wife had not reached menopause, usually selected a man of impeccable reputation with a ceremonially-qualified wife to carry the pipe to the drummer-singers.

Dancers resting behind the shelter of sheets and blankets after the sunrise ceremony. The drum was provided by the Shoshonis and was painted yellow. The pole visible to the right designated the boundary between the sacred and profane areas of the lodge. Pryor, 1941.

in place and prayed for the dancers and the welfare of the people. After taking a few puffs from the pipe, he passed it clockwise to the rest of the drum team. Hats were removed during this solemn prayer, and in returning the pipe, the drum chief told the announcer of his good wish or dream for the Crow people. He had dreamt of snow flying and wished to be with his Crow people and the dancers when the snow again fell. Such a wish always brought a chorus of thanks, "Aho!" Sponsor, assistant, and medicine man now smoked, after which the pipe was passed to the dancers on the right. When they finished, the announcer carried the pipe across the lodge to the dancers on the north side, and the pipe thus completed a counterclockwise circuit to the sponsor. Aside from these formalized moments of prayer, men of sound reputation were called forth and given a cigarette to pray, and it was hoped he would have a good dream for the Crow people.

A Dancer's Suffering and Visions

Charlie Ten Bear went to the first Sun Dance at Pryor just to look on, but wound up taking part because he found John Truhujo, his old friend, was there as the lead medicine man. As Ten Bear helped in erecting the center pole, John told him: "Charlie, you ought to go in with us tonight." Charlie protested that he was not prepared to take part, that this was the first Sun Dance he had ever seen, and he "would not know what to do." But John assured him, "Go in with me tonight and sit beside me, and I will assist you in the ceremony."

That evening, as instructed, Ten Bear bathed in Pryor Creek, ate a good supper, and then sought out Truhujo to find out how he should dress. He was told to "get a whistle, get a white plume and attach it to your little fingers." He needed a shawl to wrap around his body, a blanket on which to rest, and he should come in barefoot. Ten Bear remembered:

. . . That night I entered the lodge. John opened the ceremony part by praying and smoking. While sitting down and listening to their songs, I realized something in my own heart. I say to myself. I perhaps came into something that I did not know anything about; so therefore I must pray to God to endure the three days and three nights, and as I was thinking, John was praying and he mentioned God and Jesus, so that gave me encouragement.

After the end of his prayer, we came back to our places and sang four songs. He then advised me to lay my heavy blanket down, put the whistle in my mouth, and commence to blow my whistle as he did. So I at once start praying. I prayed for my children, grandchildren, and prayed for my friends, and when the leaders start running to the center pole I did not go. John and William Big Day started in the first run to the pole. They danced back and I was still standing back blowing my whistle. John motioned me to join him in the next dance, and I did, and I kept on dancing pretty near every song til sunrise. I commenced to know the hardships. After the sunrise ceremony I was tired. My feet commenced to ache, the soles of my feet began to hurt. I told John that I did not think I would be able to stand the two remaining nights. John said, "You are my friend. You are a man about my age, so do not give up. Keep on praying." I took his advice, and I prayed as often as I could. I studied this lodge while I was in there for the first time. John taught me many things—the way it was conducted, the way the singers were singing, the way he danced, the way he prayed for the sick when they came into the lodge.

I took interest in the ways, and I said to John, "This is very good. You ought to give me something in the Sun Dance lodge to help me along. Sometime I might go into another Sun Dance lodge like this." He said, "I will give you something that will help you along; I want you to pray with this and use it." He gave me a feather. I used that in the lodge with good results.

I knew on the third day I was getting pretty dry, and I was not feeling very good, for I was getting pretty weak. I told this to John. He said, "Charlie, get up, go to the tree. Take a cigarette and offer it to God. While you are smoking, ask the Maker for strength, courage that you may finish this dance; so you will not be so weak."

On the next song I did exactly what he advised me. I put the smoke at the foot of the pole in the dirt, and the next song I got up to blow my whistle—my throat was awful dry at that time—I saw the water drip from the tip of my whistle. My mouth began to moisten up with spit. My throat commenced to bear water, and I danced through three days and three nights with the help of John's advice. I thought that was something mysterious at that time.

In a Sun Dance at Crow Agency in 1943, Ten Bear danced most of the night, but when the afternoon sun was very hot, he began to suffer.

After going out in the sun and dancing, I laid down and took a brief rest. . . . I got up to dance, and found myself to be very dry. I had a strange notion of giving up . . . whether to stay or go out and take some water which I needed very much. I had a weak feeling covering my body. My legs were almost ready to collapse under me.

I stood back a brief time during this hot spell, and dry, I prayed for help from the great God above me, to Whom I was praying harder than ever. I took courage at the end of my prayer. I ran to the tree. The heat was terrific. The top of my head was so hot, and the bottom of my feet was just burning. I danced two or three times, and on the last attempt I was running to the tree, when a drop of water struck me in the middle of my back. That drop of water—where it came from I did not know—for there were no clouds in sight, only the heat. I thanked the Maker for that drop of water on my back, feeling relief. I started again, and again a drop of water hit me right in the same place, and I danced . . . [until] the end of the song. . . . I felt relieved as if I had had a cup of cold water.

I told John about it. He replied, "That is very good. That is the very way to conduct your prayers in the Sun Dance, that something will help you right along in this dance." I also told him of the feeling to run out and get some water. He said, "That feeling you should not practice, but stay with it. If you stay with it as you did, that will be a good omen for your prayers that you are asking." I was not dry again in that Sun Dance.

In 1944 . . . in the month of August . . . I took part in another Sun Dance. That time I was bothered very much with my rheumatism. I have been to Thermopolis hot springs and took baths . . . in hopes of some relief. The baths did me some good, but not enough. Just before this Sun Dance, my rheumatism bothered me very much. At times I have dreaded that I might not be able to walk; but I have never given up the courage to carry on in the Sun Dance.

In this Sun Dance on the second day my legs were in a very bad shape. Getting up to dance was something terrific—pains and stiffness. At times I could not step on the soles of my feet—it was just like walking among a rocky place. I was very much bothered with this pain and stiffness in the knee joints. I danced many times that day with pain. Along towards evening it seemed that my legs were getting worse, and at this point I took a smoke and prayed the harder, and with much courage I ran to the tree, and danced back as many times as I could. At one point when the singing came to an end for a brief time, I was standing on my feet, not looking at the crowd. I was looking at the forks of the tree, right above the buffalo head. In my vision, while standing there, I saw a person coming to the tree on crutches, one leg lifted up and using one leg like they do at the time when one leg is out of use. I kept on looking and this person came right to the forks of the tree, bowed his head, and prayed. After a short time of prayer, he set his crippled leg, stood up erect, threw his crutches to one side, looked at me and talked at me that I'm healed of the rheumatism in my leg. So he dropped his crutches on the ground and left the lodge. Soon after, he looked back at me and started pacing a little faster until he came to a run, and went into the tipi in front of the lodge. The singings started again and I began to run to the tree. All the pain from the soles of my feet up to my joints, I felt much relief from these pains. I danced the rest of the day in much comfort. . . . That night I took a good rest. I slept well into morning. I got up, shook my legs and exercised my legs and feet. I felt no pain in them, so I danced again like I have done in the past, and I felt good, thinking that I was healed by this vision I have seen. Sure enough I felt good after the Sun Dance and I was able to use my legs like if they were never affected by rheumatism. . . . I believe that when we fast in the Sun Dance, and go through many hardships, we do some good, if we put our prayers and worship devotedly. I am telling this from the bottom of my heart.

The Sun Dance, as Ten Bear observed, was a "hard thing" to go through because of a burning thirst and the "stomach [also] burns from being empty . . . of food." However, Ten Bear wished to worship the Maker in a way that would bring "good results." In the Sun Dance, prayers for a successful end to the war were answered. It was in the first Sun Dance at Crow Agency, in 1941, before war with Germany had broken out, that he saw an indication of the war that was to come.

. . . One night I was dancing late; it was after midnight. I wanted to dance late that night. While I was dancing, I saw a vision on the pole. There was a picture of Hitler on the tree. I tried to look at it. It was dark; but it was a picture of Hitler. I danced close to the tree to see. It never moved, but I saw that he was mad. And about the second time I went up there, they stopped singing, and I told what I had seen to John. He laughed, "Well, Charlie, it may be it means something; keep on trying." So I did. After some dancing, the picture disappeared. So I remembered that, and it was not very long until this country was in war with Germany, causing many of our young men to go across the big pond.

In another Sun Dance I reminded John, and he said, "You were right. Whatever was there was to tell you that we were to be at war with Germany." Whatever the mystery might have been, it told me about Hitler in the vision. In the next year I went into another Sun Dance. I prayed hard because we were at war with Germany, and newsflashes all over the world that France was taken over by Germany, England at a very hard point, and Italy also in a bad way [sic] . . . So I prayed hard for the safe return of our soldier boys, and this is one of the things . . . in the Sun Dance . . . that made me believe in what I have obtained from the Sun Dance.

After this Sun Dance, there was another that I was in, and I heard a song, while watching the tree and praying hard. It seemed like the song made a "joy song,"

> You look over the ocean,
> Victory will come to us very soon,
> You will have lots of prisoners.

I did not know the song very well at first, but later on the same song was sung to me in a mysterious manner. Perhaps this was the result of my prayers. I was in Toppenish, Washington, when the war was over, and I saw lots of German prisoners working. I recollected back and said, "This is the song, and this is the meaning." The war was over; German prisoners were working.

Although the Crows lost some of their young men in battle, Ten Bear felt "good in heart and soul" because victory had been won and the soldier boys had returned. He did not wish to say anything against other religions, for all the churches had done their part in praying for soldiers of this great country. For his part, however, Ten Bear worshipped the Maker in the way of his ancestors. "... I worship the Maker as best I know how ... but we do this because we are Indians. ..." Everyone had the right to worship the Maker "in the way he sees fit" and Indians were pleased with their results.

By the end of the first day, a dancer felt the sharp and continuing pains of thirst, hunger, and fatigue. The pains intensified during the second day. At this time it was a sign of a special blessing to have a dream, as Big Day did. "Toward morning I slept a little and dreamt that I was atop a mountain with openings in the pines and a little pool of water. I drank that water. In that very dream, when I drank that water, I woke up and from then on I never got thirsty or hungry."

The urge to take water and food was not always completely resisted. Dancers were tempted to suck on the damp towels which were brought for their morning toilette. A few found it difficult to resist eating available wild berries or taking water or mouth wash, but these were shamed into their responsibilities by a stern reminder that they should not have entered the Sun Dance if they could not do it right. "When them guys eat like that or drink, all the dancers suffer and become thirsty and hungry." What applied to food and water applied equally to liquor. When the dance ended, dancers were warned away from hard drinks and told to take soda. They were encouraged especially to take the traditional beef soup.

Tormenting thirst, stomach pains, and fatigue were natural preoccupations and concerns of dancers. On the second and third days, dancers during the late afternoon lined up by the tree and waited for the medicine man to doctor their weakness and give them the strength to carry on. Water drawn from the tree was splashed on the backs of dancers to help invigorate them. Truhujo gave both Jim Buffalo and David Bad Boy water-drawing whistles. Ira Left Hand related the following:

About last year [1954], the last dance, I and another guy, Ray Bear Below, were kind of weak. We were standing at the pole and an old guy came along, his name was Jim Buffalo. He used a whistle and he sucked water out of that pole and splashed water on our backs. That really made us feel good, and we didn't have any more trouble clear to the end.

Bird Horse used a flat piece of wood, a traditional Crow tool, to knead the chest and stomach area of a dancer to relieve the pain of stomach cramps. From the cattails, sage, and mentholated cigarettes brought by relatives and friends on the second day, dancers derived some relief from the searing daytime heat and the dryness of their bodies. Encouraging words from experienced dancers also brought the hope of a dream or vision and helped to put the sense of weariness out of their minds.

Five to ten per cent reportedly found the physical suffering too intense and restricted their dancing to once or twice during the day and night. However, they knew that chances for getting something "good" increased when a dancer kept going. Suddenly he might see the buffalo come to life, or a herd of them coming to "run over him." Other dancers, sensing the imminence of power, exerted more effort, and the drummer-singers increased the tempo and sang without letup. Fear must not overtake the dancer at this moment. He must dance right up to the tree if he were to get the power. If he hesitated or hung back, the power helper departed. In meeting the power person, the dancer ideally fell down, and his spirit left the body and received instructions about the medicine and its use. To fall down, however, was most unusual in the present Sun Dance. More often the power visitation came in the quiet sleep of dreams. Cummins dreamt that his "spirit" left the dance hall and ". . . went out onto the prairie with the birds. The birds were sundancing and I was among the birds. The birds told me that all the dancers that took part and all the Crow tribe would have good luck this year. There was a butterfly all through the dance in the hall, and the butterfly told me that he would get me all through the Sun Dance."

Terminating the Sun Dance

By the evening of the second day rumors circulated about the hour when the dance might end on the third day. Usually the time was not announced by the pledger more than two hours beforehand, and the condition of the dancers was important to his decision. At Lodge Grass, a few minutes after ten, Cummins asked the herald to announce that he intended to continue the dance until four o'clock in the afternoon. However, when it was revealed that someone had brought a wet towel to one of the dancers, it was decided it was not good to continue and they should stop at noon. Despite this flaw, Truhujo assured Cummins that his dance was the best held ever among the Crows, and that this Sun Dance was made for good luck.

Following the announcement, Yellow Woman, the designated "water-woman," led her three helpers to get four buckets of water. When they went for the water, the water woman offered a smoke and prayed to the Creator. When they returned, the women waited outside the lodge until the herald told them to bring the water in. At this moment, too, the order, "Don't play!" was given to the drummer-singers. With the water woman in the lead, the women filed in and deposited the buckets on the east side of the tree, two on the north and two on the south.

Cummins selected four outstanding men to pray individually over a bucket of water. To the south of the tree, John Whiteman and William Big Day faced west, while David Bad Boy and Bruce Goes Back, an Arapaho, faced east, north of the tree. Each prayed separately over the water, beginning with Goes Back on the north. In starting out, Goes Back spoke in English:

My friends, the Crow. I wish to express my appreciation for being chosen to do this honor of offering a prayer for this water. I want to thank John Truhujo who has brought this form of worship to you. I wish to thank particularly those of you who came into the lodge for your suffering.

I try to be here every year to help you, and I feel better each year. I don't want to keep you any longer. That the water may enter the bodies of the dancers and any others who wish to take it, I'm now going to offer a short prayer.

Goes Back next prayed in Arapaho, and when he ended, he took a dipper of water, spilled a little on the ground, and then took a drink. As each in turn prayed, he too offered water to the earth and then drank.

When the sanctified water was distributed, the two central buckets north and south of the tree were carried first to the sponsor and his assistant, and then circulated to the right and left respectively. Whiteman and Goes Back carried the two outer buckets first to women fasters at the south and north extremities, and then to adjacent male fasters and dancers. In deference to the sacred ground of the Big Lodge, the honored water bearers removed their shoes. When all the dancers had been given a sip of water, it was offered to the spectators. At Lodge Grass an old Crow man told the audience to use the water in the correct way, and he advised them to sprinkle some of it over themselves. Very few did so.

After the distribution of the water, the dance terminated without further ceremony. Some dancers immediately draped sheet screens before their stalls, and a few slipped into their street clothes and departed. Two summer favorites, orange soda and watermelon, were accepted eagerly from wives, children and other relatives. Paternal clansmen and prominent figures in the Sun Dance or other well known men stepped out on invitation and prayed over individual dancers. The benefactor stood in back, raised his right hand to the Sun, and prayed for the long life and welfare of his "child." In return he received gifts of money, blankets, quilts, and dress goods.

As the dancers departed to bathe and partake of broth and

Relaxing at home after the Sun Dance at Lodge Grass, 1975. *Left to right:* Mrs. Tom Yellowtail, medicine man Tom Yellowtail, and medicine man Truhujo (88 years of age). Wyola, 1975.

other liquids, young boys invaded the Big Lodge and ransacked the stalls in the hope of finding cigarettes and other items left behind.

The following day, a feast, which was defrayed principally by the sponsor, aided with funds raised by his committee and contributions by close relations and the district residents, brought the encampment to an end. Occasionally, as at Cummins's Sun Dance in celebration of war's end, a parade war dance was pledged, with participants drawn from district fraternities—the Night Hot, Big Earholes, Last Hot, and Sioux dancers. That night a "hand game" offered lively entertainment and gambling. By the second day the camp was quite deserted. Most of the visitors, aided by monies collected to defray a part of their expenses, departed.

The poles and brush of the Big Lodge were later used as firewood, or for fences and corral poles. The sponsor divested the lodge of its sacred quality. He told the Maker of All Things in prayer that they were through with the lodge and that the poles would be used for corrals and fencing. In some cases a warrior came and struck coup upon the tree and said a prayer. Usually the chief pole and rafter were left standing, and the center tree was never used again because of the association with lightning. As days turned into years, all that remained was the forked center pole with its tattered pennants, standing as a stark sentinel and witness of the sacred pledge and the sacrifices of the dancers.

CHAPTER 7

Integration of the Sun
Dance into Crow Society and Culture

Introduction

A cultural-historical point of view is useful in gaining perspective on personal and cultural factors in the borrowing of the Wind River Shoshoni Sun Dance by the Crow Indians in 1941 and its subsequent integration into Crow Reservation Culture. Individuals reenact, test and alter cultural conventions; and observing the interplay of personal and cultural factors in the actions of innovators, sometimes makes it possible to learn how special individuals emerge at a particular time and capture an historic place in the life of their societies. The historic emergence of Sun Dance leaders takes on new meaning when viewed through the interplay of surviving elements of the traditional culture and the infiltrating American culture. In the contest between the two cultures, acceptance of the Sun Dance bonded the Crows in a continuing struggle to maintain their national identity by cultural reaffirmations that allowed them a measure of control over their own destiny. It is important to discern, through comparison of the traditional Crow Sun Dance with the present Shoshoni-Crow ceremony, what has remained constant and what has changed in traditional attitudes, beliefs, and procedures, as well as in ceremonial leadership, form and pattern.

Crow anxiety over their national identity and destiny was

shared by tribal enemies and friends, for the advancing frontier destroyed Plains Indian culture. The Crows, as well as the hostile Sioux and Cheyennes, experienced the painful transition from independence and freedom to the controlled ambiguities of life on a reservation. A cultural-historical perspective requires analysis of events through a number of levels, leading from the interrelations between individuals and culture (Crow), to the interrelations of cultures in a culture region (Crow to Plains Culture), and then to the interrelations of two distinct culture-areas (Plains and American, from fur trade to frontier, and to present industrial).

Crow Culture-History and Reservation Acculturation

Faced with a deteriorating situation because of the westward movement of the Teton Dakotas and constant raiding by more populous enemies, the Crows cultivated friendly relations with whites and ultimately joined them in military alliance. Even so, they still shared in the embittered resistance and fight for independence of other tribes, such as the Dakotas, who were slaughtered at Wounded Knee in 1890. In 1887, the sudden "uprising" and equally sudden death of Swordbearer (Wraps Up His Tail) at the hands of a Crow policeman brought momentary turmoil but no disruption in Crow-American relations.[1] It was during this transitional time of

---

[1] According to White Man Runs Him, his friend, Wraps Up His Tail, fasted in the mountains and in a dream was given a "certain power and he thought he could exterminate the white people." With a sword, painted red, he was confident that he could "cut the soldiers down" and then people would be "free . . . [to] move around like in the olden times." Wraps Up His Tail was confident that he could not be brought down by bullets and that lightning would strike down the soldiers, probably when he pointed the sword and sang his medicine song. He also could blind the soldiers by throwing gunpowder in their eyes. He painted himself, the sword, and all his clothing red. See Hugh L. Scott, "Historical Notes on the Crow from White Man Runs Him," manuscript.

troubles that the last Crow Sun Dance took place about 1875, ending disastrously when the pledger abruptly abandoned his quest.

During the ensuing years, the Crows continued to carry out some of their traditional ceremonies despite the opposition of missionaries and orders from the Secretary of Interior as early as 1882 to suppress their Indian religion. To force the Crows into the "civilized" mold, new rules forbade war raids or participation in the "sundance, scalp dance, war dance, and even feasts."[2] Agents forced compliance by withholding rations, and those found guilty of infractions were threatened with imprisonment. Nevertheless, traditional religious practice, because it was bolstered by status objectives achievable through adoptive purchase of membership and ritual rights, eroded but never suffered extinction. This was especially the case for the Tobacco Society in the first two decades of the twentieth century. While the sacred tobacco was not always planted on an annual basis, it continued as the prime focus of ceremonial adoption and the purchase of rights to ceremonial privileges.[3]

Religion and Identity: The Spread of Peyotism

The spread of Peyotism between 1910 and 1925 once more merged Crow culture-history with that of the rest of the

With the red paint, Wraps Up His Tail probably indicated that the Sun, or Sun's child, Morning Star, had made him a gift of power. Red, arrows, and lightning in Crow symbolism are associated especially with the Sun and his helper, Thunderbird.

[2] C. C. Bradley, Jr., *After the Buffalo Days*, 48.

[3] Today the Tobacco Society remains the most prestigious ceremonial adoption, even though sacred tobacco can no longer be grown nor a sacred mix given to the person adopted. When Chester Medicine Crow died, the secret mix that caused the tobacco to thrive was not passed on, and efforts to put together a mix based on what was known about it proved unsuccessful. At the last planting in 1968, the tobacco shoots simply withered on the vine.

Plains tribes. Peyotism represented a more personal, reformative orientation to worship and a more accommodative
posture in relations with whites. This movement contrasted
with the nationalistic orientation of the Ghost Dance (1887–
1895), which projected an apocalyptic destruction of the
threatening white-dominated world and promised a return to
the old life of buffalo hunting and horse raiding. Both the
Ghost Dance and Peyotism reflected changes in the historic
circumstances of Indians in the Plains, and both were directed
to overcoming the demoralizing lack of control over their
own destinies.[4]

The Ghost Dance and Peyotism emphasized traditional
faith in the "medicine fathers" as a means of personal and
group identification, which assured some continuity in the
face of a life of confinement and alien control. However,
religion also served as an instrument of division within the
reservation community when missionaries stressed the "true"
faith of Christianity versus the "superstition" of traditional
belief and practice. The introduction of Peyotism sharpened
religious differences and conflicts between Crow tradition
and Christianity as well as between old-time medicine bundle
owners and those who claimed that peyote was a new way
to get power to cure disease. Within Peyotism itself, Crows
faced a choice between Christianized and traditional ceremonies.[5]

When users of the bitter-tasting peyote were fined and jailed,
the twin objectives of cultural identity and of freedom of
worship were advanced. Worshippers defended themselves
on the legal ground of the First Amendment of the United
States Constitution. They argued that the peyote cactus was

---

[4] Weston LaBarre, "The Peyote Cult," Yale Univ. *Publications in Anthropology No. 19;* James Mooney, "The Ghost Dance Religion," Bureau
of American Ethnology *Seventeenth Annual Report;* Voget, "American Indian in Transition"; Wallace, "Revitalization Movements"; also, Aberle,
Peyote among the Navaho.
[5] Kiste, "Crow Peyotism."

used in their religious worship and state legislatures and Congress were forbidden to make any law that interfered with their religious freedom.

Despite rivalrous conflicts with traditional medicine bundle practice, Peyotism made possible accommodations between past and present Crow belief and practice, as well as with Christian teaching. Although the tradition-oriented "Tipi Way" and the Christian-oriented "New Way" had doctrinal and ceremonial differences, these differences were not enough to dissuade a majority of Crow Peyotists from attending either one.[6] Each person brought to the peyote ritual whatever doctrinal and ceremonial posture fulfilled his needs. This coincided with the personal need and instrumental orientation of the Crows to a mystical world of power that lay at their doorstep. Peyotists quickly adapted their ceremony to traditional Crow organization and thereby assured its integration into the developing Reservation culture. "Clan fathers" assembled on invitation in the peyote tipi to bless and to honor their "children," who in turn warmed the backs of their "fathers" ("clan uncles") with blankets and adorned the heads of their "mothers" ("clan aunts") with silken scarves. Peyotism thus demonstrated how contemporary ceremonies, operating with traditional procedures, served present-day needs and accommodated to traditional social organization. In the Peyote meeting both the father's matrilineage and the mother's matrilineage continued the traditional protection and career guidance of their "children."

The key to the adaptive potential of Peyotism was the well-tried and simple remedy of pouring new wine into old bottles. Undoubtedly the articulation of contemporary situations using traditional social reciprocities had been going on before Peyotists adapted their ceremony to the mystical-power–material-wealth exchange. The Crow approach opened the way to the use of any instrument, Christian or tribal, that prom-

[6] Ibid.

ised success, especially when it was validated by a dream. The traditional Crow vow, in which a personal ritual sacrifice was traded for fulfillment of a need, was readily incorporated into Christian worship on a private basis. A personal search for mystic power and the formation of a small community of followers likewise was possible in the Christian context. During the 1930s a Black-Lodge district family introduced Aimee Semple Macpherson's Foursquare Gospel, with its emphasis on miraculous cures and an oil of anointment; and Harold Carpenter returned from California and established a Pentecostal-type church in the 1950s.

The spread of Peyotism in the first two decades of this century marked the beginning of a new phase in Indian resistance to the acculturative pressures eroding their national identities.[7] The resistant posture was sharpened by local antagonisms and legal challenges to the use of "narcotics" in worship, and Peyotists defended their right to worship in hearings in state courtrooms and before congressional committees. Thus they were introduced firsthand to lawyers, legal processes, legislative fact-finding procedures, and individual rights guaranteed under the Constitution. This type of resistance to pressure inevitably gave the Indian minority a broader base of experience in relation to the majority.

Peyotism found quick acceptance among tribes in the Plains and was carried into the Great Basin and Southwest by "missionaries" during the 1930s and 1940s. Since peyote doctrine stressed Indian revelation, leadership, ceremony and procedures, it became a rallying point for a modest Indian renaissance, which some ethnologists and anthropologists termed "Pan-Indianism." Peyotism united Indians in a common faith and forged an inter-tribal community of worshippers who reaffirmed their commitment to Indian worship and identity. In their separate but similar peyote ceremonies, In-

---

[7]For a thorough treatment of Peyotism and the struggle for religious freedom, see Omer Stewart, *History of the Peyote Religion.*

dians found a new medium for inter-tribal fellowship as well as a base for organizing resistance to the destruction of Indian culture.

In part, the "Indian Renaissance" stimulated by Peyotism was fed by the needs of first-generation reservation children. These children grew up without the traditional means to achieve status—marriages, wealth, and public reputation based on warfare and the possession of mystical power. Given this circumstance, the Crows, as well as their Blackfoot neighbors,[8] turned eagerly to purchasing status and mystical power by acquiring ceremonial memberships and rights, especially in the Tobacco adoption.

Among the Crows, Peyotism provided the primary arena for a legal and intellectual defense of their beliefs and practices. Among the Wind River Shoshonis, however, both the Sun Dance and Peyotism furthered the defense of Indian ways.[9]

The Crows, as their neighbors, based their intellectual defense on two pillars. First, both Indians and whites worshipped and lived their lives under the direction of the same Maker of All Things. The Creator had revealed himself to Indians, had conferred special powers on them, and had given ceremonial directions different from those passed to whites. The beliefs and practices of both stemmed from a common Creator, and therefore must be equally true and worthy. Similarities or "Correspondences" between Christian and Indian belief and practice provided the second pillar for a logical defense of Indian tradition. Christians fasted and prayed; so did Indians. The Book of Romans was cited as referring to the peyote cactus when directions were given to eat of the bitter herb.

Correspondences provided a basis for mutual acceptance

[8] Clark Wissler, "Ceremonial Bundles of the Blackfoot Indians," American Museum of Natural History *Anthropological Papers* 2:1–163.

[9] Shimkin, "Wind River Shoshone Sun Dance."

of differences in belief and practice. Despite local and state harassment, Peyotists won their right to worship in their own way. The Meriam Report[10] called for less paternalism and more independence for Indians, and by 1935, under Commissioner John Collier, the Federal ban on native worship was lifted completely. The official change in policy that accompanied elimination of the ban encouraged Indians to rely on their own values and traditions in order to cope with the hard economic realities and social problems of reservation life.

The political-legal successes of Peyotism and the reversal of the hard line government policy were all part of the background for a renewed interest in tribal custom and ceremony. Tribesmen prominent in the introduction and spread of the Wind River Shoshoni Sun Dance among the Crows had worshipped with peyote, and two had been turned out of the church for so doing. They were the ones who took trips to the Northern Shoshonis of Idaho and to the Wind River Shoshonis in Wyoming and displayed a keen interest in the ceremonies they observed. Each probably saw himself as a medicine man, although William Big Day was the only one who openly avowed this to have been a long-time goal. Whatever personal needs leaders and followers brought to the Sun Dance were submerged by the public need caused by the outbreak of World War II. The Sun Dance became the primary vehicle for overcoming the enemy, just as in the buffalo days. In those former times individual warriors fasted for power and sacrificed themselves for the public good. In 1941 a number of older men pledged themselves to fast or to dance in every Sun Dance until the war ended. As the modern warriors returned, the Sun Dance became the stage for honoring them in a victory celebration. They were called upon to recite their war deeds during construction of the lodge, or at small give-aways when they performed a ceremonial task. Like

[10] Lewis Meriam and others, *The Problem of Indian Administration.*

warriors of old, they were honored at special give-aways and received from their "clan uncles" ("clan fathers") names of illustrious warriors of old, which names they alone were entitled to bear and to confer upon others. After the war was over, personal needs and ambitions again were appropriate reasons for participation.

Peyotism and the Sun Dance in Cultural-Historical Perspective

In cultural-historical perspective, the diffusion of the Sun Dance from the Wind River Shoshonis to the Crows was part of a broader pattern of cultural resurgence among Indians in the plains. In the aftermath of the tragedy at Wounded Knee, hopes were abandoned for a return to former days of buffalo hunting and martial glory. In the medicine lodge of Peyotism, Indians met together in a ceremony made familiar by traditional forms and meanings, one that operated according to long-accepted assumptions about mystical power and the causes of things. In running counter to the administrative objective of forcing Indians into the "melting pot" mold, Peyotism drew the Crows into the same kind of conflicts that were faced by traditional worshippers of other tribes. The Sun Dance acted as another medium for a rediscovery and reassertion of cultural identity and independence, and it rejected the condition that linked morality and health, as was the case with Peyotism. The Sun Dance thus did not share the "reformative" psychology of Peyotism, but rather was a positive accompaniment to the growing political and cultural consciousness of the Crows, stimulated by new experiences during World War II.

Today's generation is much more knowledgeable and alert to what is going on in the wider American society and its meaning for the Crow tribe. Land claims cases necessitate familiarity with legal processes, and Crow representatives now accompany hired lawyers and expert witnesses to the courtroom. Some Crows recently put their legal knowledge into practice and halted the building of a new interstate highway by frustrating condemnation proceedings against their lands. They then negotiated a better settlement with the State of Montana. Crow leaders are well aware that their coal resources provide a new power-base from which the tribe can negotiate greater self-determination and respect for their cultural ways.

The Sun Dance Then and Now: Comparisons

The Sun Dance as a Tribal Event

The Sun Dance was not the only important tribal ceremonial during buffalo-hunting days. There were equally, if not more, compelling reasons for the Crows to assemble for the annual planting of the heaven-sent sacred tobacco, since it assured their integrity as a nation and helped them to be a great people.

Two factors conspired to limit the national character of both the Sun Dance and the Sacred Tobacco ceremonies. First, there was the difficulty of distances and timing as bands followed the seasonal cycle. Second, the personal need and cult (medicine bundle) emphasis in Crow worship limited the development of an annual national worship based on either the Sun Dance or Sacred Tobacco. Thus, the worship of Tobacco was organized in a number of medicine bundle chapters whose members had the right to worship together because all had been adopted and paid their fees. Serious defeats or widespread sickness quickly transformed a personal crisis into a public one, and both the Sun Dance and the Sacred Tobacco served the national interest at times in tribal performances.

Today the Sun Dance does not function as the primary event in the calendar round of the Crows. That place is taken by the annual Crow Fair and Rodeo. From the very start, the Sun Dance, even at Crow Agency, was a district enterprise, with aid solicited from other districts. This district level of organization paralleled the importance of the band-residence of the pledger in determining a primary level of organization and responsibility in buffalo-hunting days. World War II did create a sense of urgent personal sacrifice and cooperation that unified the Crows behind the Sun Dance, since it provided hope of a victory over the Iron Hats and the safe return of loved ones.

The present Sun Dance usually takes place in June or July and offers Crow families the opportunity to make certain everyone will be healthy at the time of the Crow Fair and Rodeo. People can be cured, and family dancers and relatives "sacrifice" themselves as well to assure that good luck follows their betting on the horses, their vying for prizes in Indian dress and dancing, and competition in rodeo events.

The Sun Dance today holds a place in the ceremonial calendar reminiscent of its place in historic Crow culture, since it is not always the occasion for an annual assembly of the Crows for a general tribal enterprise.[11] As of old, the Sun Dance can unify the Crows behind any threat to the nation as a whole, such as war. However, the Sun Dance is mostly a medium for working out personal needs that bear no relation to war, and this adaptability to contemporary life situations is important to its acceptance and integration into Crow reservation culture.

Sponsorship and Organization of a Sun Dance

Today, as in the past, a man who faces a crisis pledges a Sun Dance because of a supernatural directive received in

---

[11] The first Sun Dance at Crow Agency took place in conjunction with the Crow Fair and Rodeo and accidentally linked the ceremony to a tribal encampment. During the war, the fair and rodeo was suspended and Sun Dances at Crow Agency became the focus for a district encampment.

a dream or seen in a wakeful vision. However, a mourner in search of vengeance against the enemy is no longer the pledger. Today, a pledger and his fellow dancers use the Sun Dance to cure sickness, to forestall illness and early death, to prevent accidents, and to obtain a run of good luck and wealth for themselves and their next of kin.

In the absence of a chief of the tribe, pledgers usually take advantage of a public ceremony, such as a Sun Dance, to invite assistance and participation. Superintendent Yellowtail's role in the first Sun Dance at Pryor and at initial dances at Crow Agency offered a parallel to tradition. When Big Day went to Yellowtail, the head tribal officer, and solicited his permission and assistance for the dance at Pryor, Superintendent Yellowtail responded by making tribal and government resources available. The use of tribal buffalo for the feast and vehicles to bring brush and poles for the lodge lent a national quality to the initial Sun Dances. On the other hand, Superintendent Yellowtail played the role of a "chiefly" emissary of the Crow Tribe Council when he negotiated with the Wind River Shoshonis for the performance of a Sun Dance at Crow Agency.

The contemporary Sun Dance is organized on a district level. Crows consider the head of the elected social and recreational committee of the district as a "chief," but this term is a common reference for anyone in charge. The district social committee and the four dancing fraternities offer functional substitutes for the former band and military fraternity leadership. Today the formal political organization is not used to compel participation. In former times, when the poles were needed for the lodge, ten to twenty young men were honored with the task of dragging them in. In return for this honor, their parents were obligated to bring wealth to the medicine man who directed the ceremony. At the present time, everything is voluntary, other than compulsions felt personally because of kinship and friendship. Moreover, the number and variety of assigned ritual tasks is greatly diminished and amounts to about one-quarter of those formerly found in the traditional ceremony. The virtuous female tree notcher, the enemy captive, and the berdache all played important roles in the consecration and felling of the first tree but now are replaced by the medicine man, pledger, and a veteran. Veterans may or may not be called upon to scout the center tree, but they are indispensable to the prayerful marking of the tree in black, whereas in the old Sun Dance the enemy captive applied the victory color to the tree. Before lighting the ceremonial fire, a veteran today narrates a miraculous war experience and blesses the Sun Dance venture. Selection of a worthy young man, usually a veteran, to get the willows that the old women move up and down while singing, parallels tradition. However, the association of this symbol of fertility and plenty with women singers is not always accented in present Sun Dances. The willow bundle tied below the crotch of the center pole more often represents the idea of growth.

When the last of the old Crow Sun Dances was held in 1875, many ceremonial positions for men and women died with it. However, the Shoshoni-Crow Sun Dance with its Elk Lodge has provided a set of positions of honor equivalent to those found in Peyotism and has revived the traditional association of man and wife in ceremony and prayer. As women began to dance along with men, they asserted a new ceremonial role and independence. While the women's liberation movement may have contributed something to the new image of Crow women as sun dancers, the immediate stimulus came from Bannock women in Idaho, who for some time had held Sun Dances of their own, or dances in conjunction with men.[12]

The Elk Lodge brought organizational and logistic support to a pledger and members, and made medicines available for a "fee." There was no Elk Lodge at the time of the first Sun

[12] Hoebel, "The Sun Dance of the Hekandika Shoshone."

Dance at Pryor, and Big Day relied on friends and relatives to form a committee to handle routine problems and finances. Committee organization in churches and political groups served as the model. A reliable and energetic treasurer was needed to raise funds for the feast at the end of the Sun Dance. Other tasks included the bringing of poles from the mountains to the dance ground, arranging for teams of drummer-singers, and appointing policemen to maintain order.

In comparison to the traditional groups, the Sun Dance committee organized by today's pledger represents a new initiative and responsibility. In former times the bundle owner, working through chiefs and military fraternity heads, took command of the camp. The bundle owner, in accordance with his mystic power, directed the ceremony and brought the search for revenge power to a successful conclusion.

A mentor-apprentice, or "father-child" relationship was common to ceremonial leadership and instruction among the Crows. Truhujo provided medicines and instructions to Crows who wished to learn his ceremonial way, and thus followed Crow tradition governing relations between a ceremonial "father" and "child." Moreover, throughout his long association with the Crows, Truhujo never surrendered the role and rights of a mentor.

Today, according to custom, the pledger and his ceremonial father supervise consecration and construction of the lodge without performing any physical labor. The task of completing the lodge, once the center pole is up, usually is undertaken by the pledger's assistant, who may be a special clan mate or "partner." A pledger does not take control until consecration of the Big Lodge is completed. This event occurs after the singing of the four songs of the Four Winds, subsequent to the ceremonial entrance of the lodge. At this time the pledger steps forward to pray in his own behalf and for success of the Sun Dance mission. However, decisions usually are arrived at by conference with and in deference to the medicine man. The authority and direction exercised by the pledger thus is nominal, and he subordinates himself to the counsel of his ceremonial father much as in former times. Within the kinship system a sponsor relies heavily on his real and classificatory brothers-in-law for basic assistance. He is free to ask them for help, and today the brother-in-law relationship is just as integral to mutual aid as it was in the old days. The Crow fair is a prime occasion to strengthen these relationships with distributions of wealth. If one honors a daughter-in-law with a give-away at the Crow fair, he can count on his in-laws honoring his son with a give-away at the next fair. Tags showing the cost are left on give-away items to assure that the piece is not used merchandise. Blankets and shawls worn for the first time in the grand parade at the Crow Fair and Rodeo also carry cost tags, since no one knows when it will be necessary to remove a blanket on the spot and give it away to a relative or close friend who may admire it.

Clan brothers and sisters stand in a similar supportive relationship, and appeals to a "brother" or a "sister" can hardly be turned down. Assistance by a father's clansmen tends to be voluntary rather than solicited, except for special prayers and advice. The spirit of Crow reciprocity, however, is one of voluntary cooperation. Once a need is made known, it is up to the kin to step in and pick up a part of the burden.

Consecration

Much of the traditional Crow Sun Dance was devoted to consecration of the pledger and his avenging mission. The pledger, his dress, the lodge, and special paraphernalia, including the buffalo heads, the white clay bed, and the sacred tree with eagle-feather hoop and mannikin, all were ceremonially smoked with incense and prayed over by the bundle-owning "father." Every important judgment and act required a prayer smoke supported by dream communication from a spirit helper, as in the four stops along the way to the dance ground. Consecration is still a prominent element of the Sun Dance. This is seen in the narrative-blessings of veterans at "outside dances" preliminary to the main dance, which recall the four ceremonial stops of the traditional ceremony. A smoke-prayer with calumet or cigarette by the medicine man and pledger is vital before the cottonwood tree can be cut for use as the center tree. Though the pine rafters and the center tree may or may not be scouted and couped in symbolic defeat of the enemy, a veteran is invited to bring his mystic power to bear on the sacred mission by recounting an escape from death. Smoke-prayers by the medicine man and sponsor, the dedicatory singing of the songs of the Four Winds, and the blackening of the tree by a veteran are all coordinate elements in the consecration of the Big Lodge. There is nothing, however, comparable to the parade of war captains who mobilized power by prophetic visions and the dramatizations of successes over the enemy that occurred in the traditional ceremony.

When they build the lodge today, individuals voluntarily consecrate their own purposes by putting up special poles, digging the hole for the center pole, and furnishing the prayer flags attached to the arms of the center tree. An offering of two sacks of Bull Durham tobacco to the Maker is a necessary accompaniment of the prayer flags. This voluntary effort contrasts with former times, when all but the sick and aged were compelled by whip-threats of camp police to take part in getting the poles and in constructing the lodge.

Getting a dance outfit together is the responsibility of pledger and dancer alike. A skunkskin necklace and blackened moccasins, which formerly symbolized victory and the blinding and driving crazy of the enemy, are no longer part of a pledger's dress. Today the pledger and dancers conform to a more similar dress than in the past. For pledger and dancer the eagle-bone whistle, textile wrap-around kilt, eagle feather plumes attached to the little fingers, and blanket-robe are counterparts to traditional elements. According to the seriousness of his purpose, a pledger today readies himself for his moment of sacrifice by fasting, smoke-praying at sunrise, putting up a sweat lodge in which to pray to the Sun, and avoiding sexual activity and alcohol. During the war years, the Elk Lodge provided a mechanism for blessing a pledger and his venture at a "sing" or full-moon meeting. On this occasion he might be invested with a "cane" in fulfillment of a dream instruction, or according to a dream of a medicine man or other dancer noted for power obtained through the Sun Dance. At a "sing," a pledger made known the dates for his outside dances and issued appeals for help.

Pledger's Role and Authority

A mourner's revenge provided the staging for the original Crow Sun Dance. All other aspects played supportive and subordinate roles in the mobilization of mystic power behind the pledger. When the pledger received the prophetic vision of success, the ceremony came to an abrupt end. There was no waiting for those who individually sacrificed themselves by hanging from lodge poles. Their hopes for visions during this extraordinary concentration of mystic power were secondary. They were released with a prayerful blessing and took themselves home, bearing the rawhide lines as evidence of their sacrifice, to await their own power dreams.

In the present Sun Dance, the pledger is not the central figure in a vision-seeking drama. He shares the stage with others who may have visions as important as his own. For example, during the war, while in the dance lodge, Big Day had visions prophetic of victory. He saw the number nine signalling the second atomic bomb drop in August. Others saw "iron hat" prisoners working in the United States, or ships returning with victorious soldiers. In none of these instances was the visionary a sponsor of the Sun Dance. The visions of success followed traditional form.

War whoops by old men and words of praise and encouragement from relatives now substitute for coup recitations and blessings formerly spoken by war captains during breaks in the pledger's dancing. Today the Big Lodge is a pale reflection of the enthusiasm and excitement that, in former times, transformed the Sun Dance into an exultant war party. However, war-narrative blessings occurred frequently in the victory Sun Dances at the end of the war, in which veterans related to the pledger were honored. Now, as formerly, a "clan uncle" spontaneously sings a praise song in honor of the pledger, dancer, or veteran, and is rewarded with a gift of value. Drummer-singers alert themselves to a dancer's condition, and, as was true in the traditional ceremony, the beginning of a vision is marked by a song that is sung continuously.

In the old Crow Sun Dance, the pledger's entrance to the consecrated lodge was a central element in beginning the search for power. On leaving his own tipi, the pledger reenacted the gradual emergence of the Sun Dance mannikin from his medicine wrappings, as seen in the original revelation. Today the pledger and his assistant each lead a file of dancers in a ceremonial circuit and entrance of the lodge. There are no ritual stops along the way in the number of four, but one and all blow four long blasts of the eagle-bone whistle at each of the cardinal points as they circle the lodge twice and then enter, beginning at the west point of departure.

Dreams are used for introducing innovations in the Sun Dance. However, Crow sponsors have been apprentices to ceremonial mentors from the Shoshonis and Bannocks, and hence have not been in a position to innovate except in a minor way. Today a sponsor takes ostensible control of the ceremony following the songs to the Four Winds, when he makes his opening prayer. Although he may not sleep or dance on a buffalo-wallow bed prepared of clay and bounded by two buffalo skulls as of old, today's pledger does have a special place beside the chief rafter, which is lined up with the rising sun. This chief pole is forked and is fitted with an eagle, the special messenger bird of the Sun. The sponsor thus is primed for reception of messages, but he submits any messages he receives to the medicine man for wise interpretation. This, too, is old practice.

Ceremonial convention limits the authority of any pledger. Usually in consultation with the medicine man, he determines the moment when the pipe is offered to the drummer-singers, but his choice must be before midday and before midnight. If he is a cane holder, the pledger decides when to put the cane in motion. A pledger has the right to select respected dancers or old men to give special prayers. While the pledger decides whether the ceremony is to end before or after noon, he cannot stop the Sun Dance before it has run its scheduled course of two and a half days unless something extraordinary, which all perceive as a threat, takes place. Such a crisis occurred at Pryor when a leader reportedly turned up drunk and took alcohol into the lodge, prompting the pledger and dancers to walk out for a time. Confronted with exhausted dancers, or by a weakening of the power quest brought on by some taking water on the sly, a sponsor may feel compelled to end the Sun Dance before midday.

Ceremonial Pattern and Innovation

As a medicine owner, the director of a Sun Dance may seem to determine its form. However, as a public ceremony, the old Crow Sun Dance operated according to conventional understanding concerning forms and procedures, to which the separate medicine bundles added but minor variations. Similarities exhibited by recent Sun Dances in the different districts of the Crow Reservation suggest that tradition may be just as strong today in limiting ceremonial variability, together with trends beyond the control of leaders. In a first burst of enthusiasm, Truhujo, as mentor, enriched the Shoshoni-Crow ceremony with special forms of his own, such as the canes for pledgers and drum chiefs, the "little man," and the Elk Lodge with the full-moon meeting. However, by 1975 most of these innovations were gone, and the Crow ceremony in its simplicity took on the quality of the standard Wind River Shoshoni Sun Dance. Tom Yellowtail, current holder of Truhujo's Sun Dance medicines and owner of the ceremony, carries on Elk Lodge curing meetings. At times selected elders, sun dancers, and paternal relatives may be seated around an altar replete with Elk medicines and symbols of Truhujo's visitation by the Elk Person. There may be times, too, when Yellowtail and his wife are the only members present except for patients.

The trend toward simplicity suggests that both historic and evolutionary structural processes are involved. Personalized needs and crises infuse the ceremony with a structural-functional character that is linked to the satisfaction and resolution of human problems. Traditional war symbolism and coup requirements today bear no functional connection to the satisfaction of personal desires for health, wealth, protection, and career success. War symbolism thus is no longer as important in the ceremony as it was during the war years. Historic processes also reinforce change by taking aging cane holders out of circulation.

Historic and evolutionary factors also combine to account for the most striking change in Sun Dance form—the participation of women as dancers. The historic break with Truhujo led Big Day to turn to Bannock medicine men, and these contacts stimulated women, following the lead of Bannock women, to enter the Sun Dance as dancers during the fifties. Many persons, including his brother, criticized Big Day for this striking modification. However, ritual avoidance of menstruants, which was traditional to any power-quest, prompted accommodation rather than acceptance of women as equivalent participants. Following Crow convention, a man and wife may dance as a team in order to change their luck or to forestall disaster. However, women are barred from the ceremonial prayers accompanying the sunrise greeting, and their smoke-purification is carried on outside the Big Lodge at four different fires. Expulsion of menstruants from the dance is a rigid rule. Men also hold the preferred positions in the dance lodge, to the west of the center pole, while women are assigned positions toward the entrance. This corresponds to the place normally given over to fasters, with females always at the extremities.

An absence of pledger's canes and the lack of war symbolism in contemporary Sun Dances does not mean that canes and coup-striking may not appear spontaneously in future ceremonies. The inheritance-purchase of cane rights, the onset of war, or an injunction legitimated by dream could prompt a pledger to re-introduce such elements. However, they probably would be no more than momentary historic variations based on fleeting personal and situational contexts, and would have no perceptible effect on current evolutionary trends toward ceremonial simplicity.

The trend toward ceremonial simplicity and the initiative taken by women in the Sun Dance indicate that processes outside the control of Sun Dance leadership are predominant in shaping the ceremony today. Internal processes are shaping a drift toward a standardized ceremony resembling that of the Wind River Shoshonis. Processes outside the Shoshoni-Crow Sun Dance are making an equally profound impact as Crow women, taking their cue from their Bannock counterparts and the new image of women, are revolutionizing the Sun Dance and forcing ceremonial accommodations to their presence.

The division of leadership in the Sun Dance between Pryor, Crow Agency, and Lodge Grass districts presents an interesting parallel to the distribution of ceremonial power exercised by bundle owners in buffalo-hunting days. Today the possession of medicines or bundles on temporary loan, by gift, or by purchase is essential to this "factional" leadership. Big Day brought in the Bannock medicine man Charlie Bell to shore up his position after the break with Truhujo when the Bannock-born Wind River Shoshoni sun dancer Tom Compton proved unstable. The Old Coyotes retain the medicines obtained in purchase from Truhujo and thus maintain a claim to leadership. In turn, Tom Yellowtail, through a testamentary gift from Truhujo, asserts a right to primary leadership. Now, as then, medicine bundles and their owners are ranked, and from the number of dancers who accept his leadership, Tom Yellowtail is number one because of his close association with Truhujo.

World View and Personalized Worship

The view of the world expressed in Crow contemporary philosophy contains the idea that individuals are linked to the world through a personalized cause-and-effect. This concept echoes beliefs by which their forefathers lived. The world is alive with power, *maxpe*, and whatever moves, grows, and lives does so because of its special *maxpe*. *Maxpe* is a gift of the Creator, first bestowed during the creation. It is *maxpe* that makes all things and persons different in their capabilities and natures. Whether He First Made All Things holds Himself aloof in the heavens or is the same as Old Man Sun, or Old Man Coyote, is not an important issue for dispute. The important thing is that a "person" may be in anything and everything—sun, ants, bears, buffalo, rocks, streams, and trees. The world thus is made up of "persons," spiritual and human, who can talk to, influence, cooperate with, and make gifts to each other in mutual exchange and benefit.

To overcome omnipresent threats to life and limb, men need to cooperate with and seek out the protection of the power holders and power dispensers in the world. Men need the *maxpe* of the eagle, which never misses, or of the bear, which is courageous, overpowering, and smart in fighting and eluding enemies. Then there is the buffalo, the fearless and fearsome charger, ever ready to turn and bowl his enemy over, and tough to subdue even when mortally wounded. In the ant one finds the busy and tireless industry that never ends despite the work load, while the quick mobility and near invisibility of the dragon-fly is a power to have ready at any time.

Man's animal, bird, insect, tree, and rock associates are not to be ignored, but respected for their powers and solicited for assistance in living out one's natural life. In power quests and in dreams, humans "see" a power-giving person and "hear" him speak his instructions. The sensible and practical person thus is alert to inner-communications which may come in dreams not always directly sought but frequently prompted by concerns over special needs and aspirations. The power quest alerts a spirit person to the extremity of the need in the hope that he will bestow the power to satisfy that need.

At present, as in the past, Crow individuality rests on the "inner voice" and the distinctive power capability conveyed. The gift of power capability also points up distinctions between peoples. Indians and whites are different, because each was given access to different powers and ways of worshipping; and, in consequence, their natures are different. The world thus is made up of many different natures with different potentials, the gift of the Maker, and each is worthy of respect in its own right.

The Sun Dance as a Power Quest

Although a public ceremony, the Sun Dance always has been a vehicle for satisfaction of a personal need. The principle of body-suffering is unchanged. The ordeal of body-suspension favored in the past is no longer found, but fasting for two and a half days without food and water forces a dancer to "tough it out." While participants run to the tree and dance back into position instead of dancing in place, vision seekers still use the technique of fixation, focusing on the buffalo head or the "little man," who may be attached to the tree on the second day. The eagle-bone whistle and the smoking of tobacco remain the chief media for sending prayers to the Creator and other spirit persons. There is a good deal of continuity in principles and procedures between traditional practices and the present Sun Dance. In prayers by the sponsor and respected elders, personal objectives seem to merge with the public welfare. Yet even here the focus is upon the person who is sick, as well as upon fulfillment of the wishes of the individual dancers.

Interpretations for Whites: Correspondences and Legitimacy

Because of their relations with whites and their reservation experiences, the Sun Dance has a special meaning for its followers as an Indian way of worship. In validating the self through Indian religion, sun dancers assert a legal right to freedom of worship. The Sun Dance thus takes its place alongside Peyotism, the sacred tobacco, and the sacred sweat as expressions of Indian identity and cultural continuity. In the past, religious ceremonial rights and powers were dispersed among owners of medicine bundles. Crow religious organization today shows a similar dispersal of ownership of ceremonies and ceremonial rights. The idea of ceremonial ownership extends to those who introduced the Four-Square Gospel and Pentecostal denominations. Ownership may even attach itself to Christian missions if a high-ranking and politically-strong family dominates church activities.

Missionary challenges to the true and god-given nature of their worship prompted the Wind River Shoshonis to legitimate their Sun Dance by pointing out its similarities to Christianity. Such a response to challenges to traditional worship is not uncommon, and thoughtful Crows, according to their orientation, readily accepted or rejected apparent parallels between Christian and Sun Dance elements and practices. The most important of these comparisons were as follows:

1. The center tree represents the cross of crucifixion.

2. The three days of the dance correspond to the days Jesus lay in the tomb and then rose from the dead.
3. The twelve support posts and rafter poles represent the twelve apostles.
4. Fasting by Indians is like that carried out by Christ.
5. The Crow people worship the same Creator as the white man, but follow ways given to them by the Maker Of All Things, just as He bestowed different ways on the white man, including a written word as found in the Bible.

The incorporation of correspondences into the metaphysics of the Sun Dance gives it the potential to be all things to all men. Churchgoers are not forced into a conflict of conscience and, if challenged, can muster a plausible defense for involvement in the Sun Dance. Moreover, non-Indians themselves point out correspondences. Today the participation of Catholic priests and white friends in the Sun Dance forges links between Crows and American belief and practice, thereby reinforcing a composite reservation culture. Correspondences are not there just to fool white bretheren. They exist as a justification whereby individuals in their own consciences selectively accept traditional meanings, Christian meanings, or both together or separately by context.

Correspondences do not mean that the Sun Dance, or elements of the ceremony, have been reinterpreted with Christian meanings. Though an accommodation to the challenge of legitimacy of belief and of self, correspondences do not necessarily constitute a first step along the way to reinterpretation. That step may come when those with strong Christian convictions feel compelled to rationalize the Sun Dance as an Indian-Christian ceremony.

Traditional and Contemporary Symbolism

Crow customarily base their symbolism on straightforward connections. Both form and color may carry the burden of meaning, and both may hold multiple significances within a standardized system of meanings. Variability stems from the subjective experience of the visionary. Usually color tends to be more variable than form, since different colors may be associated with the same form or design. For example, the arrows carried by Morning Star were each a different color, and "lightning lines representing the Thunderbird might be yellow, blue, or green according to an individual's revelation."[13] A seasonal symbolism commonly associated green with spring, red with summer, yellow with autumn, and white with winter.[14]

The reds and yellows of the pre-dawn sky traditionally are linked to the Sun. Red set next to yellow occurs with frequency in old Crow beadwork as well as in today's rainbow designs. Red and yellow apparently recall that mystic and ecstatic moment in which the visionary experiences adoption by a medicine father and his gift of power.[15] Red is the prime color applied to the near-featureless effigy used in the Sun Dance. The half-curve of a rainbow drawn in red on the forehead of an effigy recalls Thunder. For humans, red is linked to "longevity and the ownership of property, as well as blood."[16]

A rectangular cross usually represents a star, and in this form Morning Star appears frequently on traditional Sun Dance objects and pipe bags.[17] White is especially important for those seeking a vision, whether applied as white clay to the body, or draped around the body as a whitened buffalo robe, or as a white sheet in the present Sun Dance.[18] White clay also may represent the earth. White seems especially con-

[13] Robert H. Lowie, "Crow Indian Art," American Museum of Natural History *Anthropological Papers* 21:320.
[14] Wildschut, "Medicine Bundles," 17:9.
[15] Ibid., 29.
[16] Lowie, "Crow Indian Art," 21:320.
[17] Ibid., 292.
[18] Ibid., 320.

nected with the buffalo, who washes himself with the white dirt of his prairie wallow, and on occasion appears as an albino. White thus simulates a condition of ritual cleanliness. As a primary power figure, the Sun, usually portrayed as a red circle, in former times was offered an albino robe and hailed as a "father's clansman." This way of addressing the Sun accented the role of one's own father's clansmen in the bestowal of dream blessings and power. In the round of traditional color symbolism, red, yellow, blue, green, white, and black predominated, recalling sun, sky, growth, earth, and victory over the enemy.

In the contemporary ceremony, traditional designs and color symbolism persist alongside variable interpretations by individuals. Truhujo makes use of zigzag rainbow and lightning designs in his body decoration and feather medicines. The black rings drawn on the trunk of the center tree represent the war successes of the veteran who applies them. Others interpret the rings as the days the dance will last, or both together. The blue and white pennants attached to the forks of the center tree are sacrifices, along with the tobacco, to the Sun. Blue symbolizes day, or night, while white may represent day, water, snow, and earth. The white clay plastered on the buffalo's head and used by dancers on entering the lodge, or on the first day, is the buffalo's own medicine, since he paws up the white dirt and tosses it over himself. Yellow is the preferred color on the second day, the best for getting power. The nostrils and eyes of the buffalo are ringed with yellow, and yellow paint is applied to the eagle's beak. The base drum brought by the Shoshonis to the first Sun Dances also was colored yellow.

Stellar Origins of the Sun Dance

Revelations associated with Crow Sun Dance medicine bundles linked the ceremony to the Sun, Morning Star, Moon, and the Seven Stars of the Big Dipper. In the Four Dance account, seven buffalo bulls donated the ceremony along with the moon, who presented a man-effigy. Moon, the Old Woman who adopted Morning Star, son of the Sun, turned out to be an ambiguous, if not conspiratorial, grandmother.[19] Old Woman at times worked against her grandchild as he struggled to make the earth a safer place by ridding it of cannibalistic monsters. In Two Leggings's account, a man and a woman, apparently sent by the Sun, instructed the visionary with promptings from that being. The lodge for the ceremony was dedicated to the Sun.[20]

As the Sun's child, Morning Star occupied a prominent place among the more important sacred beings of the Crows. His symbol, a rectangular Saint George's cross, appeared on Sun Dance objects, and was painted on the pledger's chest and back. In one of his exploits, Morning Star, finding himself inside a cannibalistic buffalo bull, used the Sun Dance ceremony to mobilize the power that enabled him to kill the monster and rescue people inside the bull's stomach.[21]

On his monster-killing ventures, Morning Star carried four magic arrows that watched over him. Each arrow was colored differently, red, black, yellow and white.[22] Medicine arrows were linked to the Seven Stars, but Morning Star actually made the gift to the visionary.[23] In this case the quester kept the original arrow, colored red, and made seven arrow bundles in replica, with each of the arrows a different color. During the day the medicine arrow bundle was placed on the north side of the tipi and at sundown it was brought inside and tied to the north-oriented pole.[24] This orientation related to Morning Star, who left this earth after killing the monsters

[19] Lowie, *The Crow Indians*, 152–54, 303–305.
[20] Nabokov, *Two Leggings*, 22–23.
[21] Lowie, *The Crow Indians*, 146–47.
[22] Ibid., 144.
[23] Wildschut, "Medicine Bundles," 17:48–50.
[24] Ibid.

and turned himself into the North Star. The Old Woman became the Moon.[25] Morning Star's arrows and bow were made by his father, the Sun. After rescuing four near-lifeless men from a cannibalistic buffalo, Morning Star taught two of them how to make bows and arrows. When making arrows, he instructed them to "make lightning with them and whatever you shoot at you'll kill."[26] In the traditional Crow Sun Dance, the pledger not only carried the mark of Morning Star on his chest and back but also the Sun's own painting, a zigzag lightning mark, on his forehead.[27] Thunderbird, with his lightning arrows, hail, and rainbows, was an important "helper" of the Sun, and in his earthly manifestation as an "eagle" held a prominent place in the ceremony, symbolized by the "eagle's nest" of the dance lodge.

Truhujo was "adopted" by an Elk Person and given his special powers to cure, but he considered Seven arrows to be the owner of the Sun Dance. The first thunder in the spring was the signal to begin the cycle leading to the Sun Dance. The center tree was dedicated to worship, and anyone who used it for secular ends risked being struck down by lightning. The tree itself symbolized lightning, but it also signified growing things and life. Canes possessed by Elk Lodge Sun Dance leaders attracted lightning, and so must be removed from the house during a thunderstorm.

Dwarfs, the Sun Dance, and Stellar Connections

The Sun Dance owner, Seven Arrows, was not a Crow but a Shoshoni figure. He was a dwarf who lived in the Wind River Mountains in the area of the painted drawings at Din-

[25] Lowie, "Myths and Traditions," 25:57, 59.
[26] Ibid., 53.
[27] Lowie, "Sun Dance of the Crow Indians," 16:23.

woodie Canyon. This was a favorite fasting spot for Shoshonis who aspired to become medicine men.

Crows and Shoshonis shared common ideas about dwarf people who inhabited this earth, lived very much as humans, and who have bestowed great power on needy persons. A favorite dwarf of the Crows lived inside the stone butte in Pryor Gap. His magic arrow unerringly cut the thread attached to the protective medicine feather floating above hateful Red Woman, and so he destroyed her. He then built seven sweat houses in the shape of stars and brought back to life his brothers, the victims of Red Woman. They became the Seven Stars of the Big Dipper.[28]

The dwarf at Arrow Rock in Pryor Gap at one time adopted a Crow boy-child carried off in a dog-travois runaway. He gave his adopted "child" a bow and four arrows with lightning qualities, "one red, blue, black and yellow. . . ."[29] The dwarf also made his "child's" body like stone, impenetrable. He sent him hunting for meat to feed some stones (dwarf people) on a mountain across the way. Under instructions given at this time the Crows piled stones along the Pryor Gap trail, where they are visible today. He also told his adopted child that if people gave him arrows and beads, "anything they wish they shall have."[30] The butte where this dwarf lives is known as Rocks-they-shoot, or Arrow Rock, for the Crows made their offerings to the dwarf by shooting arrows into the rock.

At another time, finding a boy and girl who fell behind the moving camp, the dwarf at Arrow Rock gave them powerful rock medicines.[31] Rock medicines made things increase in number, so they were good luck for wealth. They also brought good health, plenty of food, and success in war. Frequently

[28] Curtis, *The Apsaroke, or Crows*, 4:124–26; Lowie, "Myths and Traditions," 25:119–33, 165–71.
[29] Lowie, "Myths and Traditions," 25:169.
[30] Ibid.
[31] Wildschut, "Medicine Bundles," 17:94–97.

these medicine stones suggested human faces as well as bird and animal forms. They might be either male or female, but it was the female stones that made things increase. The discoverer of the errant boy and girl persuaded older dwarfs also living at Arrow Rock to teach them the ceremony called, Cooked Meat Singing. At the onset of spring and of winter, Crow owners of rock medicines on dream instruction met in a tipi with entrance facing the mountains where dwarf people generally lived. Their Cooked Meat Singing ceremony was designed to benefit the Crow people by ensuring that they would have plenty to eat, good health, and great successes against the enemy. The rock medicines were taken from their wrappings, passed around, and sung to with songs made powerful because they had been obtained in dreams and in visions. In mobilizing their powers they sang Sun Dance, war, and praise songs that honored the most successful warrior.[32] An outstanding war leader was invited to recite his coups, and everything was done to dramatize the happy times in camp. Plenty of meat was distributed, and those taking part gave a horse or other wealth to a father's clansman, the bestower of success and protection to a "child" through his gifts of medicine dreams. All in all it was a joyous occasion, with laughter at mistakes and good feelings all around.

Today, Crows say that they encounter dwarf people in the mountains. Little Fox is the chief of the little people around Pryor, and Seven Arrows is chief of all the little people, according to Tom Yellowtail. The owner of the Sun Dance thus is the chief of the dwarf people, and Truhujo relinquished his control when Seven Arrows told him to pass his medicine feathers and songs to Tom Yellowtail. In traditional fashion, Tom Yellowtail himself received the gift of an eagle feather from Seven Arrows and thus validated his right to the Sun Dance ceremony conveyed by Truhujo.

Crow and Wind River Shoshoni beliefs about the little peo-

---

[32] Ibid., 102–103; Lowie, "Minor Ceremonies," 21:349–55.

ple forestalled any misgivings about the ownership and origins of the Sun Dance performed under Truhujo's direction. Indeed, as members of the Without Fires clan of supernaturals, dwarfs took their place alongside such stellar figures as the sun, stars, moon, and thunder.[33] As for Seven Arrows, the Crows frequently encountered seven figures in the mystic world. Besides the seven bulls of the Big Dipper, there were seven stars, seven cranes, seven brothers, and the ceremonial use of seven feathers and of seven songs. At times visionaries made seven duplicate medicine bundles, such as the seven arrow bundles of Takes Back Twice.[34] As Tom Yellowtail observed, four medicine songs belonged to the Sun Dance and three were his very own, given to him by Truhujo for use in the prayer meetings.

Something close to a doctrinal controversy could erupt when ceremonial innovations clashed with convention. Tom Yellowtail's use of a blue-painted lodge pole with two pendant otter medicines aroused criticism from some Sun Dance leaders. Because of the two otter hides the pole was erected on the second day and placed to the right of the center pole. To some observers it appeared to be a personal source for power separate from the consecrated forked tree with its pennants, tobacco offerings, willows, and buffalo. Those with severe illnesses were instructed to take hold of the pole during doctoring. Tom Yellowtail followed Truhujo's instructions and prepared the pine pole shortly after transfer of the Sun Dance bundle. He owned the right to put up a blue pole with otter medicines because Seven Arrows had determined it. Was this a new emphasis on earth and water instead of stellar "helpers?" Yet the blue signified the sky and the otter was a fearsome helper of Morning Star, noted for his gift of powers to cure.[35]

[33] Wildschut, "Medicine Bundles," 17:2.
[34] Ibid., 50.
[35] Ibid., 11–12.

His otter medicines endowed Tom Yellowtail with a mystical affinity for these underwater animals, and he expected to find them again in nearby streams from which they had been missing for years. He possessed a closer affinity for the "spike" elk, since a young elk had thrust himself out of the lake and had become Truhujo's medicine father. Now the Elk was in Tom Yellowtail ("that's in me"). When Elk entered him, Tom felt heat, or the power. Even today, when he is curing, the power brings a tingling sensation as it enters through his fingers. One day, when Truhujo was up early and in the garden at Tom Yellowtail's, he met up with a spikehorn elk. The Elk addressed Truhujo as follows: "John, I'm not going with you anymore. I live here now" (that is, with Tom Yellowtail). Then the Elk walked off in the direction of the mountains.

In former times when a medicine father entered his adopted child and became a living member of his body, that person was something special. He (she) became a *batsirape*. The indwelling spirit showed itself in a sudden protrusion of head, paws, tail, or other part of the animal through which the spirit manifested itself on earth.[36] A screech-owl was "shot" into Four Dances's body when he was shown the effigy to be used in the Sun Dance. Truhujo shot the Elk into Tom Yellowtail.

Person-offering

The pledger of a Crow Sun Dance piped and danced before a buckskin mannikin encased in a seven- or twelve-feathered hoop with handle. The "doll" was closely associated with the screech owl, noted for its night vision and capacity to avoid being hit.[37] Fixing his gaze on the figure, the pledger danced

[36]Curtis, *The Apsaroke, or Crows*, 4:54–55; Lowie, *The Crow Indians*, 264–68.
[37]Lowie, Ibid., 247–48.

until he collapsed and received the benediction of victory when he saw the dead enemy. The effigy also carried decorations that associated it with the Sun, Morning Star, thunder, and lightning. While the effigy may have represented the enemy upon whom revenge was to be taken, the stellar symbols suggest that the figure, rudely fashioned after the human form, at times may have depicted Morning Star.[38]

The Wind River Shoshonis historically derived their Sun Dance mannikin from the Crows, but gave up its use and opposed Truhujo's efforts to bring it back into the ceremony. To Truhujo, the human effigy was the "little man" or Dwarf Person. It was possible that the "child imitation" by which the Sun Dance effigy was described among the Crows referred to the "little people." Dwarf Persons in Crow thought had multiple associations—with mountains, lightning arrows, bodies resistant as stone, the sacred sweat lodge curing, the Big Dipper, and the screech owl.[39] To Bad Boy, there was a "god" in the "little man," whom Truhujo described as the special messenger of the owner during a Sun Dance. The nine-inch figure with arms and legs but without facial features was painted red from the neck up. A sash around the waist carried rainbow and lightning designs. The "little man" represented the dwarf, Seven Arrows. Truhujo commissioned Crow

---

[38] Chief Hair on Top (d. ca. 1851) used a huge buffalo-hide rattle and sang Sun Dance songs to call the buffalo. "His medicine was the image of the Lakota used in the Sun Dance." See Curtis, *The Apsaroke, or Crows*, 4:48, 69; Ewers in Wildschut, "Medicine Bundles," 17:155. In a description by Lowie in "Sun Dance of the Crow Indians," 16:50, the pledger sees the doll paint his face black, the promise of victorious revenge. In the Four-dances origin narrative, the doll is said to represent "moon-woman." The Screech Owl, which in the Four Dances account, is shot into Four Dances in Lowie, "Sun Dance of the Crow Indian," 16:14, again is described as flying into the tree with the hoop and changing into the doll in Wildschut, "Medicine Bundles," 17:23.

[39] Curtis, *The Apsaroke, or Crows*, 4:124–26; Lowie, "Myths and Traditions," 25:119–33, 165–71.

medicine man Joe Hill to make the effigy for use in Elk Lodge ceremonies. Today, however, it is not much used in Shoshoni-Crow Sun Dances.

Buffalo versus Little Man

The present Sun Dance reverses the primary roles of buffalo and of the "person-offering" in the Crow Sun Dance. In the traditional ceremony, the mannikin was the primary instrument for a pledger's prophecy. Today the buffalo is the bestower of visions and good things.

No animal took care of Crow needs in former days as did the buffalo. The list of items prepared from a buffalo's body included food, lodging, bedding, clothing, thread, glue, war shields, and ceremonial rattles. The buffalo was omnipresent in living herds grazing in the distance and in the skeletons dotting the prairie. Since buffalo allowed themselves to be used in order that Crow people could live, it seemed fitting to power-fasters to offer a portion of themselves to the Sun and other spiritual persons. They did so by slicing a tip of a finger steadied on a buffalo skull whenever possible. Even today, Crows view the buffalo as a provider of good things for living. "It represents plenty to eat, plenty to wear, and a peaceful wholesome life," according to Ira Left Hand.

In the contemporary Sun Dance the buffalo radiates power and is renowned as a giver of good things. Dancers challenge his attention by "running at it," suffering and praying that the Buffalo Person will take notice and "run over them," bringing a dancer what he desires and perhaps something more—the gift of a power to cure. Buffalo rightfully faces west because, as the servant of Evening Star, he usually appears from that direction when coming with a gift of good luck and power.[40]

Eagle and Thunderbird

Eagle is the primary servant of the Sun and in his spiritual

[40]Wildschut, "Medicine Bundles," 17:11.

manifestation takes the form of Thunderbird. Eagle is a bearer of messages from spirit to man, and from man to spirit. The eagle-bone whistle is a traditional vehicle for prayer in the Sun Dance. With eagle's own yellow paint, the whistle concentrates the prayers of the dancer. In a sense, the spirit of the eagle is also there, ready to carry the prayerful message of needs upwards to the Sun and the Maker of All Things. Eagle plumes dangling from the little finger also are of long standing in the Sun Dance. In the traditional context of war, downy plumes evoked the idea of a fog that hid warriors from pursuers or otherwise made them invisible.[41] The lightness of eagle feathers and plumes also suggested a weightlessness that carried horses swiftly over the ground.[42] As the bearer of storms, Thunderbird, when invoked by his "child," dropped a curtain of rain and hail over the pursued. Today, eagle plumes commonly represent eagle's wings, which support a dancer in his running at the center tree and keep him from tiring. The down feathers also may suggest more abstract ideas derived from church contacts—plumes as symbols of purity and of righteousness.

Eagle-bone whistle and the seven-feather medicine fan of eagle feathers are still indispensable instruments for prayer and power. With long blast and shrill staccato the medicine man alerts the Maker, Sun, and other helpers in the direction of the four winds. The medicine feathers transmit the power, which has been directed into the center tree. As feathers touch the body, the tingling warmth felt is a sure sign that the power has been sent. It is the Winds who carry the sickness away.

Prayer Smokes and Pipes

No favor was granted by the medicine fathers without a gift, whether of flesh or of tobacco. Acceptance of the gift

[41] Ibid., 28.
[42] Ibid., 52.

of tobacco ("this tobacco") meant that the spirit being granted what was desired. Tobacco sealed the bond between petitioner and sacred person, as the pipe united a set of worshippers or those setting up an agreement.

The sacred tobacco planted by the Crows never was smoked, and this gift of the Star Persons is held in similar respect today.[43] However, tobacco smoked for pleasure and that used for praying in the Sun Dance are identical. In some degree Bull Durham tobacco is a form of sacred tobacco, for it is the preferred offering to the Sun and is attached to the forks of the center tree. Dancers currently prefer Kool mentholated cigarettes because they sooth and cool throats dried out by whistling.

A smoke-prayer with words is a more direct plea for help following breath-prayers sent through the whistle. The best times to pray are when the sun moves upward to its zenith, or at night close to midnight. The second day is the best of all, for seemingly the spirit persons are close and may accept the tobacco and confer some good thing. The second day also held great expectations for the pledger of the traditional Crow Sun Dance.

In the old Sun Dance, the bundle owner used a straight, tubular pipe and smoked and prayed at the start of each ceremonial segment. He also smoke-prayed at the end until all people had left the lodge. Then he divested the pledger of his sanctified dress and passed each piece through incense.[44] A similar pattern is followed in the present Sun Dance. Smoke-prayers are given at the center tree before cutting it down and before putting it up. The sponsor smoke-prays before the dancing starts, as well as at sunrise, and usually some time before the dance is halted. Those who bless the water before distribution to the dancers pray with cigarettes and bring the ceremony formally to an end. Sponsor and medicine man smoke

[43] Lowie, *The Crow Indians*, 274.
[44] Ibid., 325.

the familiar Plains calumet at special moments. Usually this part of the ceremony comes before noon and in the evening before the doctoring. At this time the pipe also is brought to the drum-chief who smokes before the center tree. Smoke-prayers with cigarette or pipe include motions to spirit persons above and on earth, and usually to those in the directions of the four winds.

Drumming and Singing

Medicine songs, like the smoke-prayers, have a compelling effect on spirit persons because they are their songs, given to their "children." Drum-singing is just as vital today to attainment of a vision as it was for the pledger of the traditional Sun Dance. Good drum-singers stimulate dancers and keep them going. When a dancer appears on the point of being "run over" by Buffalo, they step up the tempo to bring him into the mystic state of communication with the divine.[45] Through the drumming and singing the "words" of a song may come alive and speed to the spirit persons. For this reason, Crows often look upon the drummer-singers as a team working with the dancers and, as of old, solicit smoke-prayers by offering the pipe. Women have always been part of the singing team in the Sun Dance, and, until recently, usually moved leafy willow shoots up and down in drum time to symbolize growth and increase. In singing, women played a traditional role as assistants to the mainstream of action. In the old Crow Sun Dance, women sometimes took the lead in driving a dancer "crazy" by intensifying the singing, but today they take no such initiative.

Since the mid-sixties the rattle and cane introduced by Truhujo are no longer used by the drum chief. The band-type drum has replaced individual hand-carried circular drums of former times. A team of drummer-singers is never less than

---

[45]Lowie, "Sun Dance of the Crow Indians," 16:48.

four and preferably should be seven. The sponsor assumes responsibility for "paying" them for their services.

Old Needs in a New Setting

Persistence of and variations on traditional forms, meanings, and procedures show a striking continuity between the present Shoshoni-Crow Sun Dance and traditional Crow ceremonialism. Equally striking is the way in which the Sun Dance today satisfies basic needs expressed in Crow religious thought, which formerly were taken care of in special ceremonies. The Cooked Meat Singing ceremony traditionally drew most of these basic needs into a cooperative worship. In consenting to Two Leggings's request to sponsor the ceremony, Chief Two Belly noted that he should "pray that no sickness may befall our camp, that enemies may not come near us, and that we may continue to enjoy an abundance of food."[46] The ceremony was designed to bring the utmost prosperity and protection to the Crows during the coming season and was held as winter turned into spring and again as fall turned into winter. Rock medicines were central to the ceremony, but bundle owners and invited participants shared the strongest of medicine songs and dreams. These had been conveyed in dream and vision and were related to the Sun Dance, war, praise of successful warriors, life, growth, and increase.[47] This occasion was also a happy time to strengthen relations with father's clansmen, the success-dreamers, with gifts of horses, food, and other wealth. In turn, the giver received dream blessings that protected his life during the coming season and promised more good things through dreams passed on by a father's clansman to his "child."

The Sun Dance today can be viewed as a functional substitute for the Cooked Meat Singing, since no other ceremony

[46]Wildschut, "Medicine Bundles," 17:99.
[47]Ibid., 96, 102–103; Lowie, *The Crow Indians*, 263–68 and "Minor Ceremonies," 21:349–55.

satisfies the same wide range of personal and group needs sought. All the basic needs are represented: health, growth, increase, prosperity, and protection from enemies. While concern with sickness has turned the Sun Dance into a clinic for doctors and patients, the ceremony also is considered a medium to preserve the Crows and to increase their numbers. William Big Day, who first brought the Sun Dance to the Crows, was concerned that the Crows as a people were dying out; and a husband suffers the ordeal of the Sun Dance to make the birth of his child easy and to assure its growth.

Symbols of life and growth are found in the greenery left on the center tree, the willows attached below the crotch, and pine tufts that surround the eagle perched on the chief's rafter. Willows moved up and down by the women's chorus accent their role in the increase of the Crow people and the rearing of children. The buffalo symbolizes abundance of food and of necessities without which life would be hazardous and wearisome. The buffalo also bestows great curing powers. Thunderbird in his earthly manifestation of eagle epitomizes the dynamism of thunder and lightning. He is the awakener of earth and of its greening; he is the servant of the Sun, the giver of heat and of light. The eagle also recalls the unerring strike that accompanies success. Prosperity and wealth follow the eagle, who also may bestow the gift of curing.[48] Finally, the

---

[48] "If you see an eagle, it means [something] good," observed Frederick V. Left Hand. He had dreamt that he and his brother were on their way to a ceremony honoring his brother's nephew by marriage. A question arose concerning what they had to bring the young man, since they had no blankets or other goods for their contribution. On the way, however, Fred looked out of the car just as they were approaching the gathering and saw eagles against the dark, cloud-filled sky. On the basis of this vision he advised the mother of this nephew to give him an Indian name, which she did.

Later Fred asked a respected clan brother by the name of Red Elk to tell him what the eagle dream meant. After inquiring about the number and kinds of eagles — spotted, bald, or golden, all of which were present — Red Elk explained that Fred was going to be "showered with money some-

veteran with his war-narratives and ringing of the tree with charcoal extends the protection that only victory over the enemy can bring.

The Sun Dance as a Contemporary Institution

The Shoshoni-Crow Sun Dance holds a firm place today among the varied Christian and native-based forms of worship and thus is a functioning component of crow reservation culture. Indeed, the Sun Dance possesses advantages that other institutionalized forms of worship, including Peyotism, share only in degree or not at all. No other contemporary ceremony so thoroughly unites the past with the present in the service of both individuals and the Crow people. The Sun Dance plays upon the full range of needs around which their ancestors built their worship and ceremonies, accenting growth, abundance, increase, health, wealth, and victory over enemies. These self-same objectives are attainable in the present Sun Dance, though expressed in contemporary terms such as forestalling bad luck in the form of auto accidents, economic loss, or disease. The objectives are both old and new.

All the important religious figures, meanings, and procedures associated with Crow religious belief and practice find a home in the Big Lodge—Sun, Thunderbird-Eagle, and Buffalo. In the Big Lodge, which is made for the Sun, the world with all its earthly helpers and sky beings takes on an old-time personal quality. A dancer volunteers because of a felt need or because of instruction by a spirit person through a dream. He wears the white paint of the buffalo and the red and yellow paint of Sun and Thunderbird. Time-tried princi-

how." He might have a "long life" also, for the bald eagle lives the longest of all the eagles.

The dream took place in 1980, and Fred soon was "showered with money," for he received a loan of $250,000 to build up a cattle herd in cooperation with his brothers.

ples stress physical suffering to draw sympathetic attention to
the urgency of personal need. The dancer takes neither food
nor water, conveys his prayers with an eagle-bone whistle,
and binds the spirit-person with an offering of tobacco. Prayer
is predominantly a private matter, except for some public
references in the prayers of sponsor and medicine man. The
same private quality holds for the doctoring.

The Sun Dance recalls the old, familiar ceremonial organization. There are bundle owners who have the right to lead
a Sun Dance. They have not only purchased the right, or had
it conferred by gift, but also have fasted or otherwise received
in dream a gift of power from the spirit "owner" of the ceremony. The medicine man (director) and sponsor stand in a
ceremonial father-child relationship, and the dreams of the
sponsor, and at times of the medicine man, add further sancti-
fication and protection to the ceremony. An older dancer,
the sponsor, or medicine man may adopt a dancer and watch
over him. A dancer also can count on the support of near and
distant kinsmen, who pray for him and on the second day
bring cattails and sage to soothe his weary body. At the end,
father's clansmen, the protective success-givers, are there to
offer dream wishes and prayers. All are recompensed with
wealth, in accordance with Crow tradition, and the sponsor
and his relatives pay the medicine man for his services. Those
who have been doctored or prayed over give four different
valuables if they can. People need to go home happy and there
is no better way than to send them off with full stomachs
and food to spare. This is Crow philosophy, and the sponsor
and his relatives put on a grand feast at the breakup of camp,
thus forestalling hard feelings on the part of someone who
might do harm. The prayers of happy people bring good luck.

The subjective and rewarding experiences of Crow sun
dancers emphasize that traditional beliefs and procedures
have a special meaning for the present. There is value in
something that works—anything that gets people back to

health, that protects them from witchcraft and accidents, and that helps them get ahead in this world. When Indians feel that their traditions are ignored or ridiculed in schools, churches, and hospitals, and do not seem to count for much in the world, the Sun Dance rekindles a new confidence and pride in their nations and cultures. The Sun Dance is an Indian Way approved by the Maker, and is as legitimate a belief as any held by the white man.

The individual in any society faces the necessity of finding himself by identifying with a living tradition that maintains continuity and brings a workable past forward into the present. In national culture, the individual finds goals to challenge or accept, as well as procedures and rewards that bring a sense of fulfillment and career accomplishment. This feeling of identity with a national past and culture is found in the Sun Dance. The past resurrected in the Sun Dance ceremony is not just a counterforce into which people retreat and shut themselves off from what is going on around them. The Sun Dance, the same as Peyotism, keeps the intellectual challenge of past-versus-present alive and arouses the feeling that Crow institutions and ways have value and need to be preserved. In addition, the Crows sense that they must continue their language and bring up their children to respect traditional family relations and values, such as observing the respect behavior accorded elders, father's clansmen, and inlaws.

Elders remain the mentors of religious instruction and of power transfer, and young people find traditional ceremonies attractive and useful. A dancer's dress now is far more colorful than in the past, and there is a good chance that some are "showing off" for a sweetheart. Nonetheless, youth programs in churches languish as fasting at some distant butte takes precedence, or as prayers are offered at midnight when Star Persons radiate their splendor. In their fasting and cultivation of the spirit beings, men assure a full life and good luck for their families and themselves. This is old-time Crow practice, and, in assuming this traditional responsibility, men maintain the headship and respect of the family despite erosion of their provider role in contemporary life. Careers in the Sun Dance are socially and monetarily rewarding. By the 1930s, old-time medicine men with their tubular sucking pipes were fading. Presently some eight to ten of them practice in the Sun Dance. Dancers noted for the sincerity of their purpose also are chosen to offer prayers, and are rewarded with blankets, comforters, money, and perhaps a horse. The Sun Dance thus promotes the achievement of public reputations and the circulation of wealth along traditional lines.

Lack of an uncompromising ritual mold allows considerable adaptability and survival potential to the Sun Dance in today's world. In this regard the Sun Dance is the beneficiary of common tendencies in Crow ceremonialism. From the moment of contact with Europeans, Crows incorporated tokens of power and substituted European technology for their own.[49] In the hauling of poles for the Sun Dance lodge, the horse gave way to horse and wagon and after that, trucks took over. A match substitutes for the fire-drill in starting the ceremonial fire. The buffalo head attached to the center tree is obtained from a taxidermist, while a dancer uses lipstick for painting. Mirrors and animal-figure kerchiefs find their way into medicine bundles as tokens of the power gift. As yet there are no artificial substitutes for animal hide and feather medicines, although effigies sometimes are made from industrially-tanned hides. There is little chance that the Sun Dance will perish because ceremonial specifications cannot be met.

The new role of women is a test of the adaptability of the Sun Dance in ways not experienced in other ceremonials.

---

[49]Larocque in 1805 observed the use of a magic lantern by a Crow chief. "The figures that are painted on the glass he thinks are spirits and that they assist him. He never leaves them behind when he goes to war." See "Journal of Larocque," 3:66.

Traditionally, man and wife were partners in the quest for mystic power, although direct responsibility fell to the man. When women had medicine dreams, they were accorded respect. Women, licensed by dream, were allowed to give ceremonies like the Cooked Meat Singing, where the emphasis was on the general welfare and increase, as well as on war. These were legitimate concerns of women, including protection of the up-and-coming young warriors, who were especially invited.

The number of women sun dancers accelerated in the mid-fifties, and at Lodge Grass in 1975 they made up nearly 40 percent of the total. Although challenged, breaking of the menstrual taboo was not permitted, and women have continued to occupy a secondary status in the Sun Dance. However, their new role as dancers and their increased numbers indicate a revolutionary trend. The breakthrough for women in the Sun Dance correlated with efforts to upgrade women's place in Peyotism as well. Occasionally, and for the most part briefly, women have attempted the role of "road chief." The most recent challenger began her career in 1955, and data suggest that her support for leadership came mostly from other women, who also made up most or all of the worshippers.[50]

Challenges raised by Christianity through local denominations (Baptist, Catholic, Latter Day Saints, Pentecostal) are met largely by the principle of correspondences, along with the assertion that Indian and white worship the same Creator. The center tree in the Sun Dance lodge, with its horizontally-laced willows, even suggests the Christian cross. However, it is accepted that the Creator taught Indian and white separate ways because of their natures. Most sun dancers find the link to church a tenuous one and attend only on special occasions. Sun Dance leaders are more inclined to hold aloof from active church membership.

[50] Kiste, "Crow Peyotism."

Christianity offers no serious ideological or doctrinal bar to participation in the Sun Dance, since all denominations, Pentecostals excepted, are represented. Level of education is not important, since college youths also seek solutions to personal needs through the Sun Dance.

The challenges of hospitals and modern medicine are countered by finding a place for hospital medicine along with curing in the Sun Dance. Indeed, Sun Dance leaders make use of the hospital for particular remedies such as cough and heart medicines and salves. They also refer patients to the hospital if they get a message that their powers are not strong enough for that particular illness. At the same time, medicine men know that they have cured or prolonged the lives of people who turned to them when the hospital appeared to offer no help. Tom Yellowtail doctors patients as far away as California, Wisconsin, and New York. In serious cases he sends Seven Arrows to the sick person, who, on his return, reports that a "miracle" has happened. Such miracles naturally consternate the medical doctors on the case.

The Crow Sun Dance was, and it is today, the most democratic of the traditional ceremonies. Anyone could enter without invitation or adoption-payment. An owner of a Sun Dance medicine bundle still wields a traditional ceremonial authority, but the trend toward ceremonial simplification accents a people-centered ceremony in which personal needs are paramount rather than fulfillment of precise ritual forms or adoptive-membership. At the start, the Elk Lodge laid foundations for an organization based on adoption and fees, as found in the sacred tobacco adoption. However, this trend slowed when the return of veterans gave less cause for protective blessings, and differences between Truhujo and Crow agency leaders produced a rift. The entrance of women as dancers also broadened the democratic base of the Sun Dance.

The Elk Lodge with its full moon ceremony offers a merging of elements drawn from both bundle ceremonialism and Peyotism. Tom Yellowtail refers to the prayer meeting on or about the full moon as a bundle-opening. The altar is an elk hide on which an elk effigy cut-out and a mirror (lake) are laid out along with red streamers and an otter hide. The altar materials relate to Truhujo's adoption by the Elk medicine father. Sponsors of Sun Dances are invited to sit around the altar, where they pray to the piping of eagle-bone whistles. Tom Yellowtail also has set up medicine bundle owners at Crow Agency and Black Lodge (near Hardin), but there is no formal organization of officers such as once developed at Crow Agency. Nor is there now a water or beaver woman who serves as custodian of the medicines.

While a scheduling of meetings during the full moon follows the lead of Peyotism, the timing is traditional in Crow ceremonialism. Use of cedar incense, canes, cigarette prayers, water woman (Crow Agency), cedar man, and a tea (cedar or peyote?) links the Sun Dance with Peyotism. Indeed, some persons at Crow Agency refer to the full moon meeting as the "tipi way" (Peyotism). The bundle-altar and the eagle-bone piping may derive from a pre-peyote practice initiated by Yellow-Hand, historical founder of the Shoshoni ceremony.

The merging of Peyotist and medicine bundle elements in a monthly prayer and curing ceremony linked the Sun Dance responsively to day-to-day needs of individuals. The Sun Dance prayer meeting provided an alternative that was ceremonially familiar both to traditionalists and to Peyotists. However, the use of peyote in the Sun Dance was forbidden. This proved to be a point of doctrinal significance between the Elk Lodge as it first developed at Crow Agency and that organized later by Tom Yellowtail at Wyola under the direction of Truhujo. The combination of Peyotist and medicine bundle elements, together with the full moon meeting, contributed a versatility and modernity to the Sun Dance which other ceremonies could not match.

Along with other Crow ceremonies, social and religious, the Sun Dance is a congenial host for the exercise of kinship reciprocities. It readily accommodates the central exchange between the power-giving father's clansmen and the wealth-giving children and their maternal clansmen.

Performing a Sun Dance in late June or July in one of the districts gives the ceremony a special place in the annual calendar round, which begins right after the Crow Fair and Rodeo. No ceremony can compare with the Sun Dance in its attraction of worshippers, in the extent of kinship support, and in district and inter-district cooperation. Nor is there any ceremony which promises so thorough a mobilization of power and prayer for personal and tribal purposes. The Sun Dance thus is a fitting prelude to the Crow Fair and Rodeo in August, when the Crows look forward to the happiest of times together and the utmost good luck in their lives, for this grand encampment marks the end of the Old Year and the beginning of their New Year.

Appendix A

The Elk Lodge and the Full-Moon Meeting

Truhujo made a full moon meeting an integral part of the Sun Dance of the Crows. As a fundamental component of the Elk Lodge, the prayer meeting provided a forum for announcing and sanctioning the pledge of a Sun Dance. Elk Lodge members accounted for eleven of nineteen Sun Dances pledged between 1941 and 1946. The prayer meeting was just as versatile a social instrument as the Peyote meeting in that it was adapted to the manifold personal needs and status objectives of individual Crows. During the war, the safety of the "soldier boys" and the curing of disease provided primary considerations for holding a meeting.

In developing the Elk Lodge, Truhujo and his "outgroup" of Shoshoni followers obviously used the model of fraternities traditionally associated with the production of Sun Dances. He admitted that there was a connection between the Elk Lodge and the Shoshoni Horn Packers. However, the Elk Lodge in its organization, and the ceremonial of the full moon meeting, actually embodied novel and imaginative fusions of elements drawn from Peyotism, the Sun Dance, and traditional medicine bundle ritual. The Elk Lodge also was adopted to Crow adoption practice on acquiring medicine.

Although a meeting should be held every full moon, Elk

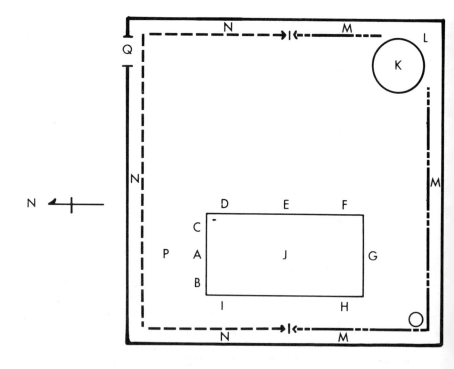

Figure 10A. Schematic View of "Full Moon" Prayer meeting at Crow Agency. **A,** Medicine man; **B,** "Beaver woman"; **C,** cedar man; **D,** assistant beaver woman; **E, F, H,** whistlers; **G,** "chief" of the meeting; **I,** younger woman assistant to the beaver woman; **J,** blanket upon which medicines are arranged; **K,** drum; **L,** drum chief; **M,** male relatives and friends; **N,** female relatives and friends; **O,** youth for whom meeting was called; **P,** position taken when being doctored; **Q,** door leading to adjacent room. The sponsor assumes no special position.

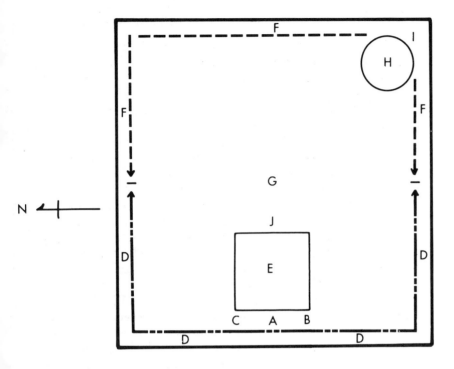

Figure 10B. Schematic View of Prayer Meeting at Pryor. **A,** medicine man; **B,** assistant; **C,** cedar man; **D,** male relations and whistlers; **E,** cloth or blanket upon which medicines are laid out; **F,** female relations, friends; **G,** area which must not be crossed during prayer, and position assumed by patient, facing east; **H,** drum; **I,** drum chief; **J,** coals. The sponsor assumes no special position.

Lodge leaders never followed this to the letter. At Pryor, "prayer" meetings directed by Big Day were held almost every week during the war, and had no connection with the moon in full phase.

Anyone, man or woman, sponsored a prayer meeting simply by communicating this intention to the Elk Lodge leaders. Usually, at this time the purpose was stated as well as whether or not a supernatural instruction for the meeting was given in a dream. Elk Lodge functionaries included a head medicine man or "water chief," a "water" or "beaver" woman, "cedar man," and "drum chief." Although others attended voluntarily or by invitation, the limited space in residences and the personal-need focus of a ceremony restricted attendance largely to Elk Lodge members and relatives of the pledger and patient.

Full moon meetings usually took place in the home of a pledger, and the ceremony began at sundown, following the models of Peyotism and the Sun Dance. A blanket furnished by the host was spread on the floor and served as an altar. Aside from leaders, those who positioned themselves around the altar were prominent figures in the Elk Lodge and Sun Dance or respected elders (see Figures 10a and b). This group constituted the "circle"—those who had been invited by the sponsor to pray and who received "pay" for their services.[1] Some of the "whistlers" were "clan uncles" of the person who was blessed because he was going away, or doctored.

In the Elk Lodge prayer meeting observed by the author,

[1] Chief Washakie reported that Yellow Hand possessed a picture of a white man, who appeared in dreams and told him to pledge a Sun Dance. See Lowie, "Sun Dance of the Wind River Shoshone and Ute," 21:396–97; Shimkin, "Wind River Shoshone Sun Dance," 151:409–10. The picture apparently was part of a medicine bundle and was brought out on request. Participants formed a circle around the picture and used Sun Dance eagle-bone whistles for their prayers. It is possible that a circle of devotees using eagle-bone whistles was a convention of long-standing with regard to Sun Dance medicine bundles, and may have served as a model for Truhujo in his Elk Lodge prayer meeting.

the water woman and her assistant arranged some ordinary tourist kerchiefs upon which an elk was depicted, in the form of a V. The point of the V was toward the medicine man, Barney Old Coyote. Medicines were laid out, with the chief of these located at the apex. The medicines were wrapped in anything from cloth to sheets of music. When the arrangement was completed, the water woman painted a red ring around each wrist and two short streaks from the corner of each eye, using a matchstick and a red lipstick.[2] She then passed the equipment in a clockwise direction, and each individual in the "circle" decorated himself in the same manner. While these preliminaries were in progress, spectators engaged in conversation and the drummer-singers softly practiced their drumming.

The prayer meeting in theory took place in the Sun Dance lodge. The medicine man and his assistants positioned themselves facing east. Drummer-singers were located at the southeast, beyond the sacred area. However, no shoes or moccasins were removed by leaders around the altar area, in contrast to the ceremonial practice observed when stepping on the sacred ground of the Big Lodge.[3]

At the start of the prayer meeting, the cedar man brought some coals in a scuttle, prayed momentarily, made a cross sign, and threw cedar incense on the coals. The cross sign was made by bringing the hand to the body and then drawing from

[2] Crow Peyotists formerly painted red circles around their wrists. Kiste, "Crow Peyotism."

[3] Big Day's description of prayer meetings at Pryor indicated that his may have been nearer the plan of the Sun Dance lodge than the ceremony witnessed at Crow Agency. With his assistant to his right and cedar man to his left, Big Day sat at the west end of the blanket altar, facing east. A sacred area beyond the altar was defined, which must not be crossed during prayer. Coals placed just east of the altar recalled the fire built up in the Sun Dance lodge. Male whistlers, representing dancers, positioned themselves along the west wall of the room on either side of the altar and extended along each wall, followed by male spectators. Beyond, women occupied the position of general spectators.

left to right. The water woman took up the chief medicine, passed it four times over the incense, and then over the other medicines, shaking the chief medicine over them. She passed the chief medicine in a clockwise direction around the circle, and each in turn fanned the incense to draw favor and power to himself.[4] When all was finished, the medicine man smoked the rattle, moved it away from himself, then from left to right, or east to west. Next the bone whistles used by the men in the circle were smoked and passed out clockwise. Not every man in the circle used a whistle, but one always did so when praying for a relative who was doctored.

The water woman kept track of all prayers requested as well as the persons who were supposed to do the praying. Occasionally the water woman kept track of over a hundred cigarettes for the smoke-prayers, but usually the number was between twenty and thirty. The first prayer was given by the "chief," Holds the Enemy, a respected elder active in the Sun Dance, who was selected by the sponsor. He prayed for the welfare of the group and the success of the meeting. The sponsor donated this prayer smoke, along with another toward his personal needs. The chief drew on the cigarette just enough to get it started, and then extended it over the medicines and prayed with head bowed. In the meantime, the medicine man signaled the drum chief, who extended the rattle over his head, rattled vigorously four times to set the beat, and then launched into the revered "water song." At the first heavy beats on the drum, which marked the beginning of the main rhythm, the medicine man and others within the circle blew a long blast, followed by four staccato notes. They then began the short blasts characteristic of the main dance. The drumming and singing continued until a prayer was completed. At a prayer's end the water woman passed an ashtray

---

[4] In traditional ceremony, medicines to be handled were passed from right to left, that is, clockwise. Peyotists followed this protocol in passing drum and leader's cane for individual drumming and singing.

clockwise and the prayer smokes were pinched out and returned to the assistant water woman. Effigy ashtrays were used. A bear was featured on the one observed. The prayer smoke butts were collected and disposed of in the coals, under the care of the cedar man.

The first part of the meeting was devoted to prayer smokes, and those in the circle fanned themselves with the various medicines that were placed on the altar. The midpoint was reached when half of the prayers had been offered, at which time the medicine man signaled the chief, who told the singers to stop playing. An informal intermission of ten or more minutes followed.

At a meeting called to offer special prayers for a youth who was about to depart for the army, the young man remained seated on a chair in the southwest corner of the room. He played no part, except that he painted himself in the manner of the Elk Lodge, was doctored and prayed over, and drank a portion of the cedar tea that had been brewed. This adoption ceremony was designed to give him courage, to relieve homesickness, to keep him well, and to bring him home safely. A special song designed to impart martial courage and protection, which was composed by a veteran in the Mediterranean Theatre, was sung. When youths departed for the army, they usually carried a medicine feather blessed by either Truhujo or some "clan uncle."

Lights were dimmed or completely extinguished during the doctoring of sick people. On these occasions prayer smokes were offered and the patient was fanned with medicines that conferred longevity and continuous health.

The last prayer smoke indicated the end of the meeting. Individuals wrapped up their whistles while the water woman smoked the chief medicine four times in the cedar incense and fanned the remaining medicines, as she had done when the meeting started. She then wrapped the medicines and stored them in a small satchel. The drum chief passed the rattle to the medicine man, who touched it to his breast, rattled it four times, and then passed it around the circle. Each person in turn blessed himself with the rattle after the example of the medicine man. Worshippers and medicine man then rose and faced in the same direction, preferably to the east, and a special sunrise song was sung by the drummer-singers. The medicine man offered a final prayer, members shook hands and thanked each other for the special prayers offered, and the meeting ended.

Refreshments provided by the sponsor then were served. The food usually consisted of a soup with meat and vegetables, bread, cinnamon rolls, highly-sweetened coffee, canned peaches, and assorted pies (peach and apple preferred). Before the assistant water woman and an aide distributed the food, the medicine man prayed and all bowed their heads. The assistant water woman distributed any leftover food.

Elk Lodge Membership

Membership in the Elk Lodge was by adoption. When he faced a personal crisis, a person vowed to join the lodge if cured, or if luck improved. When he discussed his problem with a friend or relative, the suggestion that he join the Elk Lodge sometimes was made. Someone in the lodge adopted the person, usually the water chief, Joe Hill, or the "owner" of the lodge, Barney Old Coyote. The water chief usually instructed the petitioner to gather together the makings of a special medicine.

At the adoption, the individual was painted in the Elk Lodge fashion and he and his medicine were fanned and blessed. The medicine man brushed the novice from the back of his head to his feet, then the back, front side, right side, and left side. This procedure was performed twice. Frequently a man and his wife were adopted together. During the war, a youth's parents sometimes pledged his membership if he returned safely.

A ceremonial father was always paid in blankets, quilts, money, and sometimes with a horse. The amount was never specified, but Crow parents were competitive. They tried to outdo others in making payments in public to "clan uncles" or other honored elders who blessed a "child." Following tradition, the water chief usually was given four different items. At various times individual Elk Lodge members gave a small gift to the adopted member, perhaps a blanket or money.

In July, 1946, the Elk Lodge had a membership of some 103 persons, including children and infants. Every district except Wyola had a set of officers. Three years after the end of the war, in 1948, and following the death of Old Coyote, the water woman custodian of Elk Lodge medicines transferred ownership to the eldest son. With the gradual withdrawal of Truhujo's backing, the Elk Lodge organization as constituted gradually lost its popular support. In 1975 the Elk Lodge was no longer functioning, although Tom Yellowtail, when investing Hugh Little Owl at Crow Agency and Arthur Anderson at Black Lodge with their medicines, told the people assembled that they were members of the Elk Lodge. If so, the Elk Lodge would be a replica of the small medicine bundle cult group traditional to Crow religious organization. At Crow Agency another Sun Dance medicine bundle group appears to be forming, led by Larsen Medicine Horse and Joe Hill's grandson Harold Hill. A multiplication of Sun Dance medicine bundles also would replicate traditional Crow religious organization.

Appendix B

Drummer's Cane and Rattle

Hill put some of his own ideas into the design of the four-foot tapered cane by making the upper part of ash and the lower of red willow. The ash represented the white people and the red willow the Indians.[1] He reasoned that, ". . . this generation, we are in a change. You see, we are trying to compete with the white people. By putting the two pieces together I thought that we would make some kind of hitch and get ahead some way."

Springing from the very top of the cane was an eagle plume tipped with brown, surrounded with three red-dyed down feathers. Immediately below and crowning the staff were three trimmed black tailfeathers of the eagle, each with a red-dyed down feather at its base. These tail feathers represented the eagle and the plumes, part of the tail. The three tail feathers also symbolized the "Almighty . . . the centerpole of the Sun Dance, and . . . the people." The plumes hanging from the feathers represented the down feathers that hung from the little fingers of the sun dancer. Nestled among the feathers near

[1] Kiste ("Crow Peyotism") observed two-piece and one-piece peyote canes. The idea of getting along with whites was a common theme of "moral" lectures by peyote leaders and elders.

the tip of the cane was a little buckskin bag containing a "strong medicine" to be used in doctoring a person "for whom there is no hope." Directly below the eagle feather crown were twelve prairie-chicken feathers, said to represent the "eats," for this bird was a common food of Indians in former days. Then came two wrappings of brown otter skin spaced six inches apart, with two sets of four spirals colored orange, dark green, red, and blue. These colored spirals signified the rainbow and lightning and prevented thunderstorms from sweeping over the dancers. Red generally symbolized the Indians, as well as lightning, while blue represented the thunderclouds. Green stood for anything "that is growing or wishing to grow," as children, trees, and crops, while orange symbolized the fall of the year when leaves turned color.

The handle of the elk-hide rattle was chokecherry, and small beads and pebbles were placed inside. The yellow clay on the handle held no meaning for Hill; but the three plume feathers attached to the top represented the three songs given to Truhujo at the time of his medicine adoption.

Sponsor's Ceremonial Cane

Truhujo introduced the leader's cane at the first Sun Dance at Pryor, and only sponsors of Sun Dances owned one. By war's end, Big Day, Old Coyote, Cummins, Bad Boy, and Childs possessed ceremonial canes, which others borrowed.

Since all canes in theory were the products of dream communications, each possessed its own individuality in size, decoration, and meaning. Following Truhujo's directions, Big Day made his of chokecherry. He peeled the bark and made the cane look white, just as he covered his body with white clay when dancing because the white paint represented something "clean." At the top he attached a light eagle plume, which represented the eagle in the lodge. Cummins's cane, given to him by Truhujo, was about four and a half feet long by half

an inch in diameter and made of chokecherry wood. When
the cane was in use, two dark eagle tail feathers were attached
at the top. Approximately two inches from the top were four
red bands, about half an inch broad and spaced at intervals
of nearly an inch. The meaning of the feathers and the red
bands was unknown. The cane was presented to Cummins
during an Elk Lodge prayer meeting during the winter of
1944. He recalled that "They smoked the staff, prayed for
me and for the staff, and then gave it to me. When they
gave it, they told me that it was not for everybody. I was
to handle it myself." When it was not in use, Cummins removed the eagle feathers from the cane and placed the cane
upon the wall in his room, over his bed. Such a location
corresponded to the placement of medicine bundles in tipis.

Old Coyote's cane was the result of a dream of Tilton
West, close associate of Truhujo. The cane was of red willow,
about five feet in length and tipped with a carved "stork's"
head. It was made by Joe Hill, at Old Coyote's request, for
his Sun Dance in 1944.

There was a close connection between the sponsor's cane
and lightning, and therefore the owner removed it from the
house during a thunderstorm. It also required protection from
the contamination of menstrual blood, and during his wife's
period Bad Boy hung his cane in a tree. Al Childs, evidently
following a dream communication, returned his power cane
to the medicine helper. He placed his cane in a brush hide-
out and thereby absolved himself of the restrictive responsibilities of caring for it.

Little Man or Person Offering

The "person offering" was of buckskin, nine inches in length,
with legs and arms. Facial features were not indicated, but it
was daubed with red paint from the neck upwards. Straight
black hair covered the head, and a portion stuck upright be-

hind to imitate a feather. The chest was adorned with two small strings of beads, and a sash around the middle carried the characteristic rainbow and lightning patterns of Truhujo.

The Wind River Shoshonis in their Sun Dance used a mannikin said to have been obtained from the Crows. During the reservation renovation of the Sun Dance, use of the mannikin was discontinued.

Appendix C

Crow Sun Dances by District, 1941 to 1946

Year District	Sponsor
1941 P[1]	William Big Day
1941 CA	*Gus Other Medicine
1942 P	Campbell Big Hail
1942 CA	*Charlie Ten Bear
1942 CA	Martin He Does It[3]
1943 P	Walter Chief
1943 CA	*Paul Kills[4]
1943 CA	*Barney Old Coyote
1943 SX	Walter Chief[5]
1944 P	Stanley Rides the Horse
1944 CA	*Barney Old Coyote
1944 CA	*David Bad Boy
1944 SX	*Al Childs
1945 P	Frank Hawk
1945 CA	*Barney Old Coyote
1946 P	*Francis Rock
1946 CA	*Henry Old Coyote
1946 LG	*John Cummins
1946 SX	John Half

*Designated Elk Lodge members.

[1] District abbreviations are as follows: P, Pryor; CA, Crow Agency; SX, St. Xavier (Big Horn); LG, Lodge Grass.

[2] Figures include non-Crow participants, the number of which diminished sharply beginning in 1942 and seldom exceeded two or three in 1946.

[3] Resident of St. Xavier or Big Horn district.

[4] Resident of St. Xavier or Big Horn district.

Motive	Medicine-Man	Dancers	Fasters
Sickness	John Truhujo	23	4[2]
Sickness	John Truhujo	48	6
Sickness	Tom Compton	31	10
War	John Truhujo	108	10
Sickness	John Truhujo	42	6
War	Charlie Bell	23	5
War	John Truhujo	56	12
War	John Truhujo	38	7
War	Charlie Bell	14	0
War	Tom Compton	31	7
War	John Truhujo	96	9
War	John Truhujo	78	9
War	John Truhujo	32	4
War	W. Big Day	30	8
War	John Truhujo	75	6
War-end	None[6]	30	6
War-end	John Truhujo	45	5
War-end	John Truhujo	42	4
War-end	Tom Compton	28	7[7]

[5]Resident of Pryor district. The dance was for four days, in accordance with dream instructions.

[6]John Truhujo was scheduled to lead the dance, but failed to appear, and William Big Day directed the performance without participating himself.

[7]Except for 1941 performances and the one at Lodge Grass in 1946, figures are approximate.

Bibliography

Aberle, David F. *The Peyote Religion Among the Navaho.* Chicago: Aldine, 1966. "A Brief History of the Crow Tribe." Mimeographed, n.d.

Barnett, Homer G. *Indian Shakers: A Messianic Cult of the Pacific Northwest.* Carbondale: Southern Illinois University Press, 1957.

Berkhofer, Robert. *Salvation and the Savage: An Analysis of Protestant Missions and American Indian Response, 1767–1862.* Lexington: University of Kentucky Press, 1965.

Bowers, Alfred W. "Hidatsa Social and Ceremonial Organization." Smithsonian Institution, Bureau of American Ethnology *Bulletin 194.* Washington, 1965.

Bradley, C. C., Jr. *After the Buffalo Days.* Crow Agency, Montana: Crow Central Education Commission, 1972.

Bruner, Edward. "Primary Group Experience and the Processes of Acculturation." *American Anthropologist* 58 (1956):605–23.

Bureau of Indian Affairs, Commissioner. "Programming for Indian Social and Economic Improvement." *Memorandum,* April 12, 1956. Mimeographed.

Bureau of Indian Affairs, Planning Support Group. "Draft Programmatic Environmental Statement, DES-75-2: Projected Coal Development, Crow Indian Reservation." Billings, Montana: Department of Interior, 1975.

Campbell, William S. "The Tipis of the Crow Indians." *American Anthropologist* 29 (1927):87–104.

Clark, William P. *The Indian Sign Language.* Lincoln: University of Nebraska Press Bison Book, 1982; original, 1884.

"Crow Reservation, Montana." Photocopy, n.d.

Curtis, Edward S. *The North American Indian, The Apsaroke, or Crows.* 20 vols., 4:3–126. New York: Johnson Reprint Corporation, 1970; original, 1909.

Denig, Edwin T. "Of the Crow Nation." Edited by John C. Ewers. Smithsonian Institution, Bureau of American Ethnology *Bulletin 151*:3–74. Washington, 1953.

Driver, Harold E. and Alfred L. Kroeber. "Quantitative Expression of Cultural Relationships." University of California *Publications in American Archaeology and Ethnology* 31:211–56. Berkeley, 1932.

Ehrlich, Clara. "Tribal Culture in Crow Mythology." *Journal of American Folk-Lore* 50 (1937):307–408.

Frey, Rodney. 'Sacred Symbols of the Apsaalooke Sun Dance Religion." Manuscript, n.d.

Hebard, Grace R. *Washakie: an Account of Indian Resistance of the Covered Wagon and Union Pacific Railroad Invasions of Their Territory.* Cleveland: Arthur H. Clark Co., 1930.

Hoebel, E. Adamson. "The Sun Dance of the Hekandika Shoshone." *American Anthropologist* 37 (1935):570–81.

Jablow, Joseph. "The Cheyenne in Plains Indian Trade Relations 1795–1840." American Ethnological Society *Monograph 19*. New York: J. J. Augustin, 1951.

Johnson, Thomas H. "Structure and Function in the Wind River Shoshone Sun Dance." Manuscript, n.d.

Jones, J. A. "The Sun Dance of the Northern Ute." Smithsonian Institution, Bureau of American Ethnology *Bulletin 157*:203–63. Washington, 1955.

Kiste, Robert C. "Crow Peyotism." Manuscript, n.d.

LaBarre, Weston. "The Peyote Cult." Yale University *Publications in Anthropology No. 19*. New Haven: Yale University Press, 1938.

Larocque, François. *Journal of Larocque from the Assiniboine to the Yellowstone.* Edited by L. J. Burpee. Canadian Archives *Publication No. 3*. Ottawa, 1910.

La Verendrye, P. G. de Varennes. *Journals and Letters of Pierre Gaulter de Verendrye and His Sons.* Edited by L. J. Burpee. Toronto: Champlain Society Publication, 1927.

Leonard, Zenas. *Adventures of Zenas Leonard, Fur Trader and*

Trapper, 1831–1836. Edited by W. F. Wagner. Cleveland: Burrows Brothers Co., 1904.

Lewis, Meriwether and William Clark. *Original Journals of the Lewis and Clark Expedition, 1804–1806.* Edited by Reuben G. Thwaites. 8 vols. New York: Dodd Mead & Company, 1905–1906.

Linderman, Frank B. *American: The Life Story of a Great American, Plenty Coups, Chief of the Crows.* New York: John Day Company, 1930.

———. *Red Mother.* New York: John Day Company, 1932.

Lowenthal, Richard. "Crow Indian Public Events as Documents of Ethnohistory." Manuscript, n.d.

Lowie, Robert H. "Social Life of the Crow Indians." American Museum of Natural History *Anthropological Papers* 9:179–248. New York, 1912.

———. "The Sun Dance of the Crow Indians." American Museum of Natural History *Anthropological Papers* 16:1–50. New York, 1915.

———. "Myths and Traditions of the Crow Indians." American Museum of Natural History *Anthropological Papers* 25:1–308. New York, 1918.

———. "The Sun Dance of the Wind River Shoshone and Ute." American Museum of Natural History *Anthropological Papers* 21:387–410. New York, 1919.

———. "The Tobacco Society of the Crow Indians." American Museum of Natural History *Anthropological Papers* 21:103–200. New York, 1920.

———. "Crow Indian Art." American Museum of Natural History *Anthropological Papers* 21:271–322. New York, 1922.

———. "The Religion of the Crow Indians." American Museum of Natural History *Anthropological Papers* 25:311–444. New York, 1922.

———. "Minor Ceremonies of the Crow Indians." American Museum of Natural History *Anthropological Papers* 21:325–65. New York, 1924.

———. *The Crow Indians.* New York: Farrar and Rinehart, 1935.

Mackenzie, Charles. "The Mississouri Indians, A Narrative of Four Trading Expeditions to the Mississouri, 1804–1805–1806." In *Les Bourgeois de la Compagnie due Nord-Ouest,* edited by L. R.

Masson, 1:315–93. New York: Antiquarian Press Ltd., 1960; original, 1889–1890.

Marquis, Thomas B. *Memoirs of a White Crow Indian* (Thomas H. Leforge). Lincoln: University of Nebraska Press Bison Book, 1974.

Maxo, H. E. "The Journal of La Vérendrye, 1738–39," *North Dakota Historical Quarterly* 8 (1940–41):242–71.

Meriam, Lewis and others. *The Problem of Indian Administration*. Baltimore: The Johns Hopkins Press, 1928.

Mooney, James. "The Ghost Dance Religion." Bureau of American Ethnology *Fourteenth Annual Report*, Part 2, 796–927, 1058–1078. Washington, 1896.

———. "Calendar History of the Kiowa Indians." Bureau of American Ethnology *Seventeenth Annual Report* (1895–96), Part 1, 129–445. Washington, 1898.

Morgan, Lewis H. *The Indian Journals, 1859–1862*. Edited by Leslie A. White. Ann Arbor: University of Michigan Press, 1959.

Mulloy, William T. "The Hagen Site." University of Montana *Publications in Social Science*, no. 1. Missoula, 1942.

Nabokov, Peter, ed. *Two Leggings: The Making of a Crow Warrior* (manuscript of William Wildschut). New York: Thomas Y. Crowell, Apollo Edition, 1970.

Nasatir, A. Phineas, ed. *Before Lewis and Clark. Documents Illustrating the History of Missouri 1785–1804*. 2 vols. St. Louis: St. Louis Historical Documents Foundation, 1952.

Opler, Marvin K. "The Integration of the Sun Dance in Ute Religion." *American Anthropologist* 43 (1941):550–72.

Scott, Hugh L. "Notes on the Kado or Sun Dance of the Kiowa." *American Anthropologist* 13 (1911):345–79.

———. "Historical Notes on the Crow from White Man Runs Him." Manuscript No. 4525, National Anthropological Archives, Washington, n.d.

———. "Notes on Crow History, Ethnography and Sign Language." Manuscript No. 2932, National Anthropological Archives, Washington, n.d.

Shimkin, Demitri. "The Wind River Shoshone Sun Dance." Smithsonian Institution, Bureau of American Ethnology *Bulletin 151* (1953), 397–484. Washington: 1953.

Skinner, B. F. *About Behaviorism*. New York: Alfred Knopf, 1974.

Spier, Leslie. "The Sun Dance of the Plains Indians: Its Development and Diffusion." American Museum of Natural History, *Anthropological Papers* 16:451–527. Washington: 1921.

Spindler, George. *Sociocultural and Psychological Processes in Menomini Acculturation.* Berkeley: University of California Press, 1955.

Stewart, Omer C. *History of Peyotism.* (In press.)

Voget, Fred W. "Individual Motivation in the Diffusion of the Wind River Shoshone Sun Dance to the Crow Indians." *American Anthropologist* 50 (1948):634–46.

———. "A Shoshone Innovator." *American Anthropologist* 52 (1950):53–63.

———. "Current Trends in the Wind River Shoshone Sun Dance." Smithsonian Institution, Bureau of American Ethnology, 1953, *Bulletin* 151:485–99. Washington: 1953.

———. "The American Indian in Transition: Reformation and Accommodation," *American Anthropologist* 58 (1956):264–81.

———. "Warfare and the Integration of Crow Indian Culture." In *Explorations in Cultural Anthropology: Essays in Honor of George Peter Murdock.* Edited by Ward B. Goodenough. Pp. 483–509. New York: McGraw Hill Book Company, 1964.

———. "Field Notes, Crow Indians," 1938–83.

Wallace, Anthony F. C. "Revitalization Movements," *American Anthropologist* 58 (1956):264–81.

Wied-Neuwied, Maximilian, Prinz von. "Travels into the Interior of North America, 1832–1834." In *Early Western Travels, 1748–1846.* Edited by Reuben G. Thwaites, 22:346–55. Cleveland: The Arthur H. Clark Co., 1906.

Wildschut, William. "Crow Indian Medicine Bundles." Edited by John C. Ewers. In *Contributions from the Museum of the American Indian Heye Foundation,* vol. 17. New York: Heye Foundation, 1960.

Wilson, Michael. "In the Lap of the Gods: Archaeology and Ethnohistory in the Big Horn Mountains, Wyoming." *Archaeology in Montana* 17 (1976):33–34.

Wissler, Clark. "Ceremonial Bundles of the Blackfoot Indians." American Museum of Natural History, *Anthropological Papers* 2:1–163. New York, 1912.

Index

Absaroka, Montana: 16; mountains, 4
Absarokees (Crow Indians): 14
Adoption (medicine purchase): purpose of, 63–64; initiation of, 65–66; adoption process, 66–74; childbirth theme, 69–71; ceremonial feeding, 69; ceremonial washing, 71–72; feast, 74; see also Tobacco Society
Alberta (Canadian province): 10, 12
Antlers: see Pack Antlers
Apsaroke (name for Crow Indians): 4n.
Arapaho Indians: 8, 9, 10, 11, 15, 16, 30, 77, 168n.
Arikara Indians: 9
Arrow-shooting-rock: 61, 302–303
Assiniboin Indians: 8, 9, 11, 63, 77
Atsina Indians: 8, 11, 77
Bad Boy, David: 157, 186–87, 193, 199–200, 251, 267
Band (economic-political unit of Crow Indians): 3–4, 30, 49–50
Bannock Indians: see Shoshoni Indians
Baptists: 16, 19, 21
Batsirape: 305
Bears: grizzly, 46; medicine, 62
Bear-song-dance: 61, 62–63
Beaver Dance (Tobacco Society chapter): 168n.
Beaver Woman: 153–54, 186, 189; see also Elk Lodge
Bell, Charles (medicine man, Fort Hall Shoshoni): 187, 293–94
Berdache (transvestite): 94, 119
Big Bird: 80, 83–84
Big Day, Annie (wife of William): 129, 131–32, 187
Big Day, William: 129ff., 164, 174, 186–87, 192, 202, 203, 286, 289ff., 325n.;

and dreams, 129, 131, 133, 138; contacts with Truhujo, 129, 133; reactions to Shoshoni Sun Dance, 129, 134, 139; education, 130; childhood, 130–31; traditional outlook of, 130–31; excommunication of, 131, 134, 139; concern with sickness and death, 132, 138; experiences with Peyotism, 131–34; experiences in Shoshoni Sun Dance, 133–34; and visions, 133; vows to Sun, 134, 195; and Sun Dance interpretations concerning buffalo, eagle-thunderbird, dreams, fasting, good luck, Indian-white worship, center pole, and willows, 136–38, 140–41; role in diffusion of the Sun Dance to the Crow; 142–44, 150; opposition to Sun Dance at Crow Agency, 143–44
Big Dipper: see Seven Brothers
Big Hail, Campbell: 197–98
Big Horn (district): 143, 200ff.
Big Horn Mountains: 4, 7, 15
Big Horn River: 4, 9, 11, 14, 15, 26, 30, 148
Big Horn Sheep: 148
Big-lodge (clan): 31, 143ff.
Big Lodge (Sun's lodge): 197, 236ff.
Big Shadow: Fig. 1, 99, 108ff., Fig. 3, 112–13, 114, 121, 124–25, 127
Billings, Montana: 18, 134, 140, 202
Bird Above: 255–56
Bird Horse: 208, 214, 216, 221, 224, 246–47, 255, 268
Black (color symbolism): 88ff., 101ff., 122; see also Shoshoni-Crow Sun Dance and center pole
Blackbird Well Known: 258
Blackfeet Indians: 10, 11, 15, 77, 168n.

341

Blackfoot (Crow chief): 13, 51
Black Hills: 4, 11
Blue (color symbolism): 228&n., 299
Bozeman Trail: 14
Brother-in-law reciprocity: see kinship and
  Shoshoni-Crow Sun Dance Participation
Brother-sister respect: see Kinship and
  Respect behavior
Bruner, Edward: 140
Buffalo: 3ff., 29–30, 47, 49; ceremonial
  use of, 44, 63, 70, 218ff.; hunting of,
  51, 59–60; albino, 228n.; symbolism of,
  307
Buffalo, Jim (Crow medicine man): 228,
  267–68
Buffalo skulls: see Crow Sun Dance
Buffalo spirit person: 48, 78, 136, 138,
  240ff., 299; running over dancer, 268
Buffalo tongues: see Crow Sun Dance
Bull Durham (tobacco offering): 309
Bundle owner (medicine): 42; see also
  Crow Sun Dance
Bureau of Indian Affairs: 24, 27
Calumet: pipe, 310
Camp chief: 3, 39–40, 52, 109–10
Camp crier: see herald
Camp police: see military police
Canada: 6
Captive, ceremonial use of: 95, 119
Cardinal directions: 89, 94, 100, 114–15,
  122–23, 178; Fig. 2, 106–107; Fig. 3,
  112–13; Fig. 4, 116–17; Fig. 6, 206ff.;
  Fig. 7, 233; Fig. 8, 237; Fig. 9, 239; Figs.
  10a and 10b, 322–23
Carpenter, Harold: 241, 278
Catholic Church: 134, 139, 152, 181
Catholics: 16, 19, 21
Cedar, ceremonial use of: see Crow Sun
  Dance and Shoshoni-Crow Sun Dance
Cedar man: see Shoshoni-Crow Sun
  Dance and Elk Lodge
Cedar prayer: see Shoshoni-Crow Sun
  Dance
Center pole: see Shoshoni-Crow Sun Dance
Ceremonial calendar: 283
Ceremonial circuit: see Crow Sun Dance
  and Shoshoni-Crow Sun Dance
Ceremonial father (adoptive): 40–43, 60ff.
Ceremonial fire(s): see Crow Sun Dance
  and Shoshoni-Crow Sun Dance
Ceremonial rights: 64, 70, 75–76, 296–97
Ceremonial synthesis: 318–20
Cheyenne Indians: 9, 10, 15, 16, 30, 77
Cheyenne, Wyoming: 18
Chief pole (Sun Dance lodge): 218n.,
  235–36n.
Chiefs: of clan, band, and tribe, 50–51;
  mystic charisma and power of, 51–54;

counsel of, 52–53
Chieftaincy: 39–40, 50–54
Childs, Al: 150, 187, 198, 254
Christ: see Jesus
Christianity versus Indian worship: 276ff.,
  317; see also correspondences
Clan(s), Crow: matrilineal, 30–33, 50;
  fathers/uncles, 19ff., 31–32, 34–36, 41,
  126; aunts, 22; exogamy, 50; chief, 50
Clay, ceremonial use of: see Crow Sun
  Dance and Shoshoni-Crow Sun Dance
Coal, development of: 26–28
Collier, John (commissioner of Indian
  Affairs): 18, 24, 147, 163–64
Color symbolism: 297–99; see also Crow
  Sun Dance and Shoshoni-Crow Sun
  Dance and individual colors, black,
  blue, green, red, yellow, white
Comanche Indians: 9, 11, 77, 78, 168n.
Compton, Thomas (Shoshoni medicine
  man): 164, 172, 183, 294
Consecration, ceremony of: 69, 70; see
  also Crow and Shoshoni-Crow Sun
  Dances and Tobacco Society adoption
Cooked-meat-singing: 61–62, 317; and
  dwarfs, 303
Correspondences, Indian-Christian: 174–
  75, 181–82, 279–80
Cottonwood tree, ceremonial use of: 62,
  218, 219–23, 301
Coups: as war honors: 40, 43, 48–49, 54,
  66; as blessings for success, 54, 70–71,
  223–24, 241; see also Crow Sun Dance
  and Shoshoni-Crow Sun Dance
Covers Up, Jack (Lodge Grass district
  herald): 13–14, 213–14, 225–26, 230
Crazy-dog-wishing-to-die: 56
Creator: 136–37, 174&n., 177, 228ff.,
  235–36ff., 294
Cree Indians: 9
Cross: of Morning Star, 89, 126, 298; of
  crucifixion, 253, 296
Crow Agency: 146, 199ff.
Crow Indians: population, 3, 30; trade,
  3, 9, 10–12, 15, 29; separation from
  Hidatsa, 4–8; territory, 4, Map 1;
  language, 6; treaties and land cessions,
  13; culture, 18–20; reservation culture,
  18–23; conservatism, 19–20; national
  identity, 20; pluralism, 20; pragmatism,
  20, 314–15; individuality, 38–40, 43;
  childhood of, 45; authority among, 60;
  pantheism, 138; fair and rodeo, 143,
  283&n.; attitude toward ceremony, 196;
  fair as occasion for wealth distribution,
  287
Crow Sun Dance.
——— bundle: role of owner, 42, 88, 90,

91–94, 101, 103–105, 110–11, 112–13, 115, 125; origins of, 77, 79–85; contents, 80–85; Moon Woman, 81–82; Morning Star, 81, 89, 100, 126; Seven Brothers (Bulls, Men, Stars), 82; screech owl, 82; songs, 82; number, 85; and war, 85–86; buffalo, 86, 88, 98, 108, 126–27; consecrated tongues, 87, 91, 93ff., 102, 106, 109ff., 123, 125; skulls, 88, 91, 101–102, 106, 111, 112–13, 116–17, 124, 126; ramada shade for, 91, 99, 114, 115; bull hunt, 92–93, 111–15; hides, 98, 99, 108, 109, 114, 122
—— ceremony: flesh offering: 43–44, 127; mannikin in hoop, 82–85ff., 124, 127–28; stages of, 86; eagle-bone whistle, 88–89, 103, 124, 126; drumming-singing, 89–91ff., 125; ceremonial circuit, 89, 100–101, 124–25; transfer to pledger, 90; prayer smoke, 90ff., 105; processions, 93, 118–19; wealth distribution, 95–96, 100, 103, 118, 120; tubular pipe, 97; as war party, 100, 124; skewer fasters, 102–103, 106, 111–13, 116–17, 125; termination of Sun Dance, 104, 127; mourning, 106, 127; dancers, 112–13, 116–17, 127; daily activities, 126–28
—— lodge: 82, 85, 99, 105–106, 121, 123; cardinal directions, 89, 94, 100ff., 122–23; eagle medicine man, 90n., 98–100, 122–23; role of military police, 91–93, 118; berdache and captive, use of, 94, 95, 119; covering, 96, 98–99, 108, 122; construction of, 97–101, 121–24; eagle's nest, 98, 100–101ff., 124, 127; encampment, 99, 109–11; role of chief in, 99, 109–10, 119
—— painting: black as victory, 88, 92ff., 101–102, 114, 115, 119, 127; white clay, 89, 100, 102–103, 112–13, 116–17, 124
—— pledger: 42, 78, 106, 108, 111, 114–15; dress, 83, 87–91, 126; visitants, 86, 96–97; vow, 86–87; consecration of, 86–91, 104–105; pipe offering to bundle owner, 87; painting of, 89–90, 98, 103, 118; dancing, 90, 103, 123, 125; bed, 97, 101, 103, 109n., 112–13, 116–17, 123–24; fasting, 101; visions, 104, 111, 127; war party of, 105; entrance of lodge, 124–25
—— trees: pine, 83, 92, 104, 120; purification with, 86, 89; cedar incense, 90–92, 97–98, 102, 104, 122; cottonwood, 93, 95, 105, 120; pole-notching ceremony, 94, 119; pole assignment honor, 95–96, 118, 120–21; willow, 96, 98, 118; cedar, 97, 101–102, 106, 112–13, 116–17, 123; fire, 106, 112–13, 116–17, 124; booths, 112–13; as enemy, 115, 119–21; tenders, 116–17
—— war: coup striking, 84, 92, 95, 111, 115, 119–21; scalps, use of, 88, 93, 123, 125; scouting, as enemy, 90, 92, 114, 118; no-retreat honorees, 95–96, 121; coup blessing, 98, 100, 102, 103, 111, 114; role of pipeholders, 100, 119, 124; sham battles, 102, 112–13, 116–17, 123; visions, 104, 124
Cultural identity: 273ff., 296, 313ff.
Culture processes: accommodation, 20, 23, 296–97; change, 28, 274ff.; continuity, 273ff., 311ff.; technological substitution, 316; synthesis, 318–20
Culture history: 273ff.; perspective on Peyotism and the Sun Dance, 281–82
Cummins, John: 205ff., 268
Curing: *see* doctoring
Curtis, Edward: 105, 124
Dakota Indians: 15, 16, 34, 44, 76; Teton, 9–10, 12, 15, 30, 77; Sisseton, 77; Oglala, 168n.
Dance step: 215–16
Denig, Edwin: 5, 7, 12
Devils Lake: 5, 6
Dinwoodie Canyon: 301–302
Discrimination (ethnic): 18
Division of labor: 31, 120
Doctoring: 177–78, 192–93, 199–200, 259, 267–68, 318
Doll (Sun Dance): *see* mannikin
Dream(s): mystic communication, 13, 38ff., 65, 72, 105, 108, 129ff., 181–82, 312n.–13; blessing, 51, 54, 61, 255; interpretation, 187n., 312n.–13
Drum chief: 157, 210, 236; *see also* Appendix A
Drummer's cane: 209–10, 220, 258–62; *see also* Appendix B
Drummer-singers: 88ff., 125, 236ff.
Dwarf(s): 61, 301–308
Eagle: Sun's helper and messenger, 64, 73–74, 307–308; and Tobacco Society chapter, 64; as medium for prayer, 213ff.; and medicine man, 90&n.; "nest," 98ff.
Eagle-bone whistle: 87–89, 103, 124, 126, 234
Eagle feather(s): 114, 194–95, 223; as bad omen, 183–84, 255; dreams of, 312–13n.
Earth lodge: 7–8
Education: 45–49
Effigy: *see* mannikin

Effigy hoop: 83, 93–94, 102ff., 127–28
Elk lodge: 149–50, 153, 156–57, 167–68,
    170&n., 171, 183, 186–89, 236–37,
    285–86, 318–19, Appendix A
Elk (spirit person): 192, 301; spikehorn,
    305
Entrance (Sun Dance lodge): 124–25, Fig. 7
Episcopal Church: 166, 174, 181
Excommunication: 131, 134, 139, 152,
    155
Family: 31
Fasting: 101, 133, 157
Father's clansmen: honoring and feasting,
    42, 62; as dispensers of mystic power,
    31–32, 244; see also clan uncles
Flag (ceremony): 235–36n., 251–52
Flathead Indians: 9, 11
Flesh offering: 43–44, 127
Fort Hall Shoshoni: 164, 187, 197
Forts: Raymond, 11; Union, 12; C. F.
    Smith, 14, 148; Custer, 16; Keogh, 16;
    Washakie, 129, 133–34, 146, 153, 157,
    164
Four (ritual number): 71–74, 84, 86–91,
    93ff., 132, 209
Four Dances: 80–82
Four-pole frame (tipi): 98, 106, 111–13,
    116–17, 121–23
Four Seasons: 253
Four-Square Gospel: 278, 296
Four Winds: 14, 235, 240
Full Moon meeting: 150–51, 153, 183,
    186–89; see also Elk Lodge
Ghost Dance: 16, 276
Give-away: 22, 32; see also wealth distri-
    bution
Glendive, Montana: 8
God: see Creator
Goes Ahead (Crow warrior): 43
Goes Back, Bruce (Arapaho Indian):
    269–70
Government policy: 15, 16–18, 24–26,
    171–72, 194, 276–77, 280
Grandfather: as mentor, 46–47
Grandmother Moon: see Moon Woman
Great Salt Lake: 7
Green (color symbolism): 298–99
Growth of tribe: 219; see also prayer
    smokes and willows
Hair on Top: see Long Hair (Crow chief)
Heart River: 6
He First Made All Things: see Creator
Hekandika Shoshoni Indians: 77, 163n.
Herald (camp crier): 96, 208, 216, 224ff.
Hidatsa-Crow (language connection): 6
Hidatsa Indians: 4ff., 29, 63, 124n., 128
Hill, Joe: education, 156; religious skepti-
    cism, 156–57; participation in Sun

Dance, 156–58; medicine man, 156,
    158, 205–206ff.; church affiliation, 157;
    relations with Truhujo, 157–58, 193n.;
    interpretation of drummer's cane,
    330–31
Historic innovators: factors in, 194–95,
    291–92
History and evolution: 292–94
Holds the Enemy: 192–93, 326
Homicide: 54, 60
Hoop: see effigy hoop
Horn Packers (Shoshoni fraternity): 325
Horse Dance: 63–64, 66, 73, 75
Horses (as exchange wealth): 9, 32, 37–38,
    42, 63–64, 66, 73, 119
Howe, Robert: 198–99, 214–15, 242–43
Hudson Bay: 8
Hultkrantz, Ake: 184, 185
Increase: see growth
Indian Claims Commission: 24–25
Indian Reorganization Act: 147
Individuality (how valued): 38–40, 43
Informal associations (medicine, worship):
    61–63
Iron Bull (Crow chief): 39, 51
Jesus (Christ): 177, 262
Joking relatives: 36–37
Kicked-in-their-bellies (Crow clan, band):
    4, 31
Kinship (rights and obligations): 32–37,
    42, 64, 287
Kiowa Indians: 9, 11, 30, 77–78
Knife River: 7, 63
Kutenai Indians: 77, 168n.
Lake Superior: 8
Lakota: see Dakota Indians
Larocque, François (trader): 9, 10
La Vérendrye, Pierre (explorer): 9
Leforge, Thomas: 58
Left Hand, Frederick: 312–13n.
Left Hand, Ira: 267–68
Lemhi Shoshoni Indians: 146
Leonard, Zenas (trader): 10
Lightning: 89–90, 181, 204, 253, 301
Lion Shows, Austin: 201&n.
Lisa, Manuel (trader): 9, 11
Little Big Horn (battle): 15
Little Big Horn River: 30, 219
Little man: see mannikin
Little White Bear (Crow chief): 10
Livingston, Montana: 15
Lodge Grass (Crow Reservation), town
    and district: 27ff., 133–34, 165, 225ff.,
    269ff.
Long Hair (Crow chief): 13, 30, 63,
    109–10
Lowie, Robert: 7, 104, 109, 111, 115, 120,
    123, 124

Luck (wish for good): 48, 62, 137–38, 198, 210ff., 241
Mackenzie, Charles: 11
Maize (corn): 4, 6; ceremonial use of, 73
Magpies (youth instructional group): 46
Mandan Indians: 5ff., 29
Mannikin: 78ff., 176, 184, 250–51, 295–96, 300; symbolism of, 306&n.; *see also* Appendix B
Mantannes: *see* Mandan Indians
Marias River: 10
Marriage: 18, 32, 50, 119
Maternal uncle (as "elder brother"): 47–48
Maxpe (mystic power): 38, 294–95
Medicine: "father," 13, 40ff., 52; man, 37ff., 99, 232ff.; as mystic power, 38–40, 42ff., 252–56, 268; pipe, 40–41, 52, 73–74; painting, 41, 43, 48, 70, 88, 92ff., 252–53; loan-purchase of, 41–42; songs, 41, 42, 44, 62ff., 72, 82, 114–15, 211; bundle(s), 42–44, 60ff., 85–86; inheritance of, 84–85, 172; quest, 43, 47, 132; rocks, 302–303; *see also* dreams, hoop, effigy hoop, and mannikin
Medicine Crow, Joseph: 207–209
Meldrum, Robert: 79, 105ff., 120ff.
Menard (trader): 9
Menstruants (avoidance of): 254n., 293
Mentor-apprentice relationship: 40–43, 235–36n., 286
Meriam Report: 280
Midnight (ceremonial break): 126, 241–42
Military fraternities: 52, 54–60, 96, 101; in competition, 56–58; insignia of, 55–56; recruitment, 55; judicial-political functions, 58–60
Military police: 51–52, 59–60, 91–93, 118–19
Minnesota (state): 8
Minnetarees: *see* Hidatsa Indians
Mission Creek (Crow Indian Agency): 15
Missouri River: 4, 6, 10, 11, 12
Mississippi River: 8
Montana (state): 5, 7
Moon Woman: 81, 82
Morgan, Lewis H.: 79, 105
Morning Star (deity): 81, 89, 100, 126, 168n., 232, 240, 298ff.
Mother's brother: 33–34; *see also* kinship
Mourning: 47, 55, 127
Mountain Crow(s) (band): 4ff., 30–31, 49, 51, 63, 105, 109
Mussellshell River: 30
Mystical affinity with otter: 305; *see also* batsirape
Names: as personal property, 44; conferral of, 44–45, 48–49, 67
National identity: 20; *see also* cultural

identity
Native American Church: *see* Peyotism
NaxpikE (Hidatsa ceremony): 7, 79n., 124n., 128
Newly-made-lodges (clan): 31, 143, 209
Nez Percé Indians: 11
No retreat (honor-obligation): 48, 56, 58, 95–96
North Dakota (state): 5
Northern Ute Indians: 77, 163, 235n.
North Platte River: 12
No Vitals (Crow chief): 5, 6, 8–9
Okipa (Mandan Indian ceremony): 78
Old Bear, Herbert: 146–47, 186, 192
Old Coyote, Barney: church affiliation, 152; education, 152; vow regarding daughter's illness, 152; excommunication, 152, 155; relations with Truhujo, 153; participation in Sun Dance, 153–55; Elk Lodge head, 155, 186–89
Old Coyote, Mae: 153–55, 158, 186
Older-younger relationship: *see* kinship
Old Man Coyote: 294
Old Man Sun: *see* Sun
Old Woman: *see* Moon Woman
Old Woman's grandchild: *see* Morning Star
Osage Indians: 11, 30
Otter: 56, 305
Outside dance: 204–17
Owls: 82–83n.
Pack Antlers: 170
Pan-Indianism: 278
Patrilocal residence: 31, 50
Pawnee Indians: 11, 30
Pentecostals: 19, 278, 296
Peyotism: 19, 21, 131–32; Tipi Way, 131–32, 139; ceremonial circuit, 234n.; water song, 238n.; and identity, 275–81; conflict with medicine bundle worship, 277; adaptive potential, 277–78; and Indian Renaissance, 279; and Crow Sun Dance leaders, 280
Piegan Indians (Blackfeet): 15, 16
Pine tree (ceremonial use): 218; *see also* Sun Dance lodge construction
Pipe: holder, war chief, 41–42, 49; lighter, 71; ceremonial circuit, 261
Plains Cree: 77, 168n.
Plains Indians: 16, 19, 29
Plains Ojibwa: 77
Pledger: *see* Crow Sun Dance
Pledger's cane: 209, 301; *see also* Appendix B
Plenty Coups (Crow chief): 13, 14, 46, 47, 137, 141, 149
Political-legal awareness: 23–28; *see also* Peyotism

Political organization: tribal, 39–40, 50–54; reservation, 24–25
Ponca Indians: 77
Powder River: 4
Power quest: *see* medicine quest and dreams, fasting
Prairie Dog Man: 80–84
Praise singer: 114, 115, 209
Praise song: 22, 103, 126, 214, 225, 231, 256ff.
Prayer(s): *see* prayer smoke
Prayer smoke: 42, 203, 216, 225, 226, 235ff.; gesture symbolism, 209, 214–15
Prediction: *see* dream interpretation and visions
Pretty Shield: 34, 43, 44
Pryor boarding school: 156
Pryor (district and village): 130–31, 142ff., 150, 197, 199, 201, 262
Pryor Gap: 61, 302
Pryor Mountains: 15, 30, 303
Purification: sweating, 48, 70–71; smoking with incense, 48, 86, 89, 209–11, 245–47; fasting, 101, 133, 157; sexual abstinence, 136; *see also* cedar and Crow and Shoshoni-Crow Sun Dances
Rainbow: 299
Rattle: 89, 111; *see also* drum chief and Appendix B
Real Bird, Jim: 220, 224, 226–27, 233–34, 242–43
Reciprocity: *see* kinship and wealth distribution
Red (color symbolism): 274–75n., 298–99
Red Bear (Crow chief): 51, 54, 57
Red Feather at the Temple: *see* Long Hair
Red River: 6
Reinterpretation: 297
Religion (Crow Indians): authority and organization in, 60–61, 144; corporate nature of, 74–76; personalized nature, 76, 294–95
Religion: and identity, 140–41, 275–81; and legitimatizing of tradition, 141, 296–97; and social division, 141
Respect behavior: between mother-in-law and son-in-law, 20, 33; brother-sister, 33–34; brother-in-law, 33–34; father's clansmen, 34–36; older-younger protection, 45, 47–48
Revelation: *see* dreams and visions
River Crows (band): 4ff., 30, 49, 63, 67, 110, 127
Roberts, John (Reverend): 166, 173n., 181
Rock medicines: 61–62, 301–305
Rocky Mountains: 4, 77
Rosebud creek (Agency): 15–16
Ross, Alexander: 78

Rotten Belly (Crow chief): 10, 13, 30, 57, 63
Saco, Ralph: 232
Sacred Pipe: 63ff., 73–75
Sage: 91, 97, 127, 221, 225
St. Clair, Lynn (Shoshoni Indian): 174, 183
Sarsi Indians: 77, 168n.
Scalps: ceremonial use, 88, 93, 123, 125
Scott, Hugh: 79
Scouts: 52
Scouting (ceremonial): 90, 92, 114, 118, 219
Screech owl: 82, 305
Seasonal migration: 3, 52
Sees the Living Bull: 38, 41
Seven (ritual number): 82–83, 103, 110, 300, 304
Seven Arrows (Shoshoni dwarf owner of Sun Dance): 190, 301, 303
Seven Brothers (also Bulls, Stars, Men): 5, 81–82, 229ff.
Sham battle(s): 102, 112–13, 116–17, 123
Sheridan, Wyoming: 18
Shimkin, Demitri: 78
Shoshone Business Council: 170
Shoshone Dance Committee: 170
Shoshoni-Crow Sun Dance.
——— Big Lodge construction: plan of, Fig. 8; cardinal directions, 206ff.; sacred area, 211, 233, 249, 270; chief pole, 218n., 229–30; scouting as enemy, 219; consecration of cottonwood and pine trees, 219–21, 224; prayer smoke, 219–21, 226; pledger's tipi, 220; felling of cottonwood center pole, 221; use of sap, 223–24; coup striking, 223–24; tripod altar, 224; buffalo head, 224–25; west support pole, 226; center pole, 227; willow bundle, 227; cloth offerings, 228; tobacco offering, 228; raising center pole or "tree," 229; setting uprights and stringers, 229–30; brush cover, 230; ceremonial fire, 233, 241–43
——— ceremonial synthesis: as contemporary institution, 313–20; Christianity versus Sun Dance, 232–34, 317–18; *see also* Elk Lodge and Appendix A
——— ceremony: special forms introduced by Truhujo, 196–97, 220; purification and cedar prayer, 209–10, 220, 246; religious instruments, 209–11, 220; cedar man, 220, 246–47; circuit and entrance of lodge, Fig. 7, 232–34; flag raising, 235–36n., 251–52; sunrise ceremony, 243–48; second day, 248–52; setting cottonwood supports for dancers, 249–50; mannikin or "little man," 250–51; painting, 252–53; medicines, 252–

54; water woman, 269; smoke prayers and water offering, 269–70; ceremonial circuit of water, 270; feast, 271; deconsecrating lodge and use of poles, 272
———— daily activities: drum, 207; rattle, 209–10; drummer's cane, 209–10, 220; drum chief, 210, 236; songs, 211ff., 238&n.; women's chorus, 236; dancing, 236ff.; drumming-singing, 236ff.; doctoring, 240–41ff.; wealth distribution, 241; encouragement of dancers, 255–58; drum chief's prayer smoke and luck dream, 260–62; dancers' suffering, 262–65; visions of cure, 265; Hitler and outbreak of war, 265–66; victory, 266; drawing water from center pole, 267–68; dreams of water, 268; atomic bomb drop, 289
———— dissemination among Crow Indians: shared experiences and differences among Big Day, Hill, Old Coyote, R. Yellowtail, and Truhujo, 158–62; transfer of medicine bundles and leadership, 158, 189–92
———— organizational features: Elk Lodge, 149–50, Appendix A; medicine bundles, transfer of, 158, 187–89, 294; pledger, 189ff.; assistant, 220ff.; medicine man, 232ff.; multiple leaders, 293, 296
———— participation: illness, 197, 199, 201n.; friend, 199, 262; wealth, 198; kinship, 200–202; brothers-in-law, 202, 205, 207, 210ff., 217, 219, 220–21
———— pledger: 189, 197, 219; list of (1941–46), Appendix C; vow, 197–98; dream validation, 197–98; organizational tasks, 200–203, 207, 209; district committee, 201–202; instructions to dancers, 217; consecration of Sun Dance, 203–205; thunder signal, 204; outside dances, timing of, 204–205; plan of, Fig. 6; coup blessings, 207–208; wealth distribution, 208–209; ceremonial fire, 209; cedar prayer and purification, 209–11; drumming-singing, 211ff.; initiates dancing, 212; dress, 212–13; medicines, 213; encouragement, 213–14; prayer smokes, 214–15; termination of outside dance, 216–17; entrance of Big Lodge, Fig. 7, 234–35; prayer smoke, 235–36; initiation of dance, 238; assistant, 220, 224, 226–27, Fig. 7
———— Shoshoni-Crow Sun Dance comparisons: war and visions, 280–81, 289–90; dream validation of pledger, 283–86; organization, 284–85; ceremonial roles, losses and gains, 285–86; medicine man and control of ceremony, 286ff. consecration ceremony, 287–89; coup-blessings, 288; dress, 288–89; offerings to sun, 288, 299; purification, 289; role and authority of pledger, 289–91; entrance of lodge, 290; medicine bundles and multiple leadership, 293–94; world view, 294–95; buffalo, 295; as medicine quest, 295–96; origins, 299–305; mannikin, 305–307; buffalo versus "little man," 307; eagle-thunderbird, 307–308; women's roles and place in, 316–17; wealth and circulation, 319–20
———— vows: 197–200; for relative in war, 198–99, 205ff., 221, 225, 228; avoiding evil, 238–40
Shoshoni Indians: 9, 163, 285, 290
Sioux Indians: *see* Dakota Indians
Sisseton Indians: *see* Dakota Indians
Sits in the Middle of the Ground: *see* Blackfoot
Skinner, B. F.: 140
Smoking (as acceptance of obligation): 40, 54, 56, 203
"Son" (ceremonial adoption): 31–32, 40–43
Sun Dance (Plains Indians): origins, 77; purposes of, 78
Sun (deity): 44, 71–73, 78, 85, 94, 105, 108, 114, 119, 127, 136–38, 228&n., 294ff.; as witness to oaths, 78; paints of, 89–90; offerings to, 127; sunrise greeting, 244–46; as God, 201n.; helpers, *see* eagle and thunderbird
Symbolism: 297–305
Sweating: as purification and prayer, 48, 71–72
Sweat lodge (sacred): 84
Technological substitution: 316
Ten Bear, Charlie: 193, 199, 224n., 227, 262–67
Teton Dakota: *see* Dakota Indians
Thermopolis, Wyoming: 129, 192
Three-pole frame (tipi): 111, 121–23
Thunder: 204, 298
Thunderbird: 136–37, 204, 301, 312
Tipi Way: *see* Peyotism
Tobacco: sacred to Crow Indians, 5–7, 19, 30, 70, 275n.; linked to national destiny, 5
Tobacco Society: ceremonial adoption, 63–66; recruitment, 67; stages in, 68–69; consecration of initiate, 69; adoption-lodge owner, 70; altar replica of planting ground, 70; painting and dressing, 69–70; selection of medicines by initiate, 72–73; corporate nature of, 75; status enhancement, 275n.

Tongues (buffalo): ceremonial use of, 70, 87, 91, 93–94, 96–97
Trade: 8, 11–12
Transvestite: *see* Berdache
"Tree": *see* center pole
Trudeau, Jean-Baptiste: 9
Truhujo, Joe (father of John): 165
Truhujo, John (also Treeo, Trehero, Rainbow, Two Belly): Crow relatives, 164–65; control of Sun Dance among Crows, 164–65, 187ff.; childhood, 166; education, 166; church affiliation, 166–67; lineage and Sun Dance ambitions, Fig. 5, 164–65, 167–69; inheritance of medicine bundle, 172; as historic figure, 194–95
——— Elk Lodge: origin of, 170–71, 183; establishment among Crows, 186–89; final transfer to Thomas Yellowtail, 189; recall of medicine helpers, 189–90
——— Sun Dance interpretations: associated fraternities, 167–68, 170n.; origins of, 168n.; rejection of peyote, 169, 174, 193; views of Shoshoni leaders, 172–73; Indian revelation versus Bible, 173, 181; names of Sun Dance, 174; "Indian Commandments," 174–75; Indian-Christian correspondences, 174, 176; drummer's cane, 176; buffalo, 176, 179; eagle, 176; eaglebone whistle, 177; drumming-singing, 178; cedar incense, 178–79; center pole, 179; dancing, 179–81; dreams and prophecy, 180–81, 193; Shoshoni views of, 182–85
Twelve poles: as Twelve Apostles, 234; as "moons" of year, 234
Two (ritual number): 97, 115, 123, 180
Two Leggings (Crow chief): 38, 41, 80, 114, 121, 124, 126
Ute Indians: *see* Northern Ute Indians
Virtue (ceremonial honoring of): 94, 97, 100, 118, 124
Vision(s): 38, 43, 265ff.
Vow: 65, 67, 197–98
War: status instrument: 32–33, 39–40, 43, 54
Warfare: 29, 37–40, 41, 42, 54
Warrior: idealization of, 56–57
War veterans (ceremonial role): 208, 224, 280–81

Washakie (Wind River Shoshoni chief): 324n.
Water song: 211, 238&n.; *see also* Appendix A
Water woman: 269; *see also* Appendix A
Wealth distribution: 208–209, 241; *see also* "give-away"
Wesaw, Tom (Shoshoni medicine man): 184
West, Tilton: 145, 221, 229
Whistler: *see* pledger, under Crow Sun Dance
White (color symbolism): 119, 126, 228n., 298–99
White Arm: 227
Whiteman, Blake: 217, 220
White Man Runs Him: 274n.
White Rock, Utah: 166
"Wife capture": 57
Willows: ceremonial use of, 71, 96, 98, 118, 218; as symbol of growth, 137
Willow hoop: 83, 93–94; *see also* mannikin and effigy hoop
Wind River Mountains: 4, 301
Wind River Shoshoni Indians: 11, 54, 77
Wind River Shoshoni Sun Dance: 79; diffusion to Crow Indians, 129–62; center of Sun Dance diffusion, 163; as shamanic performance, 164n., 235n.; origins, 168n.; associated fraternities, 170&n.; Christian elements in, 174, 182; punishment for disrespect toward, 182; plan of lodge, 235n., Fig. 9
Wraps Up His Tail: 274&n.
Wyola (town, Crow Reservation): 27, 28
Wyoming (state): 4
Yanktonai Indians: 8
Yellow Brow: 225, 227
Yellow (color symbolism): 181, 249, 299
Yellow Hand: 78, Fig. 5, 168&n., 170
Yellowstone Park: 7
Yellowstone River: 4, 11, 12, 28, 30
Yellowtail Dam: 26; legend of, 148
Yellowtail, Robert: superintendent of Crow Indians, 24, 147; education, 147; political career, 147–49; respect for custom, 148; church affiliations, 149; Elk Lodge affiliation, 149; relations with Truhujo, 150
Yellowtail, Thomas: 151, 165, 190–92, 218n., 294, 303–305